# Praise for
## *The Story of Millard and Linda Fuller* . . .

It was my honor as President of the United States in 1996 to present Millard Fuller with the Presidential Medal of Freedom, our country's highest civilian award. Millard and Linda Fuller have changed philanthropy. Instead of just asking for money, they asked people to swing a hammer. In so doing, they have built countless houses, strengthened communities, and empowered people of modest means to literally build a better future. This important book chronicles their remarkable quest to make a difference, one home at a time.

—William Jefferson Clinton, 42nd President of the United States

Over the past thirty years, my life has intersected with the Fullers as far back as Civil Rights days in the South and continuing through other significant junctures. I have followed with admiration as Linda and Millard expressed their love for God, each other, and humankind by creating Habitat for Humanity, an organization one of my own daughters was privileged to work with in Africa for a period of time. This comprehensive story of the Fullers is, indeed, a book whose time has come . . . to inspire more of us to give our all.

—The Honorable Andrew Young, Chairman,
GoodWorks International; former Ambassador to the
United Nations under President Jimmy Carter, Atlanta, GA

Millard and Linda Fuller have changed neighborhoods, changed attitudes, and, most significantly, changed countless lives. None of us who were part of the Renaissance Weekend 2000 Habitat Blitz Build will ever forget Millard's sunrise dedication of what had been constructed in five days, America's first new house of the new millennium. Like that house, the Fullers' lives are testimony to the power of conviction, tenacity, and friendship.

—Philip Lader, Attorney, Charleston, SC;
Former U.S. Ambassador to the Court of St. James's

Among the distilled wisdom in the Old Testament Book of Proverbs are these words that describe the life of Millard Fuller: "Without vision, the people perish." Visionary leadership is the antidote for the apathy of our world! It is the quality for which our world is starving. Millard Fuller is a man of great vision who does not believe in the word "can't." He believes that ALL THINGS are possible to those who believe. But visionaries are not always appreciated in their own time. So when Millard and his wife Linda started Habitat for Humanity, many called them foolish. But their vision inspired people of all ages to imagine a world where all human beings would have the dignity of having a roof over their heads. I have built Habitat homes with Millard and Linda and have seen firsthand the life-transforming power of their vision. I encourage you to read this poignant and inspiring story of a couple who dares to take incredible risks to follow their dreams and make them a reality. But watch out! Reading this book and getting a taste for the Fullers' vision of the world might . . . disturb you . . . keep you awake at night . . . inspire you . . . to dare to be a visionary leader right where you are . . . today!

—Bonnie McElveen-Hunter, former U.S. Ambassador to Finland;
Former Board Member, Habitat for Humanity
International; Chair, American Red Cross;
and CEO, Pace Communications, Greensboro, NC

Millard and Linda Fuller are two of the most inspiring people I have ever met . . . inspiring in what they say and in the way they have lived their lives. Their ministry of providing decent housing for poor families around the world for over thirty years is a story that needs to be heard—and understood. This book spares no detail in telling that remarkable, historical story.

—William V. Muse, former President,
Auburn University, Auburn, AL

I believe that, one day, history will conclude that Millard and Linda Fuller were among the greatest Christian giants of the twenty-first century. A resounding Amen!! to this incredible story, and one that is masterfully told!

—Bishop Dr. Gerard Mpango, Anglican Bishop of Western Tanganyika, Tanzania; Founder of Habitat in Tanzania, former International Board Member of HFHI, 1989–94

Bettie Youngs's book is a wonderful adventure with Millard and Linda Fuller. It richly tells the story of how love between two souls turned into a mission filled with love, a mission which has built homes for those in need throughout the world. We can all learn from this tale and thus enrich our lives and the lives of those around us. Enjoy this truly amazing story.

—Neil Shulman, MD, Author, *Doc Hollywood;* Associate Professor, Emory University School of Medicine, Atlanta, GA

*(reviews continued on page 379)*

# The Story of
# Millard and Linda Fuller,
# Founders of
# Habitat for Humanity
# and the
# Fuller Center for Housing

## BETTIE B. YOUNGS

burres books

Cover design by Jane Hagaman
Cover art © David Papazian/Corbis

Burres Books, a division of
BETTIE YOUNGS BOOK PUBLISHERS
www.BettieYoungsBooks.com
Info@BettieYoungsBooks.com

If you are unable to order this book from your local
bookseller or online from Amazon or Barnes and Noble, or from
Espresso, or Read How Your Want, you may order directly from the
publisher (info@BettieYoungs.com).

Library of Congress Cataloging-in-Publication Data

Youngs, Bettie B.
   The Story of Millard and Linda Fuller, founders of Habitat for
Humanity and the Fuller Center for Housing / Bettie B. Youngs.
   Published by Burres Books, a division of Bettie Youngs Book
Publishers (www.BettieYoungsBooks.com).
   Summary: "In 1973, entrepreneur Millard Fuller and his wife
Linda left behind their materialistic lifestyle and crumbling marriage
to start over as missionaries in Zaire. On returning to Georgia in
1976, they founded Habitat for Humanity and, as their personal
Christian ministry, started building houses to bring new life to the
poverty-stricken. In 2005 they were fired from Habitat for Humanity
International  and founded the Fuller Center for Housing. This is
their story"–Provided by publisher.
   Includes bibliographical references and index.
   1.  Fuller, Millard, 1935-2009 2.  Fuller, Linda, 1941- 3.  Habitat
for Humanity, Inc.–History. 4.  Habitat for Humanity International,
Inc.–History. 5.  The Fuller Center for Housing–History. 6.  Poor–
Services for–United States. 7.  Low-income Housing–United  States.
8.  Christian Biography–United States.  I. Title.
   HV97.H32Y68 2007
   363.5'858576092–dc22
   [B]

LCCN: 2013947513


ISBN: 978-0-9882848-8-3
eBook: 978-1-936332-52-6

Unless the LORD builds the house,
its builders labor in vain.

—Psalm 127:1a

# Contents

# Acknowledgments

First and foremost, to Millard and Linda Fuller: It has been my honor and privilege to be a part of this work. Certainly, it has been a monumental effort to record the journey of Habitat for Humanity's founder and life force, and to attempt to do justice in capturing both Millard the man and Millard the icon. He is a one-of-a-kind dynamo, a hero to millions, and an all-out faithful servant who serves his God with single-minded purpose. As for Linda Fuller, like so many women, her legacy is so much larger than many know. My mother used to say that the disappointing thing about housework is that no one knows what you do unless you don't do it. Linda's journey has been similar. Year after year she has walked hand in hand with Millard through continent after continent. She has found, repaired, built, and decorated homes and offices, always filling in whenever and wherever she was needed—which was everywhere. Deeply rooted in her faith, her work over the years has reflected a heart filled with love for all humanity. Linda is the founder of the enormously popular Women's Blitz Builds and can hammer a nail and put up a sheet of drywall as fast and as well as anyone. She is mother to four loving and bright children and devoted grandmother to another eight. In writing their story, I came to see their love for one another as soul-deep, and rivaled only by the love they hold for humanity as whole. Their lives and their love show us what it means to have the courage and conviction to use our time—the most precious commodity we are given—to do only that which matters—which in their estimation is to be of service to others in the years we are given. What a joy it was to write about such an inspiring legacy.

I would also like to thank my former publishers of the hardback edition (formerly *The House that Love Built: The Story of Millard and Linda Fuller, Founders of Habitat for Humanity and the Fuller Center for Housing*), Jack Jennings and Bob Friedman at Hampton Roads, as well as their talented staff, especially those with whom I worked most closely on this book: Jane Hagaman, Cindy Jennings, Sara Sgarlat, and Tania Seymour; and all the others who worked behind the scenes to give this book its wings. Thanks to the best editors in the world, Susan Heim and Elisabeth Rinaldi, for always saying, "Let's have a look . . ." My gratitude extends to Kirk Lyman-Barner, who wrote a thinking man's foreword, and to Cori Lyman-Barner, whose sensitivity in editing this work helped breathe life into it, literally. Thank you to my many friends, for the rich times in spite of my schedules, and for all the ways you prove "relationship" is what it's all about. And to the glorious friendship I have with my beloved daughter, Jennifer, and Rick and their Kendahl, for all the ways you sweeten the journey: You own my heart! And, most importantly, to the Spirit who championed and guided this work—and whose fingerprints are clearly evident upon the pages herein.

# Foreword
## Kirk Lyman-Barner, MBA, MDiv

Kirk Lyman-Barner with Millard Fuller, Shreveport, La., 2005

I first met Millard Fuller, the founder of Habitat for Humanity International, in September 1988. He was speaking to approximately two hundred seminarians, faculty, and professors at Pittsburgh Theological Seminary. Millard began his talk by asking a "theological" question. "Is it possible to build a house that is so big that it is offensive to God?" Most in the audience said or nodded "yes." He then followed up with a deeper question. "Most of you agree that it is possible to build a house so big that it is offensive. Now I want to know at what point does a house become so big that it is offensive?" One of my classmates in the back row shouted, "When the house is bigger than mine!" This brought laughter to everyone in the room, including Millard, and we often recall this story when we're together.

The housing question was motivated by Millard's observation that God has supplied the world with enough resources to house everyone in need and that all that is missing is the will to do it. The thought of a misallocation of God's resources can be both unsettling and motivating. Millard and Linda Fuller have challenged countless people to reorder their priorities, their lives, and their careers and to join in the movement to fulfill their core belief, "All of God's children deserve at least a simple, decent place in which to live."

I was so impressed after meeting Millard that I shared his message and his vision with my neighbors in Pendleton County, West Virginia, and we started the Almost Heaven Habitat for Humanity affiliate. As a young couple, my wife, Cori, and I attempted to model our local housing ministry and our lifestyle after the loving and passionate working relationship we witnessed in Millard and Linda. The Almost Heaven Habitat became very productive and successful by hosting church and student work camps. An average of two thousand volunteers from all over the nation came to our tiny community annually, and every Sunday Cori and I would orient a new group about the story of Millard and Linda Fuller, how they started Habitat, and what the ministry looked like in our Appalachian community. The visiting volunteers worked side by side repairing existing houses and building new ones with those desperately in need of better housing. While they were hammering, they made new friends and fell in love with our community.

This act of inspired community and global activism has been repeated over and over throughout the world by the building of modest and affordable housing utilizing appropriate technology and volunteer labor, and all managed prima-rily from the grass roots. Under Millard's leadership, Habitat for Humanity International grew to become the largest and most recognized nonprofit housing organization, serving in a hundred nations around the world.

But the ministry hasn't been without struggles and, at times, heartbreak and deep disappointment. On March 9, 2005, I was on the phone with Millard and Linda when they received a fax from South Africa, where the Habitat for Humanity International board of directors was meeting, announcing that they were officially fired from the organiza-tion they had started and nurtured for almost thirty years. Simply stated, the firing of the Fullers by Habitat for Humanity International was due to longstanding and deep philosophical differences between Millard and the board about how the organization should be managed.

For the purpose of understanding and healing, Bettie Youngs provides us with insights regarding the Fullers' strug-gles with the Habitat for Humanity International board of directors. But to understand the context of the struggle, you first need to meet Millard and Linda. Never before has their life story been so intimately and eloquently told. Bettie intro-duces them to us before they met and shares their incredible relationship, how they reconciled following a period of estrangement, and how they conceived what we all have come to know and respect as Habitat for Humanity International. She shares about the years of Habitat's phenomenal growth and the details that led up to their firing. Perhaps most important to anyone who has gone through a rough point in their own journey, Bettie movingly reveals how Millard and Linda have taken their firing by the Habitat for Humanity board as an opportunity to launch an exciting new global ministry, expanding the opportunity for God's love for "the least of these" to be expressed through compassion, sweat, hammers, and nails.

To illustrate the difference between Millard and the Habitat for Humanity International board in management philosophy, I'll share another point Millard made that day at the seminary in Pittsburgh. A member of the audience asked Millard, "Do you ever have trouble collecting payments from your homeowners?" Millard deferred the question to the executive director of the Pittsburgh Habitat affiliate, who hung his head and said, "Yes." Millard shouted, "GOOD! Because if you had told me 'No,' I would tell you that you are working with the wrong crowd!" Everyone in the room applauded.

The current management at Habitat for Humanity International appears determined to transform the program from a federation of grass-roots affiliates into a corporate franchise. The struggle between Millard and the board is a classic MBA-textbook example of two sides disagreeing about the merits of decentralized vs. centralized organizational structure. With the board now fully in control, the centralized management changes come with all the top-down legal restrictions concerning use of the brand and licensing protection one would expect in a for-profit corporation. If the local affiliates fail to adhere to the standards established by International's management, they risk "disaffiliation." The Habitat for Humanity International board has determined that disaffiliation is a potential outcome when mortgage delinquencies become an issue, as evidenced by their recent termination of the relationship with Habitat Jamaica. This shift away from a Christian response to a struggling affiliate (or homeowner family) is all very frustrating to Millard and those of us who believe that it is more Christian to wrap your arms around a struggling program, modeling the same kind of "hands-up" that we want to see the organizations offering their prospective homeowners.

In 1999, when Cori and I made the decision to transition on from the affiliate we had helped to start, our two full-time construction supervisors were Habitat homeowners and the person elected by the Almost Heaven board of directors to replace me as executive director was Michelle Conner. This very capable leader is herself a Habitat homeowner and was recently honored by the *West Virginia State Journal* as one of the most outstanding young business leaders in the state for her work with Habitat! We firmly believed, and continue to believe, that encouraging indigenous leaders and empowering them to do what is best for their own community is one of the key lessons to learn from the story of Millard and Linda Fuller.

Since the Fullers were fired, the value changes at Habitat for Humanity International have been implemented swiftly in some circumstances, with others being incremental and still unfolding. With Millard out of the way, executive salaries were increased. To the great disappointment of President Carter and the Fullers, Habitat for Humanity International began the process of relocating its administrative staff out of Americus to high-end real estate property in Atlanta. The organization continued downplaying the history and Christian witness on its website and in its marketing materials. "Every house is a sermon of God's love" had been prominent on the sign in front of the Americus headquarters building. Repainted, it is now practically illegible.

The importance of the Christian witness and the grass-roots management philosophy were the core values that led to the decision by Millard and Linda to choose Koinonia Farm as the location for the first meeting of the board of directors of their new organization, The Fuller Center for Housing. The symbolism of this location is easily recognizable to those familiar with Habitat's history the Christian farming community in southwest Georgia was where Koinonia founders Clarence and Florence Jordan and Millard and Linda and a few friends gathered in 1968 to launch Partnership Housing, which evolved into Habitat for Humanity in 1976. Having rejected the pursuit of corporate success to save their marriage, Millard and Linda found a new way of life through Christian service at Koinonia and through launching Habitat for Humanity. It tears at Millard's and Linda's hearts to watch Habitat for Humanity International "go corporate." At many levels they have found that the return to Koinonia to launch a new organization in 2005 has been very liberating and rejuvenating. Millard genuinely wants to see Habitat succeed, and at age seventy-two he continues to tirelessly tour, give speeches, and raise money for local Habitat affiliates.

Habitat for Humanity was built on the storytelling and Christian witness of Clarence Jordan that affirmed Millard and Linda's decision to give up their fortune and reorder their lives to work at making decent shelter a matter of conscience and action. This storytelling inspired many of us to get involved in this effort. Pushing out the articulate and inspiring storyteller and divorcing the Habitat organization from its founders and historical roots, most agree, is hardly an effective way to advance the cause. I question whether volunteers will have the same passion for Habitat for Humanity when it's more like a corporation or a bank than a grass-roots movement. Who wants to donate to a bank? If the corporate brand becomes the message, it puffs its ego and says, "Look at what the brand has done." It has been my experience that brands don't inspire people to donate their time, money, and energy. People inspire people to do those things.

Part of what makes Millard so inspiring is his faith in people and in the absolute confidence that God will join the volunteers at the jobsite. It is easy to see why so many people of all ages and all backgrounds are eager to put the Theology of the Hammer into practice. Having God supply the building materials is an off-sheet accounting practice that is bound to frustrate a more conservative-minded business manager. Clarence and Millard called the experience of divine intervention "God coincidences." When asked about how much money a community needs to raise before starting a house, Millard says, "It would be fiscally irresponsible to start a project with less than one dollar in your account." He often challenges his audience to trust in God's blessings, "Anyone can build a house with money in the bank, but it takes faith to build a house with no money at all in the bank!"

We discovered this at our Almost Heaven Habitat affiliate in West Virginia. In 1989, members of our board of directors decided to visit a man named Billy Warner whose family was living in an old school bus. Though he had been permanently disabled in a coal car accident, he was trying to build a log home using trees on his property. A proud man, Billy refused to accept any help from us until I explained the Habitat model to him. The not-a-hand-out model Millard and Linda promoted was acceptable to Billy because he would be required to pay back over time, at zero interest, the cost of any building materials that went into the house. I was pleased and looking forward to seeing his application approved by the board. Not only was Billy's project approved, it was fast-tracked by the board: "Get that family out of the school bus and into their new house before the first snowfall!" It was June. We had two unfunded projects started and no one in our community knew how to build a log house! I didn't know what to tell the family. I was thrilled they were approved, but didn't want to get their hopes up too high that we could complete the work that year. I left the board meeting and went home worried about what to do.

Twenty minutes later the phone rang. "Hello, my name is Larry Kraus. I live in Aliquippa, Pennsylvania. You don't know me, but I heard your community hosts work camps. I'm a log home builder. Our church has raised some money. Do you have a good project for us to work on?"

God sent an angel to call me that day. Then God sent many more angels in blue jeans and work boots to our little mountain community. Billy Warner's family moved into their completed log home quite literally as the first flurries of the winter started to fall from the sky.

Multiply the Warners' story by thousands and it's easy to see why Habitat for Humanity has become the biggest and best-known nonprofit housing organization in the world today. This practical solution to eliminating poverty housing is best delivered through imperfect laborers like you and me and the thousands of volunteers who have already picked up hammers and trowels knowing that God will indeed join us at the worksite.

This message and challenge continue through the work of The Fuller Center for Housing. It is my hope and prayer that the message and vision of the founders of Habitat for Humanity have a longer shelf-life than any one particular organization, that they be as "bread cast upon the water," producing abundantly to the glory of God.

Joining the effort, no matter how large or small your contribution, will certainly be an important step in continuing the journey to plant the idea in every nation and every city on earth "that everybody should have as a minimum a simple, decent place to live, so that every child will be able to fulfill his or her highest potential."[1]

Wanting the whole crowd to have a good home. I believe that's what Jesus meant when he brought good news to the poor. And certainly it is what Clarence Jordan instilled in the minds and souls of Millard and Linda. "I was a stranger and you invited me in." That is the vision and blessing they would hope for all who read this moving account of their remarkable journey.

1 Jones, *NonProfit Times* names Millard Fuller "Executive of the Year." Retrieved from www.nptimes.com/Dec03/npt1.html.

# A Word from the Author

The author with Linda Fuller at the first All-Women blitz build,
Coachella Valley, Calif., 1996

This is the story of Millard and Linda Fuller, founders of
Habitat for Humanity (and later The Fuller Center), the
largest nonprofit housing ministry in the world. Theirs is a
journey that spans more than sixty years: from Millard's
upbringing and his serendipitous first meeting with Linda,
through the crisis that almost ended their marriage but provi-
dentially led them to give away their fortune; the early years
and humble beginnings of their housing ministry, to the years

of Habitat for Humanity's phenomenal growth and then becoming a world-wide movement, and the eventual heart-wrenching takeover that led to the Fullers' dismissal from the same ministry they had birthed and nurtured. It is also the story of their spectacular rebound to establish The Fuller Center for Housing and their ongoing mission to eradicate poverty housing from the Earth.

Their story is a big one, and a remarkable one. Remarkable because they've lived uncommon, and truly inspiring, lives. Rare is the person who meets the Fullers or hears of their amazing journey and isn't inspired by them. They've built homes for a million of the world's poor, amassed more than sixty honorary doctorates between them, and won hundreds of awards. In 1996, Millard was presented with the Presidential Medal of Freedom—the highest civilian honor a person can receive in the United States of America. Also, adjacent to the U.S. Treasury building in Washington, D.C., a large bronze emblem embedded in the sidewalk bears the Fullers' images and honors them on the prestigious Points of Light Extra Mile Pathway for their pioneering work in service. But for all their recognition, they are exceptionally humble, family-oriented people. They have raised four well-educated and happy children, forging strong family ties that remain even now that the Fuller children are married and have children of their own.

Someone once said that "spending an hour with Linda and Millard Fuller is like being at a Billy Graham crusade, a Norman Vincent Peale presentation, and a rock concert—all rolled into one." Being in the Fullers' presence is electrifying. They are tremendously charismatic. Both are tall, attractive, bright, quick-witted, and energetic. Yet, behind their dynamic energy is a deep sense of calm about them. And a great joy. You develop an inkling that they know something you don't— and it makes you want to know what they know. They are permanently smiling, as if they're itching to tell you what they're happy about. If you ask, they'll gladly tell you all about it.

Their experiences are vast; their stories are rich; their friends are many. At speaking events, they often receive standing ovations just by entering the room. Being around them or being a part of any project they're promoting is captivating. Perhaps it's because they're so fully committed to what they're doing—and to their unwavering faith.

From the day Millard Fuller was first inspired to start Habitat for Humanity, he has strived to show the world that making decent shelter available to the needy is a matter of conscience and action, and he ceaselessly challenges people to join in the movement. Over the years, he has traveled tirelessly across the country and around the world to rally people into realizing that every community has the wherewithal—the talent, resources, and tools—to eradicate poverty housing, if only they have the will. The results have been no less than phenomenal. By 2005, under Millard and Linda's leadership, some two hundred thousand homes had been built, and some one million more people had a decent place to call home. But Millard was never one to gloat about the greatness Habitat has achieved nor lose sight of Habitat's mission. When some were quick to proclaim that Habitat was a smashing success, Millard would smile and say, "Habitat has work in a hundred countries, but it still isn't in ninety other countries. We may have helped a million people find adequate shelter, but some billion more people are still in need."

Despite its great success—or perhaps because of it—by 2005, Habitat for Humanity had experienced a shift in its Christian underpinning and philosophy. Millard's ministry and movement mentality no longer appealed to an increasingly corporate-minded board of directors who saw Habitat as a business—an international conglomerate with a brand value of $1.8 billion. Millard's insistence on maintaining Habitat's status as a ministry and grass-roots movement stood in the way of the international board's vision for a new order. This divisiveness would cost the Fullers the organization that was such an integral part of their lives.

Until this writing, the complete story of the Fuller's experiences has remained untold. Through understanding the crisis that birthed Habitat, as well as what happened inside

Habitat's own house—the upheaval during their final months with Habitat—you will come away with a renewed admiration for the visionary founders of Habitat for Humanity and the heart with which their organization was born. As you come to understand Millard's steadfast devotion to an organization "founded under God's direction" and driven by his commitment to working "in partnership with God," you will come to appreciate how important the preservation of Habitat as a grass-roots movement was to Millard and why he appealed to others to get involved in the struggle to end poverty housing and homelessness.

It has been my privilege to tell their story of success, crisis, and changing direction; of renewing faith, finding purpose, and fulfilling destiny; of personal courage to stand for what matters. It is my hope that this book will give you a glimpse into the lives of two remarkable people who continue to exemplify the inspiring nobility of the human spirit. May your own life be enriched by their story.

—Bettie B. Youngs, Ph.D.

# — 1 —

# Young Millard Fuller

When Millard was six, in 1941, his father gave him a pig and told him to fatten it for market, telling him he could keep the money.

His father, an independent grocer just outside a little town called Lanett, Alabama—"serving the community of Coleville and surrounding area"—sold feed to his son on credit. He helped Millard with record-keeping, showing him how to keep accurate records. When the hog was the desired weight of two hundred pounds, they took him to market. True to what his father had told him, he gave young Millard the proceeds from the sale of the hog. The profit: $11.

His father then helped Millard select a male and a female pig so that he could raise, in Millard's words, a "bunch of pigs." Motivated to repeat the success he had achieved with the first hog, Millard was dutiful about keeping the fences mended and plenty of table scraps along with bagged feed for the pigs to eat. Millard continued raising and selling pigs until junior high school. "Almost every hog I raised brought more profit and I faithfully put the money into a savings account," Millard recalls. He decided to invest in rabbits. Over three years, he built up a population of over a hundred rabbits. He sold dressed rabbits to restaurants and in his father's store, and sold live baby rabbits to children for pets. "I especially did a booming business in selling young live rabbits around Easter time," Millard would report. Still, the rabbit business had its problems. Sometimes the rabbits would develop a severe case of ear sores. Huge scaly patches would develop in both ears and the condition would cause their ears to droop. "No one wanted a droopy-eared rabbit," Millard recalls. Ever the problem solver, he discovered that if he applied a 2% solution of salicylic acid to the sore ear, the cure was complete and amazingly fast. "Almost overnight all the droopy ears perked up and I had decent-looking rabbits again," he cheerfully explained.

"Another problem with raising rabbits," said Millard, "is that stray dogs wanted to kill them." One night they ripped open a pen of rabbits, devouring fourteen of them. Millard was broken-hearted—but his father was furious. The next day young Millard came home from school to discover his father sitting on the back porch, with a rifle across his lap. In front of him was a pile of dead dogs. "I've got fourteen dogs so far," he announced. "My father had been sitting there all day with that rifle, shooting every dog that came by," Millard lamented. Then he added with a grin, "Thankfully, none of the dogs belonged to neighbors! But, we didn't have any more problems with dogs eating my rabbits."

Ear sores and predatory dogs aside, it was a rattlesnake that convinced Millard to get out of the rabbit business for good and to look for a less problematic venture. One evening as Millard was filling a pail of water behind the family home to water the rabbits, he turned on the spigot and stepped back— onto a rattlesnake. The snake bit, Millard cried out in pain, and his stepmother came running to the rescue, as did a lather-faced neighbor in the midst of shaving, straight-razor still in his hand. Millard's foot was slashed open with the razor, and his foot thrust into a pail of kerosene to draw out the poison. "I bled so much it looked like an old-fashioned hog-killin'," Millard said, "but when my father took me to the hospital, the doctor took one look and told my father, 'You've done all that needs to be done; he'll be fine now.' That pretty much killed my desire to raise any more rabbits." Millard promptly sold his rabbits and used the proceeds to buy fifteen cows.

The young entrepreneur continued to expand his experience in different business ventures with the encouragement of his father. Millard helped his father in the grocery store, delivering orders of groceries on a bicycle until he got a driver's license. "I really hated the grocery business," Millard admits, "but I loved the time with my father. He spent a lot of time with me. My mother had died suddenly when I was three and he tried to be both dad and mom to me. When I was six, my father remarried a wonderful woman and I was blessed with two half-brothers. But it was from my father that I developed a real love for business and for making money, long before I even graduated from high school. He encouraged and motivated me. He taught me to be self-reliant and self-starting and to be thrifty and saving. 'A dollar saved is a dollar earned,' he'd say. A dollar was important to my father and he worked for his. But he was generous and would open his pocketbook for any person in need. He had as big a heart as any man I've ever known. And he loved children: Hundreds and hundreds of times I'd see him pick up a child in his store and hold the child over the cookie jar he always kept on the counter and let the child take all he could hold. Always he beamed as he watched the child walk out of the store with his two hands packed full of cookies. I just loved that about him. I truly loved him with all my heart."

Millard continued to keep books and turn a dollar into two, and then into three. In high school, he joined Junior Achievement whose mission was to teach teenagers about free enterprise. Millard learned to set up a miniature corporation and go into business. He learned to produce a product, sell stock, make a profit, and liquidate the company at the end of

Five-year-old Millard with father, Render Fuller, 1940

the school year. One summer he worked the "graveyard shift" (11:00 p.m. until 7:00 a.m.) at Lanett Bleachery & Dye Works and also caught minnows in country creeks. He dug a little pool beside his father's store to keep them alive and sold the minnows to fishermen for bait.

By the end of his senior year in high school, his mind set on growing a business one day, Millard set about putting himself through college. "I knew I wanted to go into business, and I wanted it to be big, profitable, and successful," Millard recalls. "I wanted to be rich, and knew I would be." The drive to be successful motivated Millard to test the waters of various occupations the following summer.

In Detroit, Michigan, he tried his hand in one of the automobile factories, choosing the job because of the opportunity to make good money and the experience of working in a large company. His Aunt Avis lived there with her husband and family. He got a job at the Gemmer Steering Gear Factory, operating a drill press on the second shift. In this position, a gear mechanism would be handed to him from the man on his right. Millard would place it under a drill press and pull the handle down. That would drill out a hole. Then Millard would pass the mechanism on to the man on his left for him to drill a hole somewhere else. "It definitely was not the most interesting job I've held," Millard said. "As a matter of fact, it was more boring than I could stand."

A few days later he found a second job, as a door-to-door salesman of ladies hosiery and undergarments for Real Silk Hosiery Company. He did his selling in the mornings and early afternoons and then went to work at Gemmer Steering Gear Factory. "I learned a whole lot about the psychology of selling from my employment with Real Silk Hosiery Company," Millard said, "but I wouldn't say I loved this job either."

Within weeks, Millard was weary of the job at the Gemmer Steering Gear Factory. He told his Aunt Avis good-bye and thumbed his way to the upper peninsula of Michigan, hoping to get a job working on the bridge that was being built across the Straits of Mackinac. That search was unsuccessful, so he headed to Flint, Michigan. There, he worked at a bakery, helping unload flour from a railroad car.

A second job in Flint was with a small company that built houses. It was vigorous outside work and Millard loved it. "I met a real character in this job," Millard says with a laugh. "The guy's name was Bob, a guy who was long on friendliness and talking, but short on brains and memory. Seems that Bob had a problem remembering people's names, so he called everyone 'Shorty.' When he needed someone to do something, he simply yelled out, 'Hey, Shorty . . . do this or that, bring this or take that.' So every worker had to look up when he yelled 'Shorty,' because no one knew to whom the guy was talking."

As is his nature, Millard decided to help the guy out by teaching Bob to remember his name. "Bob," he said, "my name is not 'Shorty,' it is 'Millard.' Here's how you can remember that: I'm sure you've heard of Willard Batteries. So when you want to call me, think of a battery. Then think of Willard. Last of all, turn the 'W' upside down and that makes it an 'M,' for Millard. Call me by that name, 'Millard.'" Bob agreed to do that, but even so, when he wanted to get Millard's attention, continued to call out, "Hey, Shorty!" Millard decided not to answer him and so Bob would quickly say, "I mean, Hey, You!" Determined to get Bob to think deeper, Millard took to ignoring Bob completely. Frustrated, Bob then yelled out, "Okay, I know your name has something to do with a battery. Is your name Eveready?" Peals of laughter erupted from the men around, but ole Bob, no matter how hard he tried, could never remember the name "Millard." "I did not succeed teaching Bob how to remember my name," Millard concluded, "but I sure tried!"

If ever Millard needed confirmation that he wanted to "make it big" in a company of his own, that summer provided it. After a few weeks of work in Chicago delivering furniture for the Goldblatt's Department Store, Millard bought a second-hand Plymouth automobile and drove south to Alabama, thus bringing to a close his "work-travel" summer!

## Auburn University

September was upon him, and Millard turned his attention to college. He decided upon Auburn University in Auburn, Alabama, not far from where he had been raised in Lanett. He approached his college education much the way he had his employment experiences during the summer. With his eyes set on the prize of success, he was an eager student, absorbing all he could that would help him achieve his goal of wealth and prosperity. He started working toward a degree in agricultural engineering, but decided that designing farm machinery was not for him, so switched majors and would eventually earn a degree in economics with a minor in mathematics and physics.

At Auburn, Millard was characteristically involved in campus activities. He wrote a column for the student newspaper *The Plainsman*. At age nineteen, he became the program director for Junior Achievement in nearby Opelika, Alabama, making him the youngest program director of that organization in the United States. Foreshadowing his ability to make a career out of being persuasive, Millard entered into a campus-wide debate with a fellow student, William Callahan, on the topic of "Resolved, that the states shall have the right to nullify a Federal Supreme Court decision." They argued on both sides of the issue and won first place in the competition.

When he discovered there was only one political party on campus, Millard organized a new political party, the War Eagle Party, and then ran for president of the student body, organizing such a successful campaign that he came within a few votes of winning. That experience, plus taking a political science course at Auburn, whetted his appetite for national politics. With the help of a professor, Millard qualified to run for alternate delegate to the Democratic National Convention, which in 1956 was held in Chicago. Having no money, Millard had to hitchhike to Chicago to attend the convention. On his first day at the convention, the man for whom he was alternate had to leave because of a family emergency. Millard became a full delegate. He met John Kennedy along with many other political figures—quite an amazing experience for a twenty-one-year-old!

But no experience could have been more indicative of his penchant for creating business opportunities than when he got involved in a profitable enterprise with Donald Moore, a distant cousin and fellow Auburn student. Taking note that the trees on campus were loaded down with mistletoe, Donald and Millard decided to pluck, package, and sell it. They got permission to cut it, then rigged up sharp hooks on long canes and started clipping the mistletoe. Their sales were good, but limited to what they could sell personally. Mistletoe would figure into Millard's future business ventures again with a new partner and would lead to the most financially successful time of his young life.

## An Eye on the Future

On June 4, 1957, Millard graduated from Auburn University. During his senior year, he had interviewed with several companies and had seriously considered accepting a job with Babcock and Wilcox Steam Boiler Company, Creole Petroleum (in Venezuela), or a bank in Mobile, Alabama. But nothing had clicked with him. Sitting in the Student Union building one day, a fellow student, Jim Gullage, came by and told him that he'd be taking the Law School Aptitude test at the University of Alabama in Tuscaloosa the next day, and would he like to go along? Millard agreed to go with him, reasoning that law school would be helpful in either a business or political career—or anything else for that matter. Six days after graduating with an economics degree from Auburn, Millard found himself enrolled in the University of Alabama Law School.

There Millard attended a meeting of the Young Democrats and met a student named Morris Dees, a sharply dressed, fit young man with curly blond hair. The two hit it off and afterward, Morris offered Millard a ride home. Their conversation turned to business. The two young men discovered they had much in common. Both had been reared in rural Alabama. Morris, too, had raised cattle. He was interested in politics and, as a schoolboy, had engaged in various enterprises. And he had long dreamed of developing some kind of business. Idea after idea, the two students discussed various projects and how they could be made profitable. On and on they talked. Before either of them realized it, it was 2:00 a.m. Agreeing that they would be partners, the young men shook hands and said good night—neither knowing they'd be inseparable for the next eight years, but believing that they'd help one another "get rich."

Millard, delegate to the Democratic
National Convention, Chicago, 1956

Get rich they did. After years of growing a successful business with Morris, young Millard Fuller would become a wealthy, experienced businessman with an eye ever on growth and the future. This singular drive, when refocused years later, would absorb his time, passion, and commitment, and would improve living conditions for millions of people. Millard would turn his business acumen toward the pursuit of a new goal: to eliminate poverty housing worldwide. As the founder of Habitat for Humanity and The Fuller Center for Housing, he would make it his goal to convince people in every country on Earth to join in the movement that makes decent shelter a matter of conscience and action. It would not be a goal he could accomplish alone—hundreds of thousands of volunteers would be needed in this quest to build and finance simple, decent homes for all the world's poor. He would need to rely on his extraordinary charisma to persuade people, his seemingly endless supply of energy and creativity, and his unusual ability to remain focused through the most egregious distractions. All of these skills so invaluable in leading a movement would be discovered, practiced, and honed over many years and under wildly diverse conditions—from the wealthy neighborhoods of Montgomery, Alabama, to the shacks of urban Zaire; from muddy construction sites to corporate boardrooms. And from inspirational leader to slandered figurehead.

But before Millard was ready to take on an international housing movement and all that came with it, he would go through a process of growth, deconstruction, and reconciliation that would make him the man he is today, a faithful servant working in partnership with God to change the lives of millions of people around the world, and thus, one of the most revered men of the twentieth century.

# — 2 —

# Fuller & Dees

Millard's new partner, Morris Dees, loved promoting and selling. He told Millard about a couple of his most recent ventures—selling rotten cotton burrs in residential areas for spreading around shrubbery and flowers and, another moneymaker, selling lists of names of college seniors to insurance companies. He told Millard about an idea he had of selling cypress knees—root appendages of cypress trees that abound in marshy areas of South Alabama and Florida—for decorative pieces in homes. Millard told Morris about his selling mistletoe at Auburn and of an idea to sell it in quantities through florist shops. They decided to officially begin their partnership with two ideas: selling mistletoe and cypress knees.

To sell those two items, they formed a company called Fuller & Dees Heart of Dixie Products on the grounds that this would be a good name for selling "Southern" products, but later they dropped "Heart of Dixie Products" because of racial problems in the South. Morris and Millard reasoned that "Heart of Dixie" would be a liability to a company with customers throughout the nation. Within the next few years, the two would have an assortment of ventures, and an assortment of company names, from Bama Cake Service to Home-Ec Press, from Outstanding Young Americans Inc. to Favorite Recipes Press Inc., from Off to College Inc. to Fuller & Dees Marketing Group. In one of their first ventures, they decided to organize a mailing to florists to test their idea of selling mistletoe. They sent postcards to about three hundred florists around the country advertising mistletoe for sale for forty cents a pound. Within two weeks, they had orders for over three thousand pounds.

Ecstatic, and with visions of piles of money in the bank, the two celebrated the notion that money problems were about to become a thing of the past—until they realized they didn't have three thousand pounds of mistletoe. When they went out to gather some, they suddenly realized that the mistletoe was much higher in the trees than they had remembered. Since they couldn't climb up and get it, they got rifles and tried to shoot it down, only to discover that those delicate clusters of leaves and berries were porous and the bullets went right through them. Then they got cane poles and tried to knock the mistletoe down, but it tore it all to pieces. Worse, Millard and Morris discovered to their dismay that a large bunch only weighed one pound. On weekends they traveled the state looking for three thousand pounds of mistletoe. They talked to wholesale florists and others who they thought might be able to help with the problem. No mistletoe. Their first venture a failure, they wrote their customers a letter of regret and apologized and that was the end of the mistletoe business. Luckily, they concluded, they were also hard at work on the cypress knees.

Cypress knees project upward above dark swamp water. Through a special process of removing the bark, the wood surface retains a natural, velvet-smooth finish. It's a complicated process, and Morris and Millard hired an old friend of Morris's to go into "Froggy Bottom," a swamp near Morris's home, to find and cut cypress knee roots. The two rented a building near campus and built a homemade furnace and boiler. They would boil the cypress knees so they could remove the bark, leaving a smooth surface. Millard's dad loaned the two business partners his truck so they could haul the cypress knees up to the campus on weekends. By October they were deep into the production of turning the wood into bases that could be used for lamps and other decorations.

All the while, Morris and Millard attended law school full time. Millard took classes in the morning and afternoon, and in the late afternoon briefed legal cases. After dinner the two would meet at the little building to boil and peel cypress knees. After this operation was complete, they leveled off the bottom with an electric saw they had rigged up so the knees would sit up. Finally, they had to be placed on racks out back of the building so the sun would dry them.

To their great sorrow, three very unfortunate things happened in their cypress knee business. First, they found out that an acid under the bark causes your skin to peel. "It became difficult to write with a sparse supply of skin on my hands," Millard would later admit. Then, Morris wrecked Millard's father's truck one day when making a turn and getting hit by a woman he decided to pass. "The left side of my father's truck took on a rugged appearance after that encounter," laughed Millard. "And my dad wasn't too happy about the new look of his truck, but luckily for us, he didn't ask us to have it fixed." The third—and most serious—problem had to do with dollars and cents: When Millard and Morris priced their knees so that they could realize a profit, they were too expensive for most people to buy.

With great disappointment—but not enough to stop them from moving on to the next deal—the two entrepreneurial spirits readied themselves for a new venture. Now broke and with law school tuition due, they knew they had to do something to bring in money, and fast. A florist they knew suggested they sell holly wreaths that had been imported from Italy to youth groups for fundraising. Millard and Morris decided to give it a try. Soon Millard and Morris contacted local Boy Scout leaders to tout their idea. They told them they could sell wreaths for $2.50 each, keeping 50 cents for each wreath sold, and return any wreaths they did not sell. Various Boy Scouts fanned out to sell wreaths. They wound up selling nearly five thousand of them. That netted $2,500 for the Scouts and $4,000 for Millard and Morris.

Simultaneously, Millard and Morris launched another venture—selling Christmas trees. They rented a couple of empty lots at a busy intersection in Tuscaloosa and made arrangements with a man in Mississippi to put his cedar trees on their lots on a consignment basis. Huge signs were made and painted with the words, "Buy your Christmas trees from university students." Millard and Morris went into the countryside to gather wild holly, pinecones, and smilax to adorn their Christmas tree lot and offered these items for sale as well. Strings of lights were put up all over the lot. They hired two men to run the lot while they attended classes by day and, in the evenings, sold Christmas trees themselves from their lot. Racks were built for spray-painting pinecones and other items, including some of the smaller trees. They sold hundreds and hundreds of trees. Even the pinecones they'd picked up from beneath nearby pine trees and then spray-painted flew off the shelves. They even sold off the cypress knees lamps, even though they didn't stand up for long. All wreaths leftover from the Boy Scouts sales were sold.

Millard and Morris were experiencing such success and having so much fun, they could hardly stand it. "I'll bet we could even sell those old rotten china berries," Millard said, pointing up to a tree on the lot. Laughing, they grabbed a chop-axe and whacked off a small limb. They dipped it into a bucket of silver paint and hung it from a wire at the entrance of the lot. The first customer who came calling the next day looked at the painted china berries and told them they were the most beautiful things she had ever seen. "But," she said, "they look like china berries." "No, ma'am," Morris replied, "These are oriental berries!" "Well," she replied, "I want them. How much are they?" "Twenty-five cents a bunch," Millard replied. Millard and Morris chopped every limb off that old china berry tree and sold all of them for $25.

Millard and Morris were also working on other new ventures, such as the publication of a student telephone directory at the University of Alabama. Again, most of the money was made from the sale of advertising to local merchants. Additional revenue was realized from the sale of copies of the directory to students at 25 cents a copy. On the first try, they published the directory, making well above the cost of the printing. But, the next year, they wanted to increase their net proceeds, so they concentrated on selling more of the directories so that even the advertising would be clear profit to them. To accomplish this, they recruited "the most beautiful girls" on campus to take orders from students coming through registration lines at the beginning of the fall term. And they doubled the price from 25 to 50 cents. "We knew that the beautiful sales ladies would virtually ensure sales to all the male students," Millard would say. Their strategy paid off. Sales doubled, and their income quadrupled.

Publishing the directory gave them access to information about each student, such as birth date and home address. When they noticed that approximately sixteen students on campus had a birthday every day, they quickly decided to form a birthday cake service, calling it the Bama Cake Service Inc. At the beginning of each school year, postcards for all parents were addressed and stacked in chronological order according to birth dates of the students. These cards were then systematically mailed every day for all students whose birthdays were two weeks away. The parents were advised of the birthday cake service and given various options of cakes they could order. To order, they just tore off the bottom portion of the card, checked the appropriate square to indicate the size of cake they wanted, and what flavor and frostings, then mailed it to Bama Cake Service along with a check. Each day, Millard and Morris picked up the mail at the post office and called orders in to a local bakery with whom they had made a deal to bake the cakes. In the late afternoon, Millard would pick up the cakes for delivery that day, and after his studies, either he or Morris, or sometimes both, would deliver the cakes. They cleared $2 on each cake.

Always with an eye toward saving and investing, the pair had been investing their earnings in real estate. First they secured a long-term lease on a dilapidated six-room house

Millard keynotes at the Junior Achievement
National Convention, Cleveland, Ohio, 1964

near campus. The young men cleaned it up, did a bit of remodeling on the inside, painted it, and subleased rooms to students. Millard moved into one of the front rooms to manage the house. They leased the backyard out to two house trailers. Next they purchased a large two-story house and an adjacent four-unit apartment at the other end of the block from their rooming house. They renovated the large house and converted it into four student apartments. Both buildings were painted, inside and out. New shrubbery was planted, and the yard cleaned up. Next came the purchase of a vacant lot situated between the apartment house and their rooming house. On this lot they placed an old army barracks building. A professional house mover was hired to move the building from its original location to the lot. It was cleaned up, renovated, painted, and converted into three student apartments. By graduation, Morris and Millard would own almost half a city block.

Millard's next business romp would do more than pad his wallet or further his business skills. He and Morris decided that another way to make money was to sell advertising on desk pads to merchants near college campuses at four colleges in Alabama and Georgia. On a large piece of blotter paper, the size of a desk top, they would draw blocks of various sizes. In the middle of the paper, football and basketball schedules of the college teams were listed. Also listed were telephone numbers of all dormitories, fraternities, and sororities. Merchants were then solicited to purchase the blocks of advertising space that covered the remainder of the blotter surface. After all advertising was sold, a printer was hired to print two thousand to three thousand copies for each college. The last step in the process was to distribute the desk pads during the first week of class in the fall to all dormitories and fraternity houses. Since Fuller & Dees made their money directly from the advertisers, the pads were given without cost to students.

One afternoon while out selling ads in the Tuscaloosa area, Millard stopped at a movie theater and asked to see the manager. It was to become one of the most important days in his life. While he waited, he chatted with the young woman in the ticket window, who introduced herself as Joan Caldwell. He thought she was friendly and attractive and was about to ask for her telephone number, when he was told the manager was ready to see him. Upon leaving, he went to talk to her again, but Joan had left for the day and the theater had a policy of not giving out phone numbers of employees. So Millard did the next best thing. He found the nearest pay phone and tried to locate her in the Tuscaloosa phone book. There was no Joan Caldwell, but he decided to call every Caldwell in the directory until he found her. He never reached Joan, but he did happen upon another Caldwell who caught his interest, a young woman who would soon captivate him as had no other.

# — 3 —

# The Beginning of a Love Story

Seventeen-year-old Linda Caldwell was home alone one evening when the phone rang.

"Is this Joan?" the caller asked.

"No, my name is Linda," she responded.

"Do you know Joan?"

"Joan who?"

"Joan Caldwell."

The caller said he had met a Joan Caldwell briefly, and was trying to reach her.

"I've got a phone directory right here," Linda said. "Let me see if I can find her number."

Her offer bought them just enough time to get to know one another. While Linda began flipping through the phone book, she learned the caller attended law school at the nearby University of Alabama. And it turned out that they shared common acquaintances at her family's church. Millard learned that Linda was a high school student who had worked for a pediatrician in the summer and aspired to become a surgeon. A more immediate concern for Linda, however, was being able to wear heels on a date. Nearly six feet tall, it could be tough for her to find a date who stood taller than she.

"How tall are you?" Linda asked.

"Six foot four," the caller said.

This got Linda's attention! Her mind raced—her father had friends who were lawyers and they seemed to have a nice lifestyle. She thought about the man on the other end of the line—a young lawyer-to-be who stood six foot four. She shut the phone book. They talked for another thirty minutes. Millard, too, forgot about Joan. And Linda forgot what her parents had taught her about talking to strangers. When he asked if he could take her out for a soda, she gave him directions to her house.

"My first impression of Millard was that he wasn't exactly knock-over-dead handsome," Linda recalls, "but not unattractive either. And as far as I could tell, he was ambitious. He told me he was involved in some sort of venture selling advertising to local businesses, and that he was in law school, so I knew he had to be bright. And, of course, his height was a definite plus: He was tall—really, really tall—and that greatly appealed to me, and fit very nice nicely into my wanting to wear high heels without towering over some poor short guy!"

Millard's retelling of their first meeting bubbles with romance.

"When Linda came to the door I was immediately struck by her beauty," he said. "She was tall and young and looked so pure, innocent, and radiant. I felt a great sensation of excitement and love immediately upon seeing this wonderful young woman. I totally forgot about Joan and never thought seriously about her again. Linda was very much on my mind and she was the focus of my attention and affections from that moment on."

By the time Linda's parents returned home that evening, Linda had quite a tale to tell of her date with the tall law school student. Her mother wasn't happy about her taking off with someone she didn't know, and she grew even more concerned when they found out he was six years her senior. Yet Linda had a strong feeling about the man. There was just one problem: She couldn't remember his name!

The next morning, from her bedroom, Linda could hear her father in the bathroom, listening to the radio as he shaved. Familiar with his routine, she knew he would dress and sit down at the dining room table for breakfast. Linda waited until he was eating before she asked him for a favor.

"Daddy, remember the law student I was telling you and Mother about last night who called me and how we went to the University Student Center to visit for a while?" she said. "Well, it's embarrassing, but he had such an unusual name that I can't remember what it was. He said that he would come to the store this afternoon to talk to you about buying an ad for something or another. Could you please make sure you write down his name for me?"

"I guess so," Mr. Caldwell responded, "but your mother and I think he is much too old for you to date so don't be getting any ideas that you're going to."

Linda endured an agonizing wait for her father to come home from work. Her dad sensed her anxiety when he walked into the house.

"His name is Millard . . . Millard Fuller," her father said.

"Oh," Linda said, trying to sound nonchalant. "What kind of name is that . . . who ever heard of Millard? I have never heard of anyone named Millard, but it is an interesting and really nice name, isn't it?"

Linda would later learn that her future husband's parents named him after Millard Dixie Howell, a running back who helped the University of Alabama win the 1935 Rose Bowl game against Stanford. Baby boy Fuller was born three days later, and the name Millard seemed, as his father had said, "like a real winning name."

After their first date, Linda left to attend a youth camp in North Carolina, so the two didn't see each other for a couple of weeks. When she returned home, Millard wasted no time in arranging to see her again; he would later recall knowing early on that he had met the love of his life. Still, it was fall and school was starting for both, and for Linda the high school senior, dates were limited to once a week—usually a movie on a Saturday night. For Millard, the law student and businessman, time and money for "courting" were scarce.

"Dating was a rather complicated thing to pull off," Millard recalls.

"He was so busy," Linda remembers, "that finding the time to be together as much as we wanted to be was very difficult. But we did have a formal date a week, and we talked a lot at night by phone. He'd bring work projects over and I'd help with those. And we went to church Sunday evenings . . . where we sat in the back pew and passed notes between us. It was quite fun. We had to be creative—and we were!"

Time and a lack of money weren't the only things that complicated dating. "Millard's jalopy of a truck was a challenge in and of itself," Linda would say, as she discovered one evening when Millard arrived to pick her up in an old panel truck with no passenger seat—just an apple crate on which to sit. He explained the vehicle he was driving belonged to him and his business partner. "It was an ugly old thing, but other than that it wasn't too bad until Millard made a turn," Linda lamented. "I'd have to grab on to him to make sure I didn't slide off the box." As uncomfortable as his truck was to ride in, his table manners proved more difficult to deal with—as she discovered when he joined her family for an evening meal. "I'd describe them as 'a little rough,'" she said. "I had been brought up so strictly, chastised for the slightest error in etiquette. I noticed right off that his manners were quite improper, and that had to change." Linda went to the library, checked out a book on manners, and gave him lessons. "He wasn't necessarily a quick study. I suppose that I was his biggest distraction," she'd later report, "but eventually he improved." Millard says he "was more interested in holding her rather than learning the proper way to hold a fork," but agreed to the lessons because it meant spending time with Linda.

Their love grew quickly.

Reflecting back on their courtship, Linda smiled and said, "Despite his poor manners and even poorer mode of transportation, he was simply the most interesting, energetic, intelligent person I had ever met. He was one exciting man!"

# — 4 —

# Building a Personal Fortune

Knowing that Linda's parents worried about their seventeen-year-old daughter dating a twenty-three-year-old man, Millard, in his characteristically persuasive style, confronted the issue head-on. He told her parents that the age difference between them was not really that much and would only narrow as they aged. In time, her parents grew more comfortable with Millard, listening to his stories over dinner at the Caldwell home. Linda's mother, Wilma, enjoyed hearing her future son-in-law talk about his involvement at church as a boy in Lanett, Alabama. Her father, Paul, talked with Millard about the military. Millard was in the Reserve Officer Training Corps (ROTC) program, while Paul had served in the army during World War II, assigned to a procurement office in Philadelphia, and then spent many years as a Reserve Officer.

With his usual assurance, Millard informed Linda one day that they were going to get married. No getting down on his knee. No asking for her hand in marriage. True to form, he simply informed her of what he viewed as a foregone conclusion. Yet Linda did not say yes right away. When she did, Millard surprised her with a pair of high-heeled white linen shoes with rhinestone clips. They fit Linda perfectly—the result of Millard discreetly asking his girlfriend's mother what shoe size Linda wore. It was the perfect gift for a young woman who found Millard's height so attractive. He followed up that gift with a diamond ring after Linda graduated from high school.

On August 30, 1959, one of the hottest days of the year in Alabama, the strangers on the phone became husband and wife at Alberta Baptist Church. The wedding was a simple affair all around. A classmate of Linda's played the organ. A friend of Linda's cousin who lived in Birmingham sang "The Lord's Prayer." Linda arranged a special front pew adorned with pink ribbons for the ten-year-old girls she had been teaching in Bible class. Millard's stepmother had prepared, in their words, "a fine turkey and dressing lunch" for family members following morning worship services that day. After a reception and wedding cake in the fellowship hall of the church, Millard and Linda made a quick getaway to Birmingham for a three-day honeymoon—only three days because cash was short and classes were starting at

Linda and Millard Fuller's wedding, 1959

the university, where they had had their first date, first soda, and first glimpse of life together.

After the honeymoon, Linda and Millard settled into a two-room apartment that Millard and his partner Morris had been renting to students. Both Millard and Linda were students at the University of Alabama in Tuscaloosa—Millard had one semester of law school to complete, and Linda was an undergraduate freshman. The connection Linda felt with Millard changed her mind about medical school. Rather, she chose a double major in sociology and psychology but also took an elective in the home economics department with the goal of becoming a better cook. Before marrying, she had baked cakes, cookies, and cornbread, but she wanted to diversify her culinary skills. "Marriage taught me that baking and preparing meals are different matters entirely," she would tell a friend. "And I soon realized that I didn't have a handle on meat and potato fare."

Within a couple of months, the first-year student began experiencing a "terrible queasiness" in chemistry lab. Linda soon discovered she was pregnant. "It would have been nice to have my college behind me before starting a family," she says, "but there I was, expecting a baby in addition to everything else." She took it in stride, but her parents were not happy at all. Linda had promised them that if she married she would still complete her education—and Millard had promised to pay for it.

Millard and Morris were a little anxious, too, but for a different reason. A baby on the way, they hoped, wouldn't interfere with their ambitious business plan. Morris still had a year of law school to complete, with a wife and two young, rambunctious sons. After Millard finished law school, he had to fulfill his ROTC obligation. That meant six months of active duty at Fort Sill, Oklahoma. The two men planned to open a law practice together after this. In the meantime, they would continue with their mail order business, then liquidate their assets and use the proceeds to set themselves up in a law practice as partners.

Millard, University of Alabama
Law School graduate, 1960

Millard finished law school in January 1960 and spent six months in the army. Linda went to Oklahoma with him in a car loaded down with a typewriter, sewing machine, clothes, and enough fruit and canned goods to make the journey. They rented a tiny three-room house in Lawton, Oklahoma, near the army base. "There is no grass in the front yard, only a large concrete slab," Linda would write her parents. She learned soon enough that the concrete slab covered a storm cellar—a necessity in a place ravaged by tornadoes. While awaiting motherhood, Linda took a six-week course in Russian and busied herself reading up on how to care for a newborn. And, having been pronounced a "crackerjack" typist by the founders of Fuller & Dees, Linda prepared thousands of envelopes for a nation-wide sale of holly wreaths to YMCAs.

As for Millard, he spent his first three months on the base in artillery school. He was then transferred to the Judge Advocate section, where he spent the remainder of his tour as a legal assistance officer. At night, Millard taught business law at nearby Cameron Junior College.

On the 4th of July, 1960, seven weeks before their first anniversary, Linda gave birth to eight-pound Christopher Dean Fuller at the military base hospital. Linda was nineteen,

Millard twenty-five. One month later, Millard's term of active duty ended. He made plans to set up his law practice with his friend and recent law school graduate, Morris Dees.

As planned, Morris had liquidated many of their joint enterprises, such as Bama Birthday Cake Service, student telephone directories, desk pads, and student apartment properties, but selling holly wreaths and doormats by mail for fundraising was still going strong. This would be the only source of livelihood for both families until the new attorneys could get their practice established. They made $50,000 each from selling parts of their college-era businesses. Millard and Morris joked about the wisdom of graduating and laughed about the fact that maybe they should sign up for more courses since they had succeeded so well in business as students!

But moving on was a part of the plan. They hoped to set up a law practice in Montgomery, the cradle of the Confederacy and capital of Alabama. Montgomery seemed a good choice since it was a large city and had good mail and transportation connections. And Morris had grown up just a few miles outside Montgomery and had great contacts in the city. Both men had an interest in politics, and Montgomery was the political center of the state. Should either decide to run for office, Montgomery seemed the best and most logical place to start.

## The Law Practice

Millard found practicing law stimulating and exciting. He tried and won his first case in circuit court. Morris won his first case, too. "We worked diligently on every case that came to us, no matter how small or seemingly insignificant," Millard recalls. "We even saved a man's life one day." It seems a man had come into the office, distraught because his wife had initiated divorce proceedings. "I'm going to leave and shoot myself," he had said. "You don't have to leave to do that," Morris replied. "I have a gun right here in my desk that you can use." Morris handed the man a .38 pistol. It was customary

Morris Dees, right, and Millard with their products, which included holly wreaths, cookbooks, and tractor cushions, 1963

for many people in those days to keep a pistol in their office, and Morris did. Their client pushed back his chair, stood up, and closed his eyes. He put the gun to his head and pulled the trigger. Click. The gun was empty. The man dropped in the chair and was silent for some time before extending his hand to Morris and saying, "Thank you. Thank you very much. Thank you for saving my life." The man signed the divorce papers and left.

Even though the two mavericks were steadily gaining a reputation as good attorneys, their business enterprises made more money than the law practice, but also demanded more and more time. Less than two years after opening the law practice, they took down their law shingle to focus entirely on business.

## The Perfect Fit: Tractor Cushions and Cookbooks

Business boomed as Millard and Morris devoted themselves full-time to selling holly wreaths and doormats that groups could resell in fundraising campaigns. In early October, Millard met Hilliard Aranov, president of Fabrics Inc., located in Montgomery. He and Millard started talking about selling rag dolls, which Hilliard manufactured, and ended up talking about tractor cushions. Aranov told Millard that farmers wanted padding on the metal seats. That sounded logical. Millard thought about it for a few minutes, even outlining in his mind how he could sell tractor cushions to farmers through the hundreds of club chapters in high schools around the country. He strode back to the office and walked into Morris's office.

"Tractor cushions," he said. "Future Farmers of America."

Morris shot up out of his desk and banged a closed fist against his palm. "It'll work!" Morris announced. "It's a winner of an idea!"

"That's all it took," Millard says. "My saying just those few words and Morris and I agreed on a new product. That's how well the two of us worked together."

While optimistic that the tractor cushion idea would catch on, the now-seasoned businessmen wanted hard proof. They mailed an offer to select Future Farmers of America chapters throughout the country. Orders came in even better than expected. By December, Fuller & Dees was mapping plans for a nationwide promotion to all Future Farmers of America chapters throughout the United States.

The business partners contacted the Ford Motor Company and arranged to buy four Ford tractors at cost to offer as top prizes in a nationwide tractor cushion sales contest. In January, Fuller & Dees Inc. shipped ten thousand cushions to the Future Farmers of America program advisors, complete with a sales and promotion package outlining the sales contest.

Within two weeks, Millard and Morris's office was flooded with orders coming in from all over the United States. On February 18, 1961, Millard recorded in his diary, "Business is booming. As of today we have 1,000 customers. I am convinced we are going to make at least $50,000 and we may well make $75,000." On March 12 he would record, "Last month, almost 22,000 cushions have been shipped by Fabrics Inc. and our total orders including those not yet shipped are nearly 38,000."

So many orders came pouring in that Fuller & Dees had to turn down three hundred customers because Hilliard Aranov couldn't meet the demand even after adding round-the-clock shifts. Unable to meet production quotas wasn't the only crisis Millard and Morris faced. Hilliard had extended to Millard and Morris a $20,000 credit line, which was to be paid at such time when invoices would be paid by the Future Farmers of America organizations. But the maximum credit he would extend was $20,000. Though orders for tractor cushions continued to pour in to Fuller & Dees Inc., payments didn't. This meant that money was due Hilliard, but Fuller & Dees Inc. didn't have the resources to keep the credit paid down to the $20,000 limit set by Hilliard. Millard and Morris asked Hilliard to increase their credit line; after all, payment from the Future Farmers of America chapters would be forthcoming. It was just a matter of time. But Hilliard didn't budge. He didn't have extra money on hand that it would take to purchase needed materials to manufacture the additional tractor cushions. When Hilliard threatened to withhold further shipment to Fuller & Dees Inc.'s customers unless they paid down the credit line to the $20,000 balance, Millard and Morris were between a rock and a hard place—especially when Hilliard called a meeting forcing the issue.

When Millard and Morris arrived at Hilliard's office for the meeting, they were surprised to be greeted by a "committee"—who promptly offered them a deal. The "committee" would keep Hilliard's coffers paid down to the $20,000 credit limit but, in return, wanted to own 50 percent of Millard and Morris's tractor cushion business.

Both Millard and Morris said no. Seeing that their resolve was strong, and knowing business was in fact booming, Hilliard agreed to up their credit line to $60,000. Millard and Morris smiled, shook hands without so much as a word to the "committee," and walked out.

But the $60,000 credit line did not solve their problem: Fuller & Dees Inc. still couldn't move forward. Money, big money, was still needed—and it was up to Millard and Morris to raise it.

The men started by visiting their local banks, but none would loan them the needed money, saying Fuller & Dees had failed to get signed contracts from their customers promising they'd pay—so the risk was too great for the banks to chance loaning the money. Millard and Morris then headed to Tuscaloosa to the First National Bank where they had banked while running their many businesses while in college a few years prior. First National Bank offered a $25,000 loan, which was still not enough. They took the loan and continued looking. Millard went to his dad, who co-signed a note at the Alabama National Bank in Opelika, borrowing $10,000. An aunt of Millard's loaned $500, and Morris's father signed a note for the rest. "By the skin of our teeth we came through the crisis," Millard would write. "It was one happy day when all those loans were paid off."

So with loans in hand, Fuller & Dees carried on.

When the season of sales had ended, Millard and Morris had managed to bring in orders for a hundred thousand cushions, but even by working around the clock, seven days a week, Hilliard could only produce 65,000. Even after having to refuse one-third of their customers, Fuller & Dees reaped a $75,000 profit—a success they would both describe as "beyond our wildest dreams." "The Golden Boys," as they were named by the Montgomery establishment crowd, figured it would take around twenty train cars to hold all the tractor cushions they sold.

Before that gigantic success, Fuller & Dees Inc. operated out of three small rooms—one for Millard, one for Morris, and one for a receptionist, the company's only other employee. As business boomed, Millard and Morris added another desk, and then another and another. When the reception area was full, they crammed more desks and cubicles into their own offices. Soon they hired a second shift of employees to relieve the first shift. Within months, they added a third shift to relieve the second shift. "I was working day and night," Millard would later say, "and still I couldn't keep up with everything going on." When the business outgrew this arrangement, the partners bought a two-story building in downtown Montgomery, remodeled it, and moved in. In less than six months, they had outgrown it as well, even though they had already added about ten thousand feet to accommodate an ever-growing workforce.

In the summer of 1961 Fuller & Dees Inc. was busy planning for a host of new promotions they would feature for the fall. Some projects succeeded, others didn't do well. None produced sales that matched the tractor cushions.

Sitting in their offices one day, Morris picked up the recent copy of *Life* magazine and, pointing to a picture of a man with a huge stack of mail on the floor in front of him, asked his business partner, "How can we get mail pouring in here like that?" The two men agreed that having a "mile-high pile" of orders would be a good thing, and set a goal to achieve it. "We didn't want hundreds of orders," Millard said. "We wanted thousands and thousands of orders coming in our doors."

Both discussed how they could make such a thing happen. Surely the tractor cushion deal had been the direct result of having done something right . . . but what was that something?

The businessmen surmised that the tractor cushion deal had been a perfect fit between the fundraising organization and the product it sold. In other words, an organization couldn't just sell any and all products. It had to be the right product.

A week passed. Then Morris walked into Millard's office one day.

"Cookbooks," he said. "Future Homemakers of America."

Now it was Millard's turn to slap his fist against his palm and gleefully announce, "That's it! It's a winner of an idea!"

Fuller & Dees Inc. got to work. They asked home economics teachers nationwide to send in their favorite meat recipe, promising them a free cookbook in return. In January 1962, they published their first cookbook, *Favorite Recipes of American Home Economics Teachers—Meats*. Within a week, 1,000 cookbooks were sold. On the second day of the second week, 1,800 were sold, and the third day, 2,200 books sold. The orders continued pouring in.

The sales were so phenomenal that Fuller & Dees Inc. became the largest publisher of cookbooks in the country. The first edition featured meats. Next came desserts. Then volumes with recipes for salads, breads, and casseroles—five cookbooks in all. Future Homemakers of America clubs made a dollar on each book they sold, and they sold them by the tens and hundreds of thousands, which meant great return for Future Homemakers of America and even greater return for Fuller & Dees. After that, Fuller & Dees published cookbooks for other national civic clubs and organizations such as Pilot Club, Lions Club, and organizations for the wives of military officers and noncommissioned officers.

Millard and Morris identified other civic organizations and targeted publications to them. They created a directory of high school coaches, listing all coaches in the United States and indicating the sports they coached. The books were mailed free to all high schools in the country. Fuller & Dees made money by selling ads in the directories to sporting good manufacturers.

A Junior Achievement yearbook was so successful that it warranted its own division within the company. Certain sections of the book were standardized for all yearbooks sold throughout the country, with other sections customized for a specific local group. Fuller & Dees supplied kits for putting together the yearbooks, having asked local Junior Achievement organizations to supply material specific to their school or region. In the spring of 1963, toothbrushes were added to fundraising efforts, first selling some eighty thousand a month, then averaging a million a year. By late 1963, the goal created from the picture in *Life* magazine of a mountain of daily mail pouring into their office had been realized. Fuller & Dees was now sending a panel truck to the post office each day to pick up the mail.

Once again, they'd outgrown their office building with a night shift of full-time employees, not counting the staff that worked from home. They set their sights on a larger building with several thousand square feet all on one level on the outskirts of town, an office building that had once been the headquarters for Atlantic National Life Insurance Company. The property cost $100,000. Fuller & Dees wrote a check for the full amount. With a great deal of pride, Millard and Morris watched as the ATLANTIC NATIONAL LIFE INSURANCE COMPANY lettering was removed and replaced with FULLER & DEES. "For the first few days when I entered the building and left it, I couldn't help but look up at it and smile," Millard recalls. "It was pretty amazing."

Over the next couple of years as the company continued to grow by leaps and bounds, the back of the new building was knocked out and several thousand square feet of space added. Then, behind that expanded space, a separate building was erected for a printing press and other things that were needed for the ever-growing company.

The company was by then so busy that Millard and Morris hardly had time to catch their breath. Twenty-two new cookbooks were in the works and a hundred thousand sample toothbrushes were being readied to mail to prospective customers.

Advertising for the second edition of the directory of high school coaches had to be sold. A new guidance publication for high school students about how to enter college was planned. The magazine, called *Off to College*, would include articles such as "Why Freshmen Fail," "How to Study," "Should I Join a Sorority or Fraternity?" and "Campus Etiquette." It would give advice on clothing and accessories to take along to college and more. More than a million *Off to College* magazines were to be distributed free to a million-plus high school seniors planning to enter college.

Sales in 1963 totaled more than $1 million. This was the milestone they had wanted. In January 1964 Millard wrote in his diary, "Sales for the year exceeded one million dollars. Now, we want ten million! My prediction is that we'll make it within a year. 1964 should be a banner year in many respects."

## The Best Things Money Could Buy

As their company grew, so did their personal affluence. In 1960, Millard owned one old panel truck with an apple crate seat (the infamous truck he had also used while courting Linda). Now he and Morris could hardly list all they owned. In 1964 Millard and Morris each bought a new Lincoln Continental, complete with all the luxury options—elegant gray for Millard and glossy black for Morris. They paid for the cars in cash. Millard and Linda had moved from a two-room student apartment to a four-bedroom house in Montgomery, which they remodeled and filled with expensive drapes and furniture.

After settling into their new home in an elite neighborhood, Linda found a baby sitter and worked several hours a day at the office with Millard and Morris. By mid-1961, when son Chris was a year old, Linda returned to college. She hired a full-time baby sitter/cook/housekeeper and enrolled in Huntingdon College, three blocks from their home. At first she enrolled as a part-time student. Then, realizing it was going to take years to finish school at that pace, she decided to step up to a full load.

The only time she took a break was when she became pregnant with their second child. Even then, she dropped

out only one semester, and that, not entirely—she advanced
her studies still by taking a required English course by correspondence from the University of Alabama. When their
daughter, Kimberly, was three months old, Linda returned to
classes at Huntingdon, where she made the dean's list every
semester. But her devotion to her studies could not mask the
reality that her relationship with her husband was not what
she had hoped it would be.

While at first Linda told herself her husband was busy
earning the money required to maintain their lifestyle, she
was also growing resentful and feeling abandoned. Still, she
did feel lucky, privileged: She had a home with the finest of
furnishings. Millard set up a separate bank account in her
name, which he maintained at a minimum balance of $1,000.
She drove to school in a new Lincoln Continental—a big step
up from Millard's panel truck. She had the best of everything
money could buy. And lots of it: The double closet in their
bedroom became too small to accommodate her acquisitions.
Millard agreed to move his clothes to an adjoining room.

She had everything, and her family was financially secure.
They had purchased two thousand acres of farmland in the
country and stocked it with horses and cattle. They acquired a
second home on a nearby lake and bought two speedboats—
one for themselves and one for visitors. Then, when the thirteen-
room house didn't seem nice enough, they purchased a
twenty-acre lot in a prime part of Montgomery for their
"dream" house. They hired an architect to draw up plans for
the mansion. Millard thought this would especially make
Linda happy because she would soon finish requirements for
a college degree and if she didn't need to have a job or earn
money, then perhaps this house project would fulfill her and
give her something to do. They decided to retain the full-time
housekeeper.

Still, for all the conveniences and freedoms that wealth
afforded, rather than allowing them more time together, they
had less time together.

With Linda in school and Millard working fourteen to sixteen hours a day, they had little time for each other except a hurried dinner in the evenings. Often Morris ate with them since he lived twelve miles out in the country and it took too long for him to go home and come back. They did business brainstorming during meals as Linda and the children sat and listened. Linda confessed, "After they returned to the office, I felt so empty. Sometimes I loaded up the kids and went to a shopping mall just for something to do and to keep from getting depressed."

She did tell Millard how she felt. In fact, Linda begged him to spend more time with the family. Millard promised he would, and did for a while, but it wasn't long before he was back to eighteen-hour days at his office.

## Vintage Fuller . . .
### We're All Ignorant . . . Just on Different Subjects

Will Rogers, who is one of my heroes, has often said many things worth quoting. He said on one occasion, "Everybody's ignorant, just on different subjects." When I was young, I wanted to be a very successful person, and I defined that by being rich. That was my goal. And by age twenty-nine, I was rich. Very, very rich. You know in the United States, we define success and worth in terms of how many possessions you have. You've heard the question, "How much is Mr. So-and-So worth? Oh, I heard he's worth $1 million or he's worth $500 million." Or, "Have you heard about Mrs. Goldrocks? Oh, she's very wealthy. She's worth $14 million." But the people who have a lot of money may not be worth very much at all in terms of the contributions they make to the world. One of the most worthless persons I ever knew in my life had a lot of money. In fact, he inherited a bunch of money and lived in my town of Montgomery, Alabama. His favorite activity was driving people around town in his car, poking them on the knee and saying, "You see those houses over there? I own them all. You see that building there? That's mine." And he would go a little farther, and he would poke you on the knee again and say, "See all the land over there? I own it from this point all the way down to that point." And that's all he ever did. I never knew him to do anything else except drive people around, poke them on the knee, and tell them what he owned. If you ask how much he was worth, well he was worth a lot of money. But he wasn't worth a whole lot as far as I could see in terms of doing anybody any particular good. He was smart about acquiring money, but ignorant in using it to help alleviate the pitiful conditions of others.

—Millard Fuller

# — 5 —

# An Affair Changes Lives

Millard's drive to become financially successful on a breakneck timetable would take a toll on the family and gut his marriage. This surprised him. Didn't providing his family with all the things money could buy—a big house in a safe neighborhood with plans being drawn up for an even nicer one, a farm with pasture for ten saddle horses and hundreds of cattle, a couple of cars, and an extremely comfortable lifestyle—make him a good provider, and thus a good husband and father?

He wasn't completely oblivious to the problems in his relationship. Linda had begged him to spend more time with the family and even came to his office at one point to announce that the marriage was faltering. She complained that he left for work early in the morning and didn't return until late at night. They had never taken a family vacation. But Millard just figured the marital problems would eventually resolve themselves. They didn't—the estrangement from his wife and children only continued to grow.

Often lonely and feeling adrift, Linda sought solace in the attention and affections of another man. It was clearly against her Christian upbringing, and the affair filled her with shame, but she didn't know how to confess to Millard. She didn't, however, mince any words one evening when it seemed she had reached rock bottom.

Linda walked into their bedroom and saw Millard sitting on the side of the bed, preparing to retire for the night. She asked, "How do you know you love me?"

"I just love you," Millard replied. "I love everything about you."

Linda looked at him. "I'm going away for a while," she said. "I don't know if we've got a future together." She told her husband she was going to New York to talk with Dr. Lawrence Durgin, pastor of the Broadway United Church of Christ. She and Millard had attended this church a few years earlier when they had lived briefly in New York. Millard was stunned. He understood the marriage was on shaky ground, but he didn't realize how unhappy his wife had become.

After Linda left, Millard found himself suddenly responsible for the full-time care of their children, ages three and five. As he was tucking his son into bed one night, Chris looked up and said, "Daddy, it's great to have you home!" Millard never realized until then just how much the children had missed him—nor what he had been missing by not being more involved in their day-to-day care. Each night, after the children were in bed, Millard would head to his bedroom alone and cry. His eyes would wander to a document posted over their bed, an agreement he and Linda had created a week before their wedding in which they'd vowed to "outlove" each other and never keep secrets from one another.

During these quiet moments alone, in his mind Millard would recall the simpler times when they had made this promise. Why had such an important declaration, a plan the two had devised to preserve their union, been deserted? As Millard would later write: "When I first met Linda that evening in Tuscaloosa, I was absolutely captivated. I was sure

*Whereas, Linda and Millard have come to know and to love each other in a very special way, and whereas, we have since the thirtieth day of August A.D. nineteen hundred and fifty-nine openly declared our love to each other, to God, and to our fellowmen by our marriage vows, and whereas, we sincerely want to continue our love for each other so long as we both shall live,*

*Therefore, be it resolved that:*

*We shall never speak cross or harsh words to each other,*

*We shall never keep secrets from each other,*

*We shall never tell untruths – even jokingly – to each other,*

*We shall earnestly seek to minimize disagreements and misunderstandings,*

*We shall always try to give more love than the other,*

*We, together, shall always keep a right relationship with our creator,*

*We, in all these things, shall continue to work every day, every hour toward a greater love and devotion for each other.*

*August 30, 1959*

Linda Fuller       Millard Fuller

from the first day I saw her that this was the girl I wanted to marry. And our wedding on August 30, 1959, was the happiest occasion of my life."

But now she was gone, and no pain was ever greater. "The week I was without Linda was the loneliest, most agonizing time of my life," Millard would later say. "I went to work but couldn't keep my mind off my tottering marriage. And I was ashamed that I'd become a virtual stranger in my own home. I went to work before the kids got up and didn't come home until well after they'd gone asleep. And now Linda was off in New York trying to figure out how to leave me for good, and I was in Montgomery feeling miserable and desperate. I begged her to see me so we could talk things out."

But Linda said, "Not yet."

Millard thought it would make him feel better just to be a little closer. Having never been to Niagara Falls, he thought it would achieve his goal and be as good an excuse as any to leave town. So he took the children to stay with their grandparents and arranged for a company pilot to rent a plane. Off they went, flying north. As they neared their destination, the airplane ran into a bank of dark clouds. The altimeter failed and ice began to accumulate on the wings. The pilot adjusted this dial and that, working feverishly to deliver them from the storm. The radio squawked with news of a DC-7 zooming by, much too close for comfort. The plane eventually landed— but not before Millard got a dose of hair-raising fear that cast into fresh perspective all that was at stake in his marriage with Linda. More insight was to come.

That night, in his hotel room on the Canadian side of Niagara Falls, Millard flicked on the television and happened upon a movie about a woman who worked in China as a missionary. She fell in love with a soldier in the Chinese army, but the officer knew that marrying the missionary would ruin his career. He consulted an elder—a goateed, wrinkled old man—who gave him advice that would resonate with an anxious Millard. "A planned life can only be endured," he said. It seemed as if the sage were speaking directly to Millard.

"I sincerely cannot remember what was said after those words were spoken because they put my mind in a whirl," Millard said. "It was as if those words leaped out of that TV, as if God had spoken them directly to me. This young officer was living a planned life with each stage of it—from youth until retirement—mapped out and the old man told him such a life could only be endured. I was living the same kind of life. My overriding goal was to keep building up the company to make more and more money. The final stage of my planned life was to be buried in the rich part of the Montgomery cemetery. I realized if I kept on living the way I was, that would pretty much describe the way things would be."

The next afternoon, Linda agreed to see him. Millard

neared New York—and a meeting with his wife that would dictate whether their relationship would survive. Millard first saw her across the lobby of the Wellington Hotel, looking, he recalls, more beautiful than when he first caught sight of her seven years earlier. She smiled. He did, too. They embraced, and Linda told Millard she had decided she wanted to make their marriage work. They were planning to see Dr. Durgin together the next morning, but Linda suggested they see a movie that night. They headed toward Radio City Music Hall to watch a film called *Never Too Late*—a title that struck Millard as symbolic of what seemed a last-ditch effort to preserve their marriage. Once again, it seemed as if God were speaking to him, this time through the title of the movie. During intermission, they got something to drink and sat in a lounge area. Linda began to cry. When Millard touched her shoulder, her sobs magnified. "What's the matter?" he asked. She answered by crying even louder. Everything he said or did brought on the same results—more crying. They agreed to leave and go for a walk. Strolling along Fifth Avenue, crying and talking along the way, they decided to rest on the steps of St. Patrick's Cathedral. Linda knew the only way their relationship could ever have a new beginning was if she was honest with her husband about everything. Finally, the truth came tumbling out.

Sobbing, she told Millard that even though they were married, she felt alone and lonely. She explained that having all the things that money could buy was more than she could ever have dreamed, but all of that stuff wasn't making her truly happy. She told him how disappointed she was that he didn't want to spend more time with her and the children. And then, after a grueling moment of silence, she told him about her affair. She did this with fear and trembling, as she fully anticipated that he would just walk away forever. Instead, to her great relief, he embraced her. Consumed by their grief, they both cried—and cried some more. They would later recall together, "We were crying so hard standing there on the sidewalk that several people passing by asked if we needed help."

"We just cried our hearts out," said Millard, "but the tears had a tremendous therapeutic effect. They cleansed and washed away so much that was staining and discoloring our lives. I looked Linda straight in the face and told her how much I loved her. She knew I meant it. She could feel and sense it as only a close loved one can. She told me of her love for me. From that moment, reconciliation began to take place in our broken marriage." It began to rain. They hailed a taxi and headed for the hotel.

As Millard sat in the taxi, holding Linda close, he pondered the question that had plagued him—was he using his life as he should? He thought about the goals of the business and how they conflicted with the new course he believed God was charting for their lives. Together, they decided they would start over, beginning by shedding the excess in their lives: They wanted to be free to pursue whatever God had in store for them. Millard would sell his interest in the company and give the proceeds away to charity. The house, farm, lake property—all of it. It was the most fundamental way to reject the materialism that had alienated them from one another and ensure that the basis of their new beginning would be rooted in faith, purpose, and God's direction.

They awoke the next morning feeling complete and excited about their momentous decision, knowing they had a chance to begin anew. They embraced it. Then, whether a miracle or sheer coincidence, the first taxi they hailed stopped . . . and it was brand-new. They were the first to ride in it. They took it as a sign that all things in their lives were, in fact, new.

# — 6 —

# The Decision to Downsize

Making a fresh start wasn't easy. Working out the details took months and included numerous discussions with attorneys and accountants. It took a full year to sell all their properties, but the Fullers were determined. Their goal was a new beginning and to live every day according to God's plan.

Aglow in their renewed love, they returned from New York and walked hand in hand into their four-bedroom home nestled among the trees in Montgomery. The architectural plans for the mansion they had been planning to build on twenty acres of choice land outside the city were laid out on the dining-room table along with a note to call the architect. Glancing at them and then at each other, Linda and Millard confirmed what they had decided in New York. They had no interest in continuing with those plans. They called the architect and canceled the project.

As they took stock in the house around them, they suddenly realized the extent of the material gains they had accumulated. They were drowning in furniture, decorations, televisions, clothing—so much stuff. They decided to keep only some clothes and toys for the children. Everything else would be sold or given away. Linda donated many of her clothes to one of Millard's aunts who was her size. They gave furniture to his parents.

As for the business, Millard's partner, Morris, agreed to pay $1 million over ten years to buy Millard's half of the assets owned by Fuller & Dees, including farmland and livestock. When all was said and done, the Fullers kept a few thousand dollars, some of which went into a fund designed to one day pay for their children's college educations, and the rest was set aside to cover their expenses until they found a more permanent solution to putting food on the table. Everything else that came their way from liquidating their assets—several hundred thousand dollars in all—went to charity.

Friends and neighbors thought the Fullers' decision to give away all they had worked so hard for was bold, daring, and drastic—even a little crazy. They had sacrificed so much to get where they were. They had it all. Why would they give it all up?

While some understood perfectly the Fullers' new goals and were supportive, by and large, the rumor mill was churning. Relatives, friends, and business associates called daily: "Is it true? Did Millard really have a mental breakdown? Where will you live? What kind of work will you do? Where will your children go to school?" Others whispered about an impending divorce or a "family meltdown." Millard and Linda had no answers beyond saying they were putting their trust in God and enjoying being together as a family.

Despite the talk surrounding them, Millard and Linda felt as if they were on a second honeymoon. And being with the kids, five-year-old Chris and three-year-old Kim, was much more meaningful now that they were a greater focus in both their parents' lives. The family grew closer and began to rely upon one another. In the past, Millard had put money into a checking account for Linda. Now, what money they saved was deposited into one shared account.

"We forgave each other," Millard would say, "and we prayed earnestly to God to forgive us for what we had done."

They also found fresh joy in their faith. Going to church, participating in the service, singing hymns—all suddenly seemed more relevant and meaningful. "It was as if the words jumped off the page," Millard recalls. "Everywhere there was confirmation that turning our lives over to God was the right decision, and in every Scripture and hymn there was strength, power, and joy."

Linda felt it, too. "We'd be holding a hymnal together in church, and suddenly, a particular phrase or line would apply directly to our situation. I'd turn and look at Millard, and I could tell he'd just had the same 'aha moment.' Or we'd glance at each other in amazement when something was sung or said in church that made so much sense. It had never been all that pertinent before now. It was so affirming."

## A Family Vacation

Although they never had misgivings about their choice to give almost everything away, during those first weeks, they still questioned their new direction in life. Surrendering their lives was one thing, but how would the children fare? Would they still feel enthusiastic about their decision in a year? In five years? Had they heard correctly the ways in which God was directing their lives? Linda observed that Millard would "give out" and have to lie down for a while. She was sure it had to be difficult for him giving up the successful business he had worked so hard to build. Despite the questions, they remained strong in their belief that answers and a direction would be revealed. They decided to take a family vacation—something they had never done.

So while the accountants, attorneys, and real estate agents continued to dismantle the material world the Fullers had amassed, Millard and Linda packed up the car and drove to Florida for the family's first vacation—a symbolic farewell to their old life.

For nearly two weeks, the family meandered through the state, stopping to sightsee or splash in the waves wherever they fancied. In the evenings, they had supper at small diners, got a motel room, and told the children bedtime stories before tucking them in bed for the night. "That was when Linda and I began reading the Bible and praying together at night," Millard said. "We had never done that before and it gave us strength for the uncharted days ahead." They rejoiced in each other and their children, thanking God for giving them a second chance at a renewed life together.

"It was a cherished time," Linda recalls. "Every little nuance of family life was now shared with someone I loved." Including caring for a sick child. On the first day of their trip, just eighty miles from home, they noticed that Kim had red spots all over her face and arms. They stopped at a clinic. The culprit: chickenpox. Thankfully, it was a light case that cleared up in a few days, but confronting the problem together and caring for Kim as a family was a first for Linda— something she had never experienced when Millard was working all his waking hours.

As their rejuvenating vacation neared its end without any obvious answers to their lingering questions other than a resolve to trust God, Millard had a notion to visit an old friend. On a lark, he decided to take the family to see the Reverend Al Henry, the former pastor of the Pilgrim Congregational Church in Birmingham. Millard had forgotten where his friend had moved, but made a few calls and eventually got directions to a farm near Americus, Georgia, where Henry and his family were living. Though it was several miles out of the way for anyone bound for Montgomery, Millard thought it would be a nice detour and they were soon on their way. Little did they know that this simple change in itinerary would provide them with the signs they were so eagerly awaiting and set the course for the rest of their lives. And Millard would meet the mentor who was to help navigate his new future.

## Vintage Fuller . . .
## The Lord's Annual August Swing through Alabama

I was raised in an evangelistic church where we had regular revivals. I will never forget. I was probably about ten years old and we were having a big revival in our church one August (you know, the Lord makes his annual swing through Alabama in August). It was before the days of air conditioning and the fans were whirring and the preacher was going on and on. His name was Brother Gray.

I will never forget Brother Gray. I loved Brother Gray. He was preaching and he was going on and on and on and I went to sleep. I woke up, and he was standing down front earnestly pleading for people to come up. I thought he just wanted somebody to shake his hand and congratulate him on the sermon. And so I looked around and nobody was going up. I thought to myself, *That is most ungrateful.* I didn't hear it but I am sure it was a good sermon. And I am embarrassed for the man because nobody is going up and congratulating him on his good sermon. So I slipped out of my seat and I walked up there and shook his hand. I said, "Brother Gray, that was a good sermon." Well, he led me over to the first pew and sat me down and he beckoned at one deacon and beckoned another deacon. They started patting me on the head and patting me on the shoulders and patting me on the back. They got a little black book out and began to write my name in it. My daddy was sitting back several pews. I said, "Daddy, why are they patting me on my head and writing my name in this book?" He said, "Son, you joined the church." I said, "Daddy, I didn't want to join the church I just wanted to shake Brother Gray's hand and congratulate him on the nice sermon he preached."

Well, I told Brother Gray I really didn't want to join the church. I didn't have that in mind at all. And, so I disjoined. I told them to scratch my name out of the book. A couple of years later, I managed to stay awake during the whole revival and I did go up and I joined the church when I knew what I was doing.

—Millard Fuller

# — 7 —

# One Month at Koinonia

Millard turned off the highway near Americus, Georgia, for what he thought would be a pleasant brief visit with a friend he hadn't seen in years; it turned out to be a life-changing month.

Reverend Al Henry, who had been dismissed from his church in Birmingham because he advocated the admission of blacks, his wife, Carol, and their three young daughters lived at an integrated Christian community called Koinonia (pronounced *coin-o-NEE-a*) Farm.

Koinonia, from the Greek word for fellowship, was a small community of dedicated Christians whose goal was to witness to their faith in daily living. They were guided by three principles: peace, sharing, and brotherhood. The farm was founded in 1942 by Clarence Jordan, a farmer with a PhD in Greek New Testament who served as spiritual leader of the community until his death in 1969.

In the early years, Koinonia residents supported themselves by operating a poultry business, selling eggs and other products. With hundreds of customers, business was booming. Despite being an interracial community in the deep South, for many years the farm had enjoyed good relations with the surrounding white community. But in 1954, when racial tensions flared nationwide in the wake of the U.S. Supreme Court's landmark ruling ordering school desegregation, the relationship between Koinonia residents and the larger community became strained. The Ku Klux Klan had started harassing the families who lived at the farm, demanding that both blacks and whites leave the area. When the Koinonia residents refused, a caravan of ninety carloads of Klansmen drove into the community in a show of force. Unruffled, Clarence Jordan confronted them, stating that he and the other farm residents owned their land, had a right to live there, and had no plans to leave. During the next five years, the Klansmen did their utmost to intimidate the farm's residents: Attackers shot into Clarence's house on twenty-three separate occasions; a roadside market and other buildings were torched. After Koinonia rebuilt the market, it was blown asunder by dynamite. A total boycott was instituted against the farm. When one merchant in Americus sold some items to Koinonia in violation of the boycott, his store was promptly dynamited and he was put out of business. It wasn't long before the farm lost its customers and slid into debt. Some white families left the farm. Black families left, too, in some cases because relatives living outside Koinonia faced harassment and threats because of their connection to someone who lived on the integrated farm.

Yet Clarence Jordan and a handful of others remained to rebuild the shattered community, despite continued pressure to disband. Since conducting business with locals seemed impractical, Clarence decided to sell pecans and pecan products by mail-order around the nation. He located some used pecan-processing equipment and started soliciting orders. It was a vision that put Koinonia on the road to recovery. Bypassing the local boycott under the federally protected postal system, the ever humorous Clarence came up with the marketing phrase, "Help us ship the nuts out of Georgia!"

By the time Millard and Linda visited, the community was almost out of debt. The farm was doing a brisk business selling pecans, pecan candy, fruitcakes, and other products all over the United States, and even to a few customers abroad. Still, due to a shortage of workers, farm residents had trouble shipping orders in a timely fashion, particularly around peak seasons like Christmas, when orders came pouring in from across the country.

When they arrived at Koinonia, the Fullers explored the farm with their old friends, noting the simplicity of the place. Residents lived cooperatively, sharing what each produced.

The Fullers were invited to join the residents for lunch. It was a Koinonia custom for everyone to eat the noon meal together. This provided a time of fellowship and reporting of news around the farm. Just before the blessing was said, a man dressed in overalls and work boots entered the communal dining room. Al introduced Linda and Millard to Clarence Jordan. "He looked very much like a typical South Georgia farmer but I quickly learned that he was anything but typical," Millard would say. From this chance encounter, Clarence Jordan would become the most influential person in Millard's life, and a spiritual leader who would help Millard redirect his life.

After the meal, a group including the Fullers gathered around a table with Clarence. Koinonia had two other visitors that day—a retired navy chaplain and a reporter from *The Ledger-Enquirer,* a newspaper out of Columbus, Georgia, about sixty miles northwest of Americus. The reporter asked Clarence about racism, materialism, and the escalating war in Vietnam. The reporter crafted his questions to address his readers' interest in issues pertaining to dealing with enemies and whether the Bible can justify killing. Millard was himself interested in social change and listened intently as Jordan responded with real solutions guided by biblical direction. Millard would later write that Clarence's answers "spoke to

Clarence Jordan and Millard, Koinonia, 1968

me. I felt strengthened by simply being there to listen. I grew so much spiritually."

## "Millionaire Gives It All Away"

Before the discussion ended, Linda and Millard shared with the group the monumental decision they had recently made to give their wealth away. Now it was Clarence's turn to be impressed. He slapped his knee. "You all are just like the rich young ruler in the New Testament who built bigger barns and Jesus challenged him to give away his riches and follow him—except you are really doing it!" The reporter returned home and wrote a story that appeared under the headline "Millionaire Gives It All Away."

The philosophy of Koinonia resonated with Linda and Millard. They were inspired by the way Clarence had spoken, grounding biblical lessons into everyday life. They looked around themselves and saw happy, contented families—people who were prospering spiritually, forsaking the desire for material gain. In Jordan's presence, the Fullers had both felt something stir inside of them. Before the gathering broke up, Clarence told them, "God has brought us together for a reason, even if we don't yet know what that reason is." Millard and Linda stepped outside the dining hall to talk about their unexpectedly profound experience. "We need to stay here for a while," Millard told Linda. "I believe God sent us here to learn from these folks—and I think they could use some help packing up pecans and fruitcakes."

Linda agreed. They unloaded their suitcases and settled in—kids and all—and quickly took to their "jobs." Millard helped Al and Clarence in the shipping room while Linda cared for the children and helped process orders in the office. The children had plenty of other children with whom to play. An abundance of work occupied the adults. Millard helped Clarence milk the farm's only cow and pack up orders in the shipping room, and Linda sometimes helped in the community kitchen, cooking pan after pan of food. It was a simple life, and they liked it.

## The Cotton Patch Gospel

At lunchtime and in the evenings, Millard would tell Linda about the new insights into Jesus and his teachings he had learned from Clarence. Clarence particularly focused on the Sermon on the Mount (Matthew 5:7) starting with the Beatitudes. He had authored a book entitled *Sermon on the Mount* as well as his renowned "Cotton Patch" translations of the Bible, which used colloquial vernacular to make the Scriptures relevant for twentieth-century Georgians. For instance, he had Mary giving birth to Jesus in Gainesville, a town about fifty-five miles northeast of Atlanta. In place of first-century Jews and Samaritans, Clarence wrote about "Whites" and "Coloreds." Clarence delighted in translating original Greek Scriptures using familiar places and "down-home" language that could be well understood by fellow

Southerners. (The popular off-Broadway stage musical *Cotton Patch Gospel*, written by Harry Chapin and performed by Tom Key, was based on Clarence's translation of Matthew's Gospel.)

In these writings, Clarence proclaimed the simple truth that Jesus "really meant the things he said" and had contempt for so-called Christians who "watered down," ignored, or misinterpreted Christ's messages to make them acceptable within the prevailing culture. "The good news of Jesus Christ must be proclaimed and incarnated in real-life situations," Clarence would say, explaining that he felt all too often that values and actions in some cultures conflict with God's aspirations for his children. "We don't need more 'God boxes,'" he'd preach, using his term for church buildings. "We need more people doing God's work." This concept of faith in action would become a primary tenet of Millard's own work later.

Clarence especially inspired the Fullers as to the importance of doing God's work on Earth, that tolerance and acceptance incarnate God's universal love for all—which Millard would later translate into "All of God's people deserve at least a simple, decent place to live." Clarence reminded Millard that God calls mankind to faithfulness and obedience rather than success. "There is nothing wrong with success, in and of itself," he said, "but do not compromise your faithfulness to God in order to achieve it. The world judges success, but God judges a man's faith." To illustrate this difference, Jordan told about a reporter who came out to interview him during the height of the trouble with the Ku Klux Klan. The reporter asked about all the damage that had been done and the burden on the community as a result of the boycott, shootings, and burnings. At the conclusion of the interview the reporter half-sarcastically asked, "In summary, Dr. Jordan, how successful would you say Koinonia has been?" Jordan's answer was classic: "About as successful as the crucifixion."

Clarence's words and example were exactly what Millard and Linda needed—proof positive that the path they had embarked upon was the right one. He helped them reel in the teachings of Jesus and apply them in their newly directed lives. "The trouble with so many Christians today," he said, "is that they try to push Christ back up into Heaven. But if we would serve God, we must do it in the world. We must meet and serve people where they are—just as Christ did in his ministry."

Clarence had harsh words for many established church leaders in the area. "A group of people get together, erect a building, write up some rules about the kind of God they want," he said. "The trouble is, God doesn't come—because they are not operating by God's rules, and that won't work."

The days of December passed quickly for the Fullers. Christmas was approaching. No one at Koinonia decorated the outside of houses or buildings, and only fresh-cut branches with candles were used inside their homes. The Fullers delighted in this emphasis on simplicity, even remarking on how "authentically spiritual" it seemed. They helped Chris and Kim decorate a small cedar tree with popcorn garlands and snowflakes made of construction paper. The Fullers would later describe this Christmas as "richer than we'd ever known."

The month at Koinonia had confirmed for Millard and Linda that their resolve to divest themselves of their wealth and to rebuild their family—and their marriage—had indeed been the right decision. Inspired by the example of the families at Koinonia, and especially Clarence Jordan, the Fullers no longer viewed the future with uncertainty. They were sure that their renewed devotion to one another and to God was all the wealth they would ever need. To celebrate, Millard and Linda made a trip to town to look for new wedding rings. They wanted something to signify their renewed love and devotion, something to signify the break with their former lives of material success. The Fullers found what they were looking for in two matching bands. They were simple and plain, and cost a total of $60.

# — 8 —

# A Growing Awareness of Injustice and Need

After their stay at Koinonia, the Fullers drove back to Montgomery to finish clearing out their house. They traded in their sedan for a station wagon, packed it with their remaining belongings, and set out for the two-hour drive east to Cusseta, Alabama, where Millard's father and stepmother lived. They had given Millard's parents their furniture and were going to help them arrange it. But Linda and Millard also had something else in mind for their visit: They were going to remodel his parents' house. In addition to many small repairs and renovations that were needed, an inspection revealed rotted floor joists. The house had to be jacked up to replace the under-girding.

As they tackled the renovation, they thought and prayed about the next steps in their lives. At the suggestion of Dr. Lawrence Durgin of Broadway United Church of Christ in New York City, who had counseled Linda during her marital strife, Millard took a job with Tougaloo College, an African-American institution near Jackson, Mississippi. Durgin was a member of Tougaloo's board of trustees, and he convinced Millard that his fundraising skills were sorely needed at the struggling college. Meanwhile, Linda and Millard were interested in learning more about Christian missionary work abroad. Millard wrote to Jim Waery of the Stewardship Council of the United Church of Christ concerning a trip to Africa. Jim had proposed such a trip nearly two years earlier, suggesting Millard visit missionaries in several countries. At the time, Millard had decided against it on the grounds that it would take him away from his company for too long. Now that he was no longer spending all day at work, he had plenty of time for a trip to Africa.

As they waited for a reply to Millard's letter, Millard and Linda drove from Georgia to visit Linda's sister, Janet, and her family in Indio, California. Along the way, they toured a Civil War battlefield in Vicksburg, Mississippi, explored the Carlsbad Caverns in New Mexico, and visited the Grand Canyon. They even took the kids to Disneyland. Before long, the Fullers got word that church officials would indeed send them to Africa for six weeks. The United Church Board for World Ministries organized their itinerary to visit five countries. In exchange, once they returned, they would visit churches in the United States and tell of their experiences, the goal being to raise awareness of the church's needs and generate financial support for the church's mission work.

## Congo Brazzaville

Both Millard and Linda's parents agreed to keep the two children while the couple was in Africa for six weeks. So, with all the details ironed out, Millard and Linda set off on their grand adventure in June 1966, a trip they would later describe as "the most exciting and rewarding adventure of our lives." The excitement started the moment they arrived in Congo Brazzaville.

Along with other passengers, they were transported by van to the bank of the wide Congo River, where a large number of people were standing around or tending flimsy crates of goats and chickens. Through improvised sign language, some teenage boys helped Linda and Millard understand that they were waiting for a ferryboat.

Aboard the boat, Linda got out her movie camera and tripod. When they landed on the opposite shore (called Congo, Kinshasa—the Democratic Republic of Congo now), soldiers promptly informed the Fullers they were under arrest. They had mistaken the tripod for a machine-gun mount! Linda eventually cleared up the confusion by demonstrating that the tripod supported a sixteen-millimeter movie camera, not a machine gun. The soldiers released the Fullers, but not the film.

Their travels that summer carried them over twenty thousand miles and into five other countries—Tanzania, Kenya, Rhodesia, South Africa, and Ghana. They saw beautiful, modern cities such as Nairobi and Johannesburg with super highways contrasted by sparsely settled jungle villages with thatched roofs, and mud and dobble houses. They went to a few game parks and visited large numbers of missionaries—mainly doctors, nurses, teachers, and pastors in villages reachable for the most part by narrow dirt roads and paths. Their accommodations varied from a plush hotel in Kenya to a straw hut in Congo. They flew in big commercial jets, but also in tiny planes piloted by missionary aviators.

In Ghana, they visited with a judge of the country's highest court. They were exalted in some places and held at gunpoint at military checkpoints in others. They ate Western dishes prepared for them by American and European missionaries in some areas, while in others they enjoyed meals made with locally available fruits, vegetables, fish, and poultry prepared by local hosts. They even attended a traditional wedding. They saw healthy, energetic children as well as some who didn't have enough energy to play due to starvation and disease. Some children even had premature gray hair caused, they learned, by malnutrition. They saw that the Gospel was taken to people wherever they were, be it to far-off huts in remote parts of the jungle or to cities, in people's homes or in their workplaces, such as the gold mines.

Their trip left Millard and Linda determined to focus their lives on helping people in need. They returned to the United States still uncertain of just how they would end up contributing in the years to come, but they had plenty of time to sort that out. First, though, they had to pay the bills. Millard went to work in earnest for the development office of Tougaloo College, which he headquartered in New York City. His main job was to raise money from churches, corporations, foundations, and individuals as part of the college's $10 million capital campaign. Given the obstacles facing blacks in the United States in the 1960s, Millard was glad to do what he could to help. "As a Southerner and a Christian," he would later write, "I am happy to take on this task as a means of doing something concrete to improve the lot of my black fellow citizens."

## "A Sad State of Affairs"

For several years in the 1960s, as the civil rights movement gained steam in America, Millard had been increasingly aware of the racial problems dividing the country and incensed by the injustice he saw. He had been at the bus station in Montgomery when a group of Freedom Riders arrived in 1961. "It was a sad spectacle," he wrote. "They were met at the station by a mob, and two people were severely beaten. Newsmen and cameramen were also attacked and beaten. Police did not show up until twenty-five or thirty minutes after the violence had erupted, and when they did come, they made no real effort to stop any of the mobsters." Later, when the mob couldn't find the Freedom Riders, they turned on innocent black bystanders. "They beat one old crippled black man," Millard recorded in his diary. "I think the action of this mob is senseless and utterly crazy. That no action was taken by the governor, the sheriff, and the police department is inexcusable. They could have, and should have, been present to prevent the violence that erupted. The fact that they condoned the action of the mob is clear evidence that the authorities here in the city have no regard for human rights unless it is connected with getting votes in the next election. We are in a sad state of affairs."

Whites who tried to do the right thing found themselves at the mercy of the Klan and other white supremacist groups. Millard had his own experience in that regard. The law firm of Dees & Fuller had represented a Klansman in a legal proceeding. But this repelled Millard, and shortly after that experience, he pushed for equality, beginning in his business dealings.

In 1965, when thousands of marchers descended on Alabama to participate in the Selma to Montgomery march, he and Morris drove two pastors from Montgomery to Selma. As a result, several neighbors stopped speaking to them and they received threatening phone calls. Rumors started circulating that Millard printed communist literature in his basement at night and disseminated it by day. Worse, every business and community group stopped doing business with Millard's company. But he was not to be deterred: The suffering experienced by blacks in the South had convinced Millard of the moral imperative to grant equal rights to all people, and he was determined to do his part to right the wrongs.

"I have come to believe that the race problem in America is the greatest single moral, ethical, and religious dilemma facing us today," Millard would write. "Unless we can solve it, we make a mockery of the democratic and Christian heritage of the nation. Someone once said that we do Christ a disservice if we preach the Gospel when bread is needed." To Millard, a quality education represented the "bread" that Southern blacks needed most. That and, he would discover, affordable housing.

## Vintage Fuller . . .
### The Worth of a Home

We built a house for a woman whose husband had been killed in an automobile accident. He left her with this house full of little boys. She was not in good health, and they were living in pitiful conditions—big holes in the floor and roof, no toilet facilities, only a spigot outside. She was so grateful when she learned that Habitat for Humanity was going to build a new decent home for her and her boys that she wrote a letter to our paper and addressed it to Jesus. The letter said, "Dear Jesus, thank you for sending these folks to me to build me a decent house for myself and for my boys." After she had moved into her new house, I saw her one day and asked, "Annie, what is it about this house that means the most to you?" Without any hesitation whatsoever, she said, "My boys are no longer ashamed for their friends to know where they live." Can you just imagine what it means to a little boy every day of his life to be ashamed of where he lives? And can you imagine what a difference it makes in a young life to be able to move into a decent place that belongs to their family? That is the worth of a home.

—Millard Fuller

# — 9 —

# The Idea of
# Partnership Housing

Millard worked for Tougaloo College for the next two years, organizing a development office in New York and traveling around the country to speak on behalf of the college and the $10-million fund drive for new buildings and faculty salaries. As much as Millard enjoyed the job in the beginning, it grew to involve more proposal writing and he became less and less enthusiastic about it. He began to talk of doing something else. Linda was by now restless herself. She was accustomed to short, mild winters, while the winters in the North had been long and cold. Along with her caring for three children, one a newborn, she was more than ready to return to the South. They began to ponder their next move.

While on a flight to a speaking engagement, Millard scribbled a note to his good friend Clarence Jordan at Koinonia, informing him he was thinking about leaving Tougaloo.

Millard concluded by asking, "What do you have up your sleeve?" Clarence wrote back in a matter of days, telling Millard he didn't have anything up his sleeve, but maybe God had something up his sleeve "for the both of them." What Clarence really had in mind was discussing his ideas about "partnership." He told Millard that he yearned to be God's partner, to act from His perspective—and live his life accordingly. This very desire had been brewing within Millard for years, especially after his two-month trip to Africa. Millard felt excited about the concept of living life "in partnership" with God. But how? Clarence and Millard met at a church in Atlanta to discuss their future together. As usual, the time with Clarence would be insightful. As they were meeting, the pastor of the church came to see Clarence. "There is a situation concerning an excellent janitor at the church," the pastor explained. "He is required to work seven days a week, but we pay him only $80 a week. This is just not a decent wage. He lives all the way across town and has to drive about twenty miles round-trip each day. We pay no transportation allowance. He has a wife and eight children to support. He cannot live on $80 a week. I have pleaded with the deacons to raise his salary, but they will not because they refuse to increase the church's operating costs. What can I do?"

Clarence had an immediate solution. "You say the deacons refuse to raise his salary because there's no money. Maybe they don't have to. You make more than the janitor. Why not just swap salaries with him? That wouldn't require any extra money in the church budget. You live right here by the church, so you don't have any commuting expenses, and you only have two children while he has eight. Surely you could live more easily on his salary than he can."

The pastor didn't know what to say. Clearly, he hadn't expected that kind of solution. But Clarence had seen the problem from God's perspective, teaching the full measure of what Jesus meant when he said to "love your neighbors as you love yourself." It was this sort of thinking outside the box by Clarence that greatly appealed to Millard. It was decided that the Fuller family would move to the farm as soon as possible.

Millard found that Koinonia had deteriorated a great deal from the time he and Linda had stayed there a few years prior. Crops hadn't been planted and the land was being rented out for pasture. The only active industry was the mail-order business of pecans and fruitcakes. In fact, the farm was at its lowest point in its twenty-six-year history. Harassment and economic boycott had taken their toll. From a high of about sixty residents during the 1950s, now only two families remained: Florence and Clarence Jordan and their youngest son, Lennie; and Will and Margaret Wittkamper and their youngest son, Danny.

Few people and no money. But things were about to change.

## Partnership Housing

Late that summer (1968), Clarence and Millard called together a group of friends from around the country to talk about their ideas for living and working "in partnership with God." As a result of that meeting, Clarence, Millard, and the others decided that a principle focus of the new venture would be Partnership Housing (which would lay the groundwork for Habitat for Humanity). The housing idea involved creating a Fund for Humanity. Farm residents would generate revenue by raising and selling various crops, and put that money into the new fund. In addition, people with sufficient resources would make gifts or no-interest loans to Koinonia. The money in this Fund for Humanity would pay to build decent houses for low-income people in the area. The houses would be simple, but with electricity, plumbing, heating systems, and modern kitchens. They would vastly improve the standard of living for those who were currently living in shacks.

Perhaps the most uncommon features of Partnership Housing were that the houses would not be built at a profit

Millard at Koinonia, 1969

and the residents would be charged no interest on their twenty-year mortgages. Under the Bible Finance Plan, charging no interest on money loaned to the poor (Exodus 22:25: If you lend money to my people, the poor among you, you shall not deal with them as a creditor; you shall not exact interest from them [New Revised Standard Version]), money that residents paid on the loans would be put back into building more houses for more people. Though they would charge no interest, Clarence and Millard would encourage people who moved into the new homes to pay off their loans in less than twenty years—or even contribute more than their monthly payment to the Fund for Humanity. They hoped this would offset the loss of interest income.

## Koinonia Village

The first lots were laid out in late 1968. Millard did the surveying. At first, the venture lacked money to build even one house, but money soon came in to support the newly christened Koinonia Village. Initial plans called for forty-two lots and a park. The project wasn't without controversy, including opposition from local white residents, but in time the criticism was replaced with acceptance and even encouragement as people saw that the imagined problems hadn't materialized.

The progress at Koinonia energized the residents, the Fullers, and the Jordans. Millard took over the business and fundraising operations. He tore down an old chicken barn and replaced it with an economical metal-frame office building. Not only were there offices in the building, but also a new place for shipping and a huge walk-in refrigerator for storing large quantities of pecans. A pecan cookbook was published to help raise additional money for operations. Volunteers and visitors started arriving in a steady stream. The farm sprang back to life.

Poor families living near the farm found more jobs available. As orders increased, seasonal employees started working earlier in the fall and continued through December, shelling and bagging pecans and making fruitcakes and candy. Most of the employees had formerly been either unemployed or underemployed.

In the meantime, the most critical need—for housing—was being met under Millard's leadership. He was particularly excited about working on the houses because he had seen so many sharecropper families living in deplorable shacks with no heat, poor lighting, no indoor plumbing, tar-paper siding, newspaper glued to the walls for insulation, and numerous holes in roofs and floors. The new houses planned for Koinonia Village would be built with concrete block. Three brothers from Ocilla, Georgia, drove three hours round-trip each day to construct the houses at a reasonable cost. A number of volunteers who lived at the farm also helped. The dream Clarence and Millard had envisioned during their meeting in Atlanta was finally becoming a reality. Unfortunately, Clarence would never see Koinonia Village completed.

First house under construction in Koinonia Village for the Bo and Emma Johnson family, 1969

## Clarence Goes Home

It was during the building of the first house when Clarence died, or as everyone at Koinonia said, "when God called Clarence Jordan home." He was in his small, one-room "writing shack" preparing a speech he would give at the chapel of Mercer University, seventy miles away in Macon, Georgia. His latest book, *The Cotton Patch Version of Luke and Acts,* which Linda had typed, had just come off the press. A high school student had come to see Clarence that afternoon to have her book autographed. She was there only a few minutes when Clarence suddenly leaned his head back and fell silent. The student ran to Millard and Clarence's wife for help, but when Millard arrived, Clarence had no pulse. Everyone, particularly Millard, was devastated.

Millard contacted the county coroner, who refused to come to the farm, suggesting instead that Clarence's body be brought to the hospital in an ambulance. Millard knew that Clarence would not approve of this expenditure on what he would surely call a "vacated body," so Millard placed Clarence's body in the back of a station wagon and drove his beloved "brother" to the hospital. Linda found someone to stay with the kids and joined Millard at the hospital. It was past midnight before the body, covered in a sheet, was returned to them on a gurney. A paper sack containing Clarence's clothes was handed to Linda—no doubt, clear evidence of the contempt certain local people had for this "agitator," who had dared to mess with the three most prominently ingrained Southern values of his time: militarism, materialism, and segregation.

Clarence had talked with Millard, Linda, and others a number of times about his desire to be buried on the farm with no embalming. He thought it "un-Christian" to spend so much money to preserve a dead body when that money could be used to help the living poor. Linda went into town first thing next morning to the county health department in order to obtain an official burial certificate, giving permission to bury Clarence's body within twenty-four hours on Koinonia land. Already men from the community were digging a six-foot-deep grave in the hard-packed Georgia clay back in a pine grove where a few other of Koinonia's deceased had been buried. (One was a week-old infant born to the Jordans years earlier.) Millard went to a casket factory in town and purchased a pine shipping crate. Florence lined it with a quilt, and a few dozen people walked behind the pickup truck as Clarence was carried to his final resting place. Florence asked Millard to conduct a simple burial service. When Millard inquired about a particular Scripture she would like read, she responded, "Millard, you can read from any part of the Bible. Clarence loved it all." As they lowered the pine box into the grave and began to throw in the dirt, the Fullers' two-year-old daughter, Faith, stepped up to the edge of the grave and started singing: "Happy birthday to you, happy birthday to you . . ." It fit the situation perfectly.

## The Partnership Grows

The Fullers had been living at Koinonia for a little over a year and already it looked like a new community. The first house was under construction and would soon be complete. The farm was looking forward to an unprecedented number of mail orders. The community dining room had to be doubled in size to accommodate the influx of partners and short-term volunteers. In the summer of 1970, a group of young people with an organization called Young Life came to install swings and other equipment in the new park of Koinonia Village. Linda initiated and oversaw the building of a child development center. Koinonia was coming to life again—and was about to welcome a new life as well.

Just two weeks after the child development center opened, Linda gave birth to their fourth child. The birth was a particularly shared event for the people of Koinonia. Linda went into labor around 9:00 p.m., just after their three older children had gone to bed. Millard contacted one of the midwives

Millard moves furniture for new homeowners in Koinonia Village.
Two helpers, Kim and Faith, are in the bed of the truck, 1970.

from the Granny Midwife Program in which Linda had enrolled and arranged for someone to make the twenty-mile round trip to Plains to bring Ms. Gussy Jackson to the Fuller home. She helped Linda birth the healthy ten-pound girl. Someone rang the community bell to announce the new arrival. A group of residents showed up under the bedroom window to sing "Happy Birthday" to Georgia Ailene. It was one of the pinnacles of the four-and-a-half years the Fullers had spent at Koinonia Partners.

With new and capable people arriving every day, the success of the Partnership program seemed ensured, and the Fullers thought it time to see where else their talents were needed. They especially wanted to test the housing concepts birthed at Koinonia on a much larger scale.

# — 10 —

# Partnership Housing
# Goes to Africa

After much prayer and consultation, Millard and Linda took a bold step. They and their four children would leave the integrated Christian farm that had been their home for the last four years and would travel thousands of miles, across the Atlantic Ocean, to the heart of an impoverished nation in the middle of Africa. As missionaries with the Christian Church (Disciples of Christ) and in association with the United Church of Christ, the Fullers would implement Partnership Housing in parts of Zaire.

After telling relatives and the folks at Koinonia about their decision to work in Africa, the Fullers began making preparations for the complicated move overseas. On the advice of missionaries who would soon be their colleagues, Linda packed a couple of china barrels with items unavailable in their future home, such as kitchen essentials, linens, and sewing supplies to ship by boat to Zaire. Suitcases and an old

wooden military chest outfitted with a removable top parti-
tion were packed with clothes and a few toys. Millard made
arrangements with his brother, Nick, to store other belongings at his house in Alabama.

Within a few months, by early January 1973, they were
ready to go. Linda and Millard said good-bye to their many
friends, partners, and homeowners at Koinonia and relocated
to a missionary training center in Stony Point, New York.
There they spent three months reading and orienting themselves for working in the heart of Africa, and studying French,
since that was the official language spoken in the formerly
Belgian-colonized country of Zaire. To further prepare for
their stay in Zaire, the Fullers spent three months taking language courses in Paris.

## Zaire

Millard and Linda were well aware of the enormity of needs
in Africa, having spent six weeks visiting church representatives
there in 1966, but there was a big difference between touring
Africa for a few weeks and living there full time—as the Fullers
were about to discover.

Zaire's people had suffered greatly during the days of the
slave trade and later during the colonial period, when
European powers scrambled to conquer territories on the
African continent. In the late 1800s, King Leopold II of
Belgium administered the territory as his own private kingdom, using forced labor to extract rubber and ivory for the
financial benefit of the king and fellow countrymen. The king
ruled with terror, and his forces were blamed for mass killings
and atrocities. Those excesses paved the way for the end of
Leopold's rule and gave control of the colony to the Belgian
government, which improved conditions dramatically but
maintained a paternalistic attitude toward people who were
born and raised in what was then called the Belgian Congo.
The country gained independence in 1960, renamed itself
the Republic of the Congo, and went on in later years to

Clockwise, from top left: Chris Fuller; Millard and Georgia; Faith with pet, Licorice; Fuller family: (front left to right) Kim, Georgia, Faith, (back) Millard, Linda, Chris; Millard, Kim, and Faith with two friends from Switzerland; Faith and Georgia whitewash concrete block walls at housing project site change its name again. It was known as Zaire when the Fullers did their mission work in the mid-1970s. Leaders in Zaire had done away with old Belgian laws that had limited the rights of people to move from rural areas to cities unless they had a job. As a result, thousands of people were streaming into Zaire's towns and cities, even though jobs and decent housing were in short supply.

Shortly after arriving in Zaire in July 1973, Millard and Linda toured the house that was supposedly being readied for their occupancy. It was in a beautiful location on the banks of the wide Zaire River. A lovely covered veranda extended around three sides of the downstairs. But, still, the house disgusted Linda—and for good reason. There had been very few occupants since the Belgians left the country, and it was explained to the Fullers that the last inhabitants had been Peace Corps volunteers who liked living "back to nature." Goats and chickens had had free reign of the house. Manure covered the floors. Chickens had roosted over the bathtub. Linda noticed what she could imagine was once a fairly nice-looking light fixture in the dining room. It was thick with spider webs.

Linda tried to figure out how they could make the house decent and sanitary, and get rid of the stench in the house. The church had sent over a couple of men to paint, but the Fullers knew it needed a lot more than that. So, they spent the next few days with a shovel and pail, removing the manure. They were surprised to find beautiful ceramic tile flooring under the filth, although it took multiple scrubbings with soap and bleach to uncover it. As walls and ceilings were painted, the terrible smell faded a little more each day. Yet it remained a far different everyday life from what their contemporaries experienced in the United States. To get hot water, they had to heat it on the stove. They took cold showers. Electricity came and went because generators at the local power plant were continuously breaking down. And there was no readily available source of drinking water. The city supply came directly out of the river and was pumped up to the water tower with no processing. Sometimes the Fullers had to do without some of the most basic supplies such as toothpaste and toilet paper. Baking soda, brought from the United States and mixed with table salt, was a good substitute for toothpaste and deodorant. Doing without toilet paper was more challenging.

They lived in a city called Mbandaka alongside about 150,000 people, most of whom lacked jobs. Only the educated people spoke French in Mbandaka. Others communicated in one of two local languages. The Fullers enrolled six-year-old Faith in a Belgian elementary school, and two-year-old Georgia attended a nursery school run by Belgian women, but the couple could find no decent classrooms for their two oldest children, sixth- and eighth-graders. They made the difficult decision to send Chris and Kim to The American School of Kinshasa, in the nation's capital, five hundred miles south from where they were living and working. The children lived in mission hostels with other children of missionaries and adapted well. Life was challenging. Everyone in the Fuller family except Linda contracted malaria.

First houses and homeowners in Zaire (Equatorial Africa), 1974

Linda bought staples such as flour and sugar in fifty-pound sacks and tended to a garden at the house. The Fullers acquired several dozen chickens because buying eggs from neighbors was unpredictable and expensive. Vendors with vegetables such as spinach, green beans, eggplant, and occasional celery came by the house almost daily. Sometimes, men would come by to take orders for frog legs to be delivered the next day after a night of "gigging." An outdoor market was situated a half-mile away where fish, bananas, pineapples, mangoes, papaya, and freshly made peanut butter could be purchased, as well as smoked monkey, crocodile, and, sometimes, elephant. Linda learned quickly that vendors at the market tended to charge foreigners more than locals, so she sent her cook to do the shopping.

Linda and Millard also struggled to learn to drive on streets crowded with pedestrians. Except for employees driving trucks for foreign-owned businesses, few indigenous citizens owned cars. If they had "wheels" at all, it was either a bicycle or small motor scooter. Many people in Zaire believed that evil spirits possessed motorists who hit pedestrians or other cars. Thus, friends told the couple that, if they were involved in a wreck, they should not stop but, rather, keep driving until they got to a police station. Otherwise, they risked being beaten to death by an angry mob. In addition, few road signs or traffic signals advised drivers what to do, making it easy for authorities to cite motorists for various violations. Linda and Millard were arrested at least twenty times the first month they were there—sometimes two or three times in one day—but they finally figured out that the locals just wanted to get to know the newcomers and angle for some cash. If they gave in to a bribe, police would pull them over more frequently—so they learned quickly never to pay bribes. The arrests eventually dwindled and then went away entirely.

# Bokotola

Everything was in disarray. The church had about a dozen development projects in the works—all in desperate need of assistance. The three agricultural projects were in poor shape. A garage was no longer operating because all the tools had been stolen. A theater was closed because it lacked a working projector. The bookstore and print shop were barely operating. The guest house's septic tanks had overflowed, giving the area a terrible smell, and the rooms were barely habitable.

One effort that had impressed the Fullers during their visit in 1966—called a block-and-sand project—had fallen into disrepair. The program aimed to convert sand and cement into concrete blocks and then use those blocks in construction. Other than a nearby beer factory, it was about the only industry in town. No concrete blocks had been produced in two years, however. Only one of two block-making machines worked, and it functioned only because workers had scavenged spare parts from the second machine. Employees had not been paid for months. Finding good workers was a challenge because many men were in poor health, weakened by malaria, intestinal worms, and malnutrition.

Millard made the block-and-sand project his top priority. He got a $5,000 grant from the United Church of Christ in the United States to begin getting the project operational again. It wasn't an overnight success, but after many setbacks, they were able to regularly pay the workers and even earn a small profit. With spirits buoyed by this accomplishment, Millard turned his attention to building houses.

He started with a proposal to the government asking for land and assistance to build at least a hundred houses. The project would be under the Disciples Community of the Church of Christ in Zaire with grants coming from the Fund for Humanity of Koinonia Partners that the Fullers had helped establish in Georgia, as well individuals, churches, and other organizations. Each house would be made of concrete blocks with a concrete floor, a tin roof, a connected but separate kitchen to keep smoke out of the house, and an outdoor latrine. Indoor plumbing was not affordable for most Zairian families. The cost of each house would be approximately $2,000. Each family would provide a down payment of about $100. They would pay approximately $8 a month for twenty years, without interest. They were also encouraged to pay off their mortgage sooner so as to help other families. As Millard had hoped, money began to trickle in from various churches and individuals in the United States. A huge boost was realized when he received a $25,000 gift from the Lilly Endowment in Indianapolis, Indiana. That grant was made at the request of Sam Emerick who, unknown to Millard, worked at the Lilly Endowment at the time. Sam had been a part of the group that created and set up Koinonia Partners in 1968. And the government granted land for the project in a part of the city center called Bokotola, which means "man who does not care for others," as this had been the dividing section between the Africans and white settlers during the years of Belgian rule.

Early on, they faced a major hurdle when the government billed them an outrageous sum of $50,000 for building permits! After Millard protested, the government agreed to lower the charge, but they wouldn't name a figure. The wait for information and permits dragged on for weeks, and the project stalled. At long last, Millard got tired of waiting and ordered workers to begin building a storage building and the first house. They kept waiting for news about the permits, but it never came. So, they kept on working, building 114 houses in all without ever getting a permit.

The new neighborhood was more than just a place to live; it was a community. It had a playground with a soccer field, a pyramid for climbing, and a sand pit. An open-air communal building was used for worship services, preschool classes, women's sewing and cooking classes, and many other things. The families were extremely proud of their community, adding forty-eight houses and a park in 1975. For most people at Bokotola, the new houses represented a dramatic improvement. Many had lived in shacks with mud walls and thatched roofs that often fell apart during rainstorms and were infested with all kinds of parasites and vermin, like worms, rats, snakes, bats, and mosquitoes. Although the new houses were very simple, they were well built and wouldn't require repairs every few months, like the mud and palm-leaf huts. With concrete block walls and a tin roof, the homeowners could focus their scarce resources and energies on better things.

In fact, the Bokotola project introduced many building techniques that were later used in other projects, such as building schools and churches. The Bokotola houses rarely had glass windows, as glass was hard to find and expensive, so they were shuttered with wood that could be opened during the day for ventilation and locked at night for protection from mosquitoes and thieves. The homes had no pipes for plumbing or wiring for electricity, although some families had wiring installed in hopes that the city would one day make that service available to the subdivision. A year after the project was started, the city's water and electricity department installed water mains in the area streets, but they abandoned the project before the houses were ever connected into the system. The kitchen was always separate from the house, either connected to the main house by a covered walkway or physically connected, but could only be entered through an outside door, not through the house. This was done because the women cooked over an open fire on the ground or floor. The house would have been black with smoke within a few weeks if the kitchen had been connected. Ventilation blocks were installed at the top of the kitchen walls to allow some of the smoke to escape. There were no countertops, cabinets, or drawers, since these amenities would add too much cost to the houses, making them unaffordable to most. A little storage room in the back was all they needed. Homeowners often moved into the kitchen before their houses were finished, doing their cooking outside, because they were so anxious to start living in their new homes.

Other projects, started and administered by the Fullers, blossomed to meet the needs of the people. For instance, the

Fullers found out that people were unable to obtain eye-glasses, so they used the Koinonia mailing list to solicit used glasses. About four thousand pairs packed in metal barrels came pouring in, which they sold for $2 to women, $2.50 to men, and $1 to people in prison. This income enabled the construction of three more houses. Millard and Linda never hesitated to get out their typewriter and ask for financial assistance when funds got low.

Yet for all the progress, one of the most difficult tasks the Fullers faced was changing attitudes. Many people in Zaire believed that the white man, called a mundele, had all the money, owned everything, and knew how to do anything. Centuries of oppression had convinced them that God preferred whites, giving them all the intelligence and money, and Africans were inferior. Thus, they felt no connection to the housing project. They didn't think of it in terms of their project, and thus they were only motivated to work for the sake of collecting money to support their families. Workers often failed to show up for work. Millard spoke with them over and over again about taking pride in their efforts. He reminded them that they were free, and it was up to them to build their lives and communities. He told them that God had made them and loved them just as much as He did whites. To feel inferior was to criticize God's wisdom in making them. It was insulting to God not to use the talents they had been given. Slowly, it seemed his words began to sink in for some people. But it was difficult to reverse attitudes that had been passed down for generations.

## The Rise Up and Walk Project

When the Fullers first arrived in Zaire, they noticed quite a number of one-legged men and women hobbling around. In an area of the world with a year-round tropical climate and limited medical care, even a small cut could become infected and require amputation of a limb. On Saturdays, the amputees would come as a group, slowly making their way from house to house to beg because they could not work. The Fullers recalled a visit they had made in 1966 to the mission hospital at Kimpese in lower Zaire where wooden legs were made, but getting measured for and obtaining a properly fitted prosthesis required candidates to travel approximately six hundred miles to the hospital. The whole process would take at least two months' time, and they would need some money for food. But when the Fullers' investigation revealed that they could get legs for $200 or less (including transportation to the hospital and other costs of measuring, making casts, etc.), they created the Rise Up and Walk project through which many amputees were finally blessed with life-changing prostheses.

## Becoming a Community

As the Rise Up and Walk project required less of Linda's time, she began working with the women now living in the rapidly expanding community. By mid-1975, there were approximately thirty homeowner families. There was no thought about women participating in construction of the houses at that time, but some of the women volunteered to work with Linda in painting doors and shutters. Linda would often bring them snacks, and they really loved her banana cake! The women asked Linda to show them how to bake it, as well as bread. Then, the women learned that Linda knew how to sew. They asked her to teach them how to make clothes for their children. None of the women had a sewing machine, so all of the stitching was done by hand. Some of the women started making cakes, bread, and clothes to sell in the open-air markets to subsidize the family income. Linda was also asked to teach English to seminary students for six months because the regular professor had been called back to the States for a family emergency. Coupled with her responsibilities for composing fundraising letters and answering correspondence, as well as taking care of her two children at home, Linda was engaged in constant activity.

Meanwhile, Millard had his own share of challenges. Every Sunday, after the family attended church, he visited a prison with Pastor Lokoni, the religious leader of Bokotola. It was in dismal shape. Five hundred men, including the mentally ill, were housed in a single facility. Some were in prison because they simply lacked a few dollars to pay their taxes. Due to a lack of medical care, prisoners died of diseases that weren't commonly life-threatening in the United States, such as diarrhea. The highlight of the prisoners' existence was attending Sunday afternoon services. Millard came to find joy in his Sunday visits at the prison, often delivering an uplifting sermon. Unfortunately, the government forbade religious services in prisons in 1975, although prison administrators allowed the distribution of new Bibles when they arrived several months later.

As the housing project neared completion, church leaders, new residents, government officials, businesspeople, and the Fullers gathered to mark the occasion with a dedication ceremony on July 4, 1976. The community was also given a new name. "To form a prosperous and unified community of people coming from different tribes and from different religious confessions; to break down the barriers which separate the whites from the blacks; to form a society which knows no sort of discrimination—that is the aim of the Fund for Humanity," the pastor said. "Therefore we now propose to the authorities of the subregion to change the name of Bokotola, which signifies 'the person who does not like others,' to Losanganya, which means 'reconciler, reunifier, everyone together.' Furthermore, we propose to give this park where you are now gathered the official name of Tosalisana, meaning 'let's love each other.' From this day on, the spirit of our project in Mbandaka will be expressed to everyone who hears its name."

The Fullers' experience in Africa would live on in their hearts forever. The Christian housing ministry had taken hold. In its wake, a dream for a better life and a more comfortable one had come true for the people of Zaire. Indeed, a local education official who had attended college in the

United States planned a similar development for three hundred families in another part of Zaire. If the housing concept

## Vintage Fuller . . .
## Mpaka Mola

Linda and I worked in Zaire for three years, and we built 114 houses in the city of Mbandaka. I'll never forget one man that we got to know as a friend. His name was Mpaka Mola. One night we brought him to our house and gave him ice cream. Never in his life had he had ice cream. He thought it was the most awful stuff. He couldn't believe that anybody would put that kind of cold stuff in their mouth. But Mpaka Mola was probably one of the most talented block layers I have ever met. He had absolutely calibrated eyeballs. He didn't use a level, a plumb line, or anything. I'd go up to him and say, "Mpaka Mola, how do you know that wall is straight? You're not even measuring; you're not even putting a level down." He said, "It's straight." I said, "How do you know?" He said, "Put the level on it." I put a level to it and, sure enough, it was level.

He was so skilled and for that reason he would always do the corners on our houses. If he were in the United States, he'd be making a terrific salary because of his skill. But because he lived in Mbandaka, Zaire, where the economy was so bad and where jobs were so few, even though he was an incredibly skilled man, he lived in almost abject poverty. He lived in a house that was made out of mud and sticks. And his house had a mud floor in it. He applied for a house soon after he came to work with us. And as we would do periodically, the family selection committee got together and chose Mpaka Mola and his family to have a new house. I happened to be the first person to see him after the committee meeting was dismissed. I met him at the construction site and said, *"J'ai la bonne nouvelle pour vous. Votre famille etaient choisi d'avoir une maison"* (I've good news for you. Your family has been chosen to have a new house). He just fell over. I thought I'd killed him! Then he got up on his knees and took my hand in both of his with tears flowing down his cheeks. And he said, *"Merci, merci, merci"* (thank you, thank you, thank you). Then he got up and walked away. That's what a house means to somebody in a place like Mbandaka, Zaire.

—Millard Fuller

worked in Bokotola, why wouldn't it work in another part of the country? And if it could work in those two locations, wouldn't it also work around the world? The Fullers mulled these questions as they said good-bye to their friends in Zaire and returned to the United States in August 1976.

# — 11 —

# Habitat for Humanity
# Is Born

When the Fullers left Zaire in July 1976 to return to the United States, eighty families had already moved into new houses and were making monthly payments at the Mbandaka Housing Project. Plans were underway for a second project in a village about ninety miles to the south. Confident the partnership housing concept had taken hold and that local folks could keep up the momentum of the housing ministry, the Fullers were ready to head back to the United States.

Home for the Fullers was Koinonia Farm. Encouraged by the success they had had with the application of partnership housing in Africa, and excited about the possibility of building homes for the poor in other regions, the Fullers were surprised to find little support among the Koinonia Partners for their idea to take the housing ministry worldwide. Residents at Koinonia let the Fullers know they were only interested in continuing to build homes in Sumter County. They felt that to divert attention from their community priorities would put too much stress on Koinonia.

But with four years of building at Koinonia, and three more in Zaire, the Fullers were convinced the principles of the Fund for Humanity could work anywhere. "If it can work in Georgia and Zaire, it can work in San Antonio," said Millard. Convinced that partnership housing was in some way a solution to providing housing for the poor, the Fullers were eager to show others its potential for communities in any number of settings.

## Faith Lytle—San Antonio, Texas

To determine how they might proceed, Millard assembled a group of twenty-seven people from various places, including Sam Mompongo from Ntondo, Zaire, who was the organizer of the project there. For three days they brainstormed and prayed together. Also among the group was Mary Emery and Rod and Patti Radle, sent to the meeting by Faith Lytle, from San Antonio, Texas. Faith and her husband, Bill, a Presbyterian pastor, had visited Koinonia in prior years and met the Fullers there. Both Faith and Bill donated to the housing project in Mbandaka and were eager to try the partnership housing model in their hometown for inner-city families who were in dire need of housing. They had written the Fullers in Zaire, asking what they thought about initiating a Fund for Humanity–type project in that area of San Antonio.

The idea struck the Fullers as exactly the thing to do, and they had encouraged Faith to begin such a project. Buoyed by the Fullers' support, Faith got to work. She assembled a group to discuss what might be done to address the poverty housing in her city. Laying out a map of the most urgent housing needs for the poor in and around San Antonio, the group decided to start in one area of town, and then go on to another, and then another. "Our goal," said Faith, "was to build cluster-like oases, starting with The Devil's Triangle—an area of town so named because locals considered it the worst and most dangerous part of town—and then build decent housing wherever it was needed within the city." By the fall of 1978, the San Antonio Fund for Humanity was incorporated as an independent nonprofit (it would later become the first affiliate of Habitat for Humanity). The group Faith assembled began to raise money that bought the site of the first home built by the new San Antonio Fund for Humanity Inc. Ernesto and Sylvia Torres and their four children were chosen to be the homeowners. The work within The Devil's Triangle area met with much public applause, so much so that the locals renamed it The Triangle of the Holy Spirit, as the development surely represented hope to resurrect the neighborhood.

Over the next few years, the San Antonio Fund for Humanity would build more than ten houses. In 1998, Linda and Millard would pay a visit to San Antonio Habitat for Humanity to celebrate this affiliate's twentieth anniversary. To commemorate the anniversary, volunteers would build twenty houses in two weeks.

Meanwhile, back in Americus, the group Millard had assembled endorsed taking the partnership housing ministry worldwide. They set about planning the next steps. Millard would need to secure approvals from the state and federal governments so that contributions would be tax-deductible. That would require a name, but what?

Millard shared that, in Zaire, he'd heard on Voice of America that the United Nations had hosted a conference in Canada pertaining solely to human shelter; they had called the conference "Habitat." He was intrigued by the name since "habitat" mostly referred to natural surroundings of various kinds for wildlife or sea creatures. Mulling over "Habitat," a member of the group pointed out that Koinonia Farm founder Clarence Jordan had created the Fund for Humanity to encourage donors to pledge support for buying building materials, and that if the word "Habitat" were combined with "Fund for Humanity," the outcome would be "Habitat for Humanity."

The name resonated with the group. Everyone agreed the new organization should be named Habitat for Humanity. The goal would be to eliminate poverty housing and homelessness from the face of the Earth by building basic but adequate housing. Furthermore, the words and actions of people involved with the organization would call attention to poverty housing and homelessness in such a way that they would become socially, politically, and religiously unacceptable.

As for its mission, "Habitat for Humanity would be a Christian housing ministry, working in partnership with people everywhere, from all walks of life, to develop communities for God's people in need by building and renovating houses so that people could live in decent houses in decent communities and grow into all that God intended."

Habitat for Humanity would be thoroughly ecumenical and keep overhead costs low. Local affiliates would be self-governing and raise their own funds. House payments would go into a revolving Fund for Humanity. In addition, the organization would link up with other organizations. For example, a local church might sponsor the building of a home or support the travel of persons in conjunction with a project abroad, and so on.

The founding group also decided that residents of Koinonia would train builders and community development workers since many future volunteers would lack the skills to build a home. To that end, volunteers could come and work in the established housing program at Koinonia, making a contribution even as they got training for some other project—all at little or no cost to Habitat.

With these big decisions in place, plans were made to hold a formal organizational meeting the following March in Stony Point, New York, to develop the articles of incorporation and bylaws and to elect the first directors.

## Vintage Fuller . . .
## Carpenter's Circle

Recently I was in Indianapolis building a home for a mother and her two children. This family had fallen on hard times, and the mother suffered from clinical depression. They lived in a dilapidated two-story house in a run-down neighborhood. Nearly three-quarters of her monthly income was consumed in rent for this dump that offered less than substandard living conditions. (Her new Habitat home would require half that amount.) I had toured the house and was warned not to touch certain light switches because I could get an electrical shock. The stair rail was missing, and in the bathroom downstairs, there was a big hole in the ceiling over the bathtub where waste came down every time the toilet upstairs was flushed. Some of the floor in the kitchen was rotten because of chronic plumbing problems. The back door of the house could not be secured properly because the hinges were broken. Can you imagine the stress of living in such a situation? Helping this family build a new home was a total joy, knowing how much it would improve their lives.

As with all Habitat homes, much pre-planning and family nurturing takes place before construction begins. Once completed, we do a dedication ceremony where we present the keys, displayed upon a Bible, to the family. On this day, just one day away from the dedication ceremony, I stood back and assessed the progress: sod was being laid; a tool shed was being completed in the back yard; the final coat of paint was being applied to the front porch; and shrubs were being planted. It was a beehive of activity—as was the entire community, since the home we were building with this woman and her family was one of many Habitat homes being constructed in this neighborhood. And then I saw something else that made my heart leap: Someone had seen to it that the street be named "Carpenter's Circle." Jesus had been a carpenter, and here we were, his "hands and feet"—doing what Jesus would have done.

—Linda Fuller

# — 12 —

# Financing Houses:
# The Economics of Jesus

B ig ideas, lofty goals . . . but how to finance them? The
group had decided that Habitat affiliates would establish a Fund for Humanity. Each Fund for Humanity
would be supported through voluntary gifts (in cash and in-
kind contributions), grants, and interest-free loans from individuals, churches, groups, and foundations. All repayments
from housing loans would be returned to the local Fund for
Humanity.

Furthermore, Habitat's founders chose to adopt a radical
financial plan, straight from the Bible—an economic theory
called Kingdom Economics that runs completely counter to
modern economic theories, which tell us that business ventures won't be successful if interest isn't charged and profits
aren't made. Explains Millard, "The Bible says in Exodus
22:25 that if you lend money to the poor, you should not
charge interest. And we follow that ancient biblical idea. We

do not charge any interest and do not add any profit, selling houses at a price that the poor can afford to pay."

## The Economics of Jesus

"This radical mortgage plan stresses we're to trust in God to help us meet our needs and the needs of others. Scripture says that Jesus can multiply that which is given in love for those in need," Millard would say. Always colorful and to the point, Millard explained this theory in a presentation to a room of executives like this: "Jesus was preaching on the hillside to thousands of people. Evening time came, and the disciples approached him and said, 'These people are hungry. They need to be fed. But how can we feed all of these people? There's no food.' Jesus said, 'Don't we have anything?' They replied, 'Well, there is this boy here with five pieces of bread and two fish, but that couldn't possibly feed all of these people.' But Jesus said, 'Bring the bread and the fish to me.' And they brought it to him. And he did not do what so often we do. He did not say, 'You're right, this is awful little. I don't think this will be enough. We ought to just send these folks home.' Jesus did not complain a minute about the meagerness of the resources. Instead, he took what he had, turned his eyes heavenward, and thanked God for it. And then he did what any good leader would do, he delegated. He said as we would say down South, 'Y'all feed 'em.' And he passed out the bread and the fish. I'm sure he gave it to Peter. Peter was always the one who was an eager beaver disciple, always closest to Jesus. I'm sure Peter got the bread and the fish first and could hear all those stomachs growling. Then he looked back at Jesus and said, 'What did you say, Jesus?' Jesus responded, 'I said, y'all feed 'em.' And I'm sure at that point Peter called Andrew, James, and John and all the others and said, 'Boys, y'all feed 'em. I'm going to watch.'

"And Jesus said, 'Look, I did not say, have a committee meeting about this problem. I said feed the people.' And he almost had to push them out in the crowd. But finally they went, and it was not only enough, it was too much. The job got done; all of the people got fed. There you have a dramatic and classic example of Kingdom Economics—taking whatever you have and beginning to work with it, instead of complaining about the meagerness of the resources. I have been to literally hundreds of towns, cities, and communities that were considering forming a Habitat for Humanity project where people always ask me, 'How much money do we need to start a new project?' And you know what I tell them? I say, 'You have to have at least a dollar. It would be fiscally irresponsible to start a project with less than a dollar. But if you've got a dollar and you've got committed folks, you can start, and God will bless your meager resources. If you give out of what you have and don't complain about what you don't have, God will bless it. You will be amazed at what God can do with so little."

When the first Fund for Humanity was established at Koinonia, there was no money—just land, dreams, and great need. But when the community of Koinonia used their meager resources, thanked God for what they had, and got organized, great things were accomplished. The key component was faith. Millard says, "The Bible teaches that when we act in faith, God moves in and multiplies what we have to fill the need and accomplish great things." Thus, Habitat's ministry would be entrusted to God and built up by faith.

## Released from the Shackles of Interest

Whenever Habitat builds a house, the owner typically gets a twenty-year loan, at no interest. The theory is that if Habitat homeowners have to pay interest on their loans, they will become locked into difficult financial situations. The more interest they have to pay, the more difficult it will be to break free of poverty. Habitat for Humanity is more concerned with people than with profit. Its mission is to meet human need.

"Ironically," Millard has observed, "if a poor person were to go to a standard lending institution, the lender would consider him 'high risk' and charge an even higher interest rate than a person of moderate or higher means would pay. But this goes against biblical directives. Leviticus 25:35–37 (NIV) instructs: 'If one of your countrymen becomes poor and is unable to support himself among you, help him as you would an alien or a temporary resident, so he can continue to live among you. Do not take interest of any kind from him so that your countryman may continue to live among you. You must not lend him money at interest or sell him food at a profit.'

"Habitat's philosophy has always embodied the principle that each and every human being is priceless. We are to share what we have with 'our neighbor,' especially those in need. We are not to look down upon the poor. Scriptures are full of examples in which Jesus places enormous value on people whom society considers lowly. God's grace extends equally to all humanity, whether they are considered 'useful' to us or not. The parable of the laborers in the vineyard, for example, says that all the workers were paid the same wage at the end of the day, regardless of the time of day they had started. Each person's contribution was worth the same as everyone else's."

## The Theology of the Hammer

The Theology of the Hammer is the notion that God expects his people to do more than sing and speak of their love for the Lord; they have an obligation to put love into action and to care for one another.

Millard is fond of explaining: "Chapter 15 of the Book of Deuteronomy is very important to Linda and me because it is the basis on which this ministry is built. Verse 4 says, 'There will be no poor among you, since the LORD will surely bless you in the land which the LORD your God is giving you as an inheritance to possess' (NASB). God's idea is that there shall be no poor among us—a wonderful goal toward which to work with all of our endeavors in life. We all know that there are poor people among us, and the Scriptures give us explicit instructions on what to do about dealing with the poor. 'If there is a poor man with you, one of your brothers, in any of your towns in your land which the LORD your God is giving you, you shall not harden your heart, nor close your hand from your poor brother; but you shall freely open your hands to him, and shall generously lend him sufficient for his need in whatever he lacks' (Deut. 15:7–8, NASB). Does he lack food? Does he lack clothing? Does he lack shelter? Then provide it. 'You shall generously give to him, and your heart shall not be grieved when you give to him, because for this thing the LORD your God will bless you in all your work and in all your undertakings. For the poor will never cease to be in the land' (Deut. 15:10–11a, NASB).

"In response to this, I often hear people say 'therefore you should do nothing. It's an act of futility to try to help the poor if the poor will always be with us.' But there's not a period after that sentence. There is a semicolon. And after the semicolon, we read these words: 'Therefore, I command you, saying, "You shall freely open your hand to your brother, to your needy and poor in your land"' (Deut. 15:11b, NASB).

"John says in Luke 3:11 (NIV): 'The man with two tunics should share with him who has none, and the one who has food should do the same.'" Says Millard, "John doesn't say, 'The man who has more than enough for his needs should give some away.' He instructs even the man with a mere two shirts to share with the man who has none. Therefore, when Habitat receives funds, they are immediately spent on building more houses—not put in investments or endowments."

## John the Bulldozer

In a 1979 speech delivered in Chautauqua, New York, Millard read from Clarence Jordan's Cotton Patch version of the Bible—something that Millard does frequently—reminding them of a passage in Luke where John the Baptist quotes the prophet Isaiah: "A voice shouts, 'Make a road for the Lord in the depressed area and make it straight. Every low place shall be filled, and every hill and high place shall be pushed down, and the curves shall be straightened out, and the washboard roads shall be scraped smooth. Then every human being will share in the good things of God.'" John the Baptist urged people to "do something."

Millard wants us to think about the fact that many people live in decent houses while so many of our neighbors in the United States and around the world do not. "I bet you if ole John were preaching today on the banks of Lake Chautauqua," Millard continued, "he'd talk about houses and cars and bank accounts and all of those other material possessions which we own and which we control. He'd talk about it because if you're going to give yourself to the Kingdom, that's all of you. And that includes your possessions. Kingdom Economics has a lot to do with our things.

"If you read Acts 2 and 4," says Millard, "you'll learn that the disciples came together and said, 'We are brothers and sisters in a new family, the family of God. We share all of our things together.' They understood The Economics of Jesus."

## A Radical Plan That Actually Works

Millard emphasized the following as proof that Kingdom Economics works. "When we started in Koinonia, building houses in 1968, we had the land, but we didn't have any money. We had a vision and a dream and an idea. We saw homeless people, and we said, 'God is not happy with people living like that, and we want to do what we can with the little we've got.' And we asked God to bless it. And it's amazing. We've never missed a day, unless it was raining or Sunday, that we didn't work, that we didn't build houses. We build homes with the poor. Just God's people helping God's people in need. We spend all the money we take in. We stay broke all the time. All the money that comes in, we spend it. If more money comes in, we just work harder. We just buy more lumber. We buy more bricks. We work harder. We work faster. We build more houses. And the endowment is the home in which people live. And they live there, and they make their payment, no profit, no interest. But in a miraculous way, and of course with Kingdom Economics, we instill in people that this is God's project. We say, 'God's people furnish the money. God's people built the houses. You are God's people. You join the revolution. You make your payments. You help your neighbor build a house.' And a tremendous spirit begins to build up among the people. And they pay, and they work. And in eleven years, we've never foreclosed one house."

By the time Millard gave that speech, the concept first known as Partnership Housing had taken root and demonstrated its power to change lives, first at Koinonia, then in Zaire, and later around the world. The idea of Kingdom Economics had put Habitat on the path of life-changing growth. More people were joining the movement. By stepping out in faith, trusting God, and sharing without need for profit, God had magnified what started as meager offerings. Those blessings were just the beginning.

## Kingdom Economics with a Twist— The Greater Blessing Box

Years later, in 2005, the Fullers would found The Fuller Center for Housing, and the ministry would work with the "poorest of the poor." In addition to using Kingdom Economics to build houses, The Fuller Center for Housing would also employ a strategy for repayment called The Greater Blessing Box for smaller repair or renovation work. When a home renovation was complete, the recipient family would be given a Bible with the keys atop, along with a box containing a certain number of envelopes that corresponded with the number of months to make "payments" (donations) back to The Fuller Center. The number of envelopes inside would be determined with the homeowner based on a realistic timetable for repayment of building materials. For example, if a renovation cost $6,000, the homeowner would agree to monthly "payments" of $167 for three years (sometimes more or less, depending on the family's monthly expenditures for food, medical needs, and so on). Thirty-six envelopes would be placed in their box. No profit or interest would be involved, no legal obligations, no banks, and no collection efforts. The family would know that while the home renovations they received were certainly a blessing, their payments would make repairs to another family's home possible. The "payment" would be their gift to others—an even greater blessing.

Millard believes that The Greater Blessing Box preserves dignity for homeowners and is a way to mobilize millions of additional dollars that can be used to continue building homes for those in dire need. "People don't want a handout," Millard says. "They just want help getting on their feet." The Greater Blessing Box allows people to stand shoulder to shoulder, helping one another as equals and furthering the biblical ideology that it is blessed to receive, but even more blessed to give.

The first home I ever built in this ministry was in south Georgia for a really needy family headed by Bo and Emma Johnson. With their five children, they lived in a falling-down, pitiful shack, with no insulation or paint. They used an outdoor toilet, and exposed light bulbs were hanging down in the middle of the room. The house was on somebody else's land, so there was no security about where they lived. So, we announced the good news to that family: "We will work with you and build a house, not as a gift, but on terms you can afford to pay using the Bible Finance Plan." And so we built them their house, and they moved in. Since I'm a lawyer by profession, I closed the sale on that house. Bo was an intelligent man, but he couldn't sign his name on the mortgage, so we just had to put an X. They paid off that mortgage a few years ago, six months ahead of time, so we decided to have a big mortgage-burning ceremony in the Johnsons' front yard. We sang songs and had a Scripture reading. I made a speech, and some other folks made speeches, and then we got to the magic moment when Bo and Emma were called up front. The woman at Koinonia who was in charge of collecting the house payments brought the mortgage forward very dramatically, held it up, and said, "Now this mortgage has been paid off, and we've marked it satisfied at the courthouse, so all that remains to be done is to burn it up!" She struck a match, put the match to the mortgage, and, boy, it started going up in flames! She dropped it in a bucket that had been placed there in readiness to receive the burning mortgage. And then she handed the deed to Bo, now unencumbered by the mortgage, free and clear. He finally owned his own house. He put the deed above his head and said, "We did it, we did it, praise God, we did it!" And everybody jumped to their feet, shouting and screaming and applauding, and began to hug everybody. It was one of the most exciting things I had ever been a part of. This man who could neither read nor write now has a daughter who's a lawyer. He has another daughter who's a psychologist, and another daughter who's a nurse. All five of the children have turned out to be wonderful adults, all engaged in productive, useful activities. And a big part of that was because they had a good place to live, a place where love could grow. You see, love makes things blossom and allows little children to become all that God intended them to be. Children given the opportunity to grow up in a decent home, like Bo and Emma's children, may even change the world.

—Millard Fuller

# — 13 —

# Habitat's Childhood

Their mission in place, the Fullers got to work. They were living at Koinonia Farm and set up an office in a room that had once been used to dry pecans. Millard lived on the phone with donors, trying to keep a flow of money coming in to further the work being done at both Mbandaka and Ntondo. But with four kids and a new venture—launching Habitat for Humanity—Millard needed to practice law to bring in a steady income. He also felt called to represent the legal needs of low-income people. His practice often focused on personal injury cases, and Millard and his associate, Ken Henson, Jr., of Columbus, Georgia, tried about twenty personal injury cases over the course of the next ten years, winning every one of them.

Millard often tells the story of one of his most memorable cases involving a woman who had been injured in a car wreck. She and her husband had gone to church on Sunday morning out in the country near Jimmy Carter's boyhood home of Archery. Typical of African-American services in Georgia, worship had extended into Sunday afternoon.

The couple was driving back toward Americus on a country road at about 2:00. Another man, a deer hunter in his pickup truck, was driving on a road that intersected with the road the couple was on. Instead of looking out the windshield as he should have been, he was looking out the passenger window for deer tracks and thus did not notice that he was coming up on an intersection. He collided with the couple's car, injuring the woman's knee severely as it was rammed into the dashboard of the vehicle.

Millard speaks on the phone to a law client, 1982

After Millard took the case, the deer hunter's insurance company simply would not settle, so the case went to trial. Evidence was submitted by various witnesses. Finally, it came time for Millard to give his closing argument to the jury. He told them that his client and her husband had been coming back home following a church service and driving in a lawful manner down the road. The defendant, on the other hand, had not been in church on Sunday. He had been out in his pickup looking for deer tracks. "Now," Millard said, "there is nothing wrong with looking for deer tracks, but there is something wrong with it if you are driving a car. You should be watching where you are going because if you don't, you might run into somebody and injure them, which is exactly what this man did." And then, with considerable emotion, Millard said that what had happened was not right.

An older juror in the front row of the jury box bolted right up out of his seat and exclaimed, "Amen!" Millard could tell

## Vintage Fuller . . .
### "Is This Lawya Fuller?"

When Linda and I returned from Africa in mid-1976, we had virtually no resources but we had four children who needed to be educated. The two older ones were approaching college age. So I opened a law office in the spring of 1977 and one room of that law office was the first official office of Habitat for Humanity. In addition to providing for my family, I wanted to practice law in order to represent the legal needs of low-income people. I made myself available to defend murder cases involving people who were facing a possible death sentence. I traveled far and wide, all over the state of Georgia, trying murder cases. In many instances, there was no doubt about the guilt of a person. I and my associates were simply trying to save them from the electric chair. We did so in every case but one. I'll never forget the day I got a phone call from a lady needing assistance: "Is this Lawya Fuller?"

"Yes," I replied. "What can I do for you?"

"Is you the lawya that works for nuthin?"

"Yes, I suppose I am. What can I do for you?"

It pleased me that I had gotten a reputation in the community for being available to people who did not have any resources. And as I recall, as a "work for nuthin" attorney, I was quite busy!

—Millard Fuller

from the body language of the other jurors that they agreed with him. The lawyers for the defendant could also see that Millard had gotten through to the jury.

When Millard finished his closing argument, the judge called for a recess. The defense lawyers came over to his table and said, "There is no reason to prolong this misery. We see you've won the case. We'll just write you a check for the policy limits so we can go on home!" That was not the only time Millard ever had a juror say "Amen!" in response to an argument he was making.

Now that Millard's law practice was taking off, and Habitat

for Humanity was underway, new living and working arrangements were desperately needed.

## Habitat Gets a Home

Thus, the Fullers bought a 1,200-square-foot house in nearby Americus where Millard could establish a law office and develop Habitat for Humanity. They paid $4,000 for an old house with a broken-down porch, which would become Millard's office. In addition, they agreed to pay $12,500 for an old house that would be their residence for the next twenty-three years.

It pretty much fell on Linda's shoulders to turn a rundown house into a presentable law office on a very low budget, and to make another old home a decent place for the family to live. She involved the children in basic home repairs, such as painting and other chores. Millard continued working at Koinonia until Linda had completed the renovation on the

Habitat for Humanity's first headquarters
in front room of Millard's law office, 1977

new office. He had two phones on his desk—one for Habitat and one for the law practice. Linda's desk was up front in the waiting room. She greeted clients and ran the office. She typed up all the legal documents and prepared letters for Habitat for Humanity to solicit or acknowledge donations. *Habitat Happenings* newsletters were printed on an old cylinder lithographing machine. These newsletters had to be folded, stuffed in envelopes, sealed, and stamped. The Fuller children often helped after school and in the evenings.

As word spread, people began calling Millard Fuller to ask for help with their own plans for building housing for impoverished neighbors or within a neighborhood. In January 1977, three young pastors asked the Fullers if the partnership housing concept would work in the hills of Tennessee. The Morgan-Scott Project—named for two counties it served— had worked for five years to aid low-income residents in rural Appalachia. Housing was among the greatest needs in the area. In fact, some 40 percent of the houses in Morgan and Scott counties had been classified as substandard. Enthusiastic about the application of partnership housing in Appalachia, and feeling it would succeed, the Fullers encouraged and supported the Morgan-Scott effort. John and Mary Hawn and their four children were chosen to be the first family to receive a Habitat for Humanity home in Appalachia. Many people in the community and from other states helped the Hawns build their home, lay grass, plant shrubs, and move in. With the Hawn home barely completed, two more homes went up—one in a nearby neighborhood in Morgan County and the other in next-door Scott County.

## Affiliates Are Created

In community after community, the idea of partnership housing caught on. It seemed a natural thing to do—building homes for people in need. When word got out there was going to be an old-fashioned "barn-raising"—building a home—people in the community, young and old, turned out. People even traveled from other states, taking a week's vacation to help someone have—as was the Fullers' vision—a simple and decent place to live. There was something for everyone to do, from making generous financial contributions, to engaging in smaller efforts to raise money, such as having car washes or rummage and bake sales to help buy nails, cement, lumber, doors and windows. Most people found that building a home was not only a good thing to do for a family, but it was fun, too. And when the house was completed, it instilled community pride resulting in folks patting themselves on the back for months and months. Many wanted to repeat the experience. If they could build one or two homes, why not more? If they could raise money for one home, why not another? From this enthusiasm emerged affiliates of Habitat for Humanity, local groups that would focus on providing homes for the poor in their own communities. Eventually Habitat would encompass more than 1,700 affiliates in the United States and hundreds more in a hundred countries.

In 1978, at the suggestion of a national church leader, Millard made a trip to Guatemala to visit an American missionary. He planned to see if a second international project was feasible, and he was excited about its potential. The missionary, Bob Stevens, had just read Millard's book, *Bokotola,* and was inspired to start Habitat in Guatemala. Discussions ensued, and Habitat for Humanity Guatemala would become Habitat's first project in Latin America and its second project outside the United States. The operation in Guatemala would build twenty-five thousand houses in the next twenty-seven years.

Another person who had read Millard's book, the Reverend Jack Takayanagi of the Almaden Valley United Church of Christ in San Jose, California, was so moved that he gave a copy to every member of his congregation, challenging them to do something about the great need for housing for the poor. At that time, there were no Habitat affiliates in California. Eight years later, in the spring of 1986, there were six Habitat projects in California. One of these was in Fresno, which had become Habitat's 100th affiliate the year before.

## Habitat Outgrows Its First Home

Habitat's staff outgrew its offices. Both Habitat and the law business had increased to the extent that it was time to find more space to house volunteers and make more work areas. Also, the need for a full-time administrator became critical, especially with Millard traveling the country, recruiting more and more volunteers to help with the ever-expanding Habitat ministry. Millard bought two houses adjacent to the law office for $13,000. Jim Prickett, a semi-retired pastor from Evansville, Indiana, took over as administrator, and wife Janette served as volunteer bookkeeper.

During the first few years of Habitat's existence, the long hours and hard work started paying off. Habitat for Humanity

Second Habitat headquarters, next to Millard's law office, 1979

Fuller family members join a visiting team of volunteers by the first HFHI headquarters sign, 1980

was bringing in donations and building homes—and improving neighborhoods. Communities were being transformed. Sturdy new homes replaced shaky shacks. As more and more neighborhoods got facelifts, word began to circulate—a term that also characterized Habitat's tireless, relentless crusader, Millard Fuller. A dynamic person, powerful speaker, avid correspondent, and serious crusader for God's people in need of "a simple, decent place to live," Millard accepted every speaking engagement he could with the goal of attracting more and more donors and volunteers so they could continue to build more and more houses. "There are fifty states in the United States, and some 190-plus countries," Millard would say, "and Habitat will build homes in every one of them."

At the beginning of 1986, Habitat for Humanity had modest projects underway in twenty-five locations in fourteen developing countries, including Zaire, Uganda, Peru, India, and Papua New Guinea. And, in every case, people had contacted Habitat headquarters requesting assistance in starting Habitat in their town, their state, their nation.

In the United States, Habitat partners were inspired to form regional centers. Each regional center covered several states and offered speakers, guidance, and resources of all kinds to Habitat affiliates and other interested groups. They also promoted and encouraged support for the worldwide work of Habitat for Humanity. Habitat Midwest Regional Office, covering nine states, was formed in Chicago. Mary Brock of Dallas, Texas, formed Habitat Southwest, covering the huge territory of Texas and Oklahoma. In Acton, Massachusetts, Ron and Barbara Yates formed Habitat Northeast, devoting enormous energy throughout New England and New York.

## "Infectious Habititis"

When Millard's book *No More Shacks!* was published in 1986, Habitat had expanded to all but fifteen of the fifty states of the United States, with houses going up in 145 locations.

Work overseas was continuing to go strong. Habitat for Humanity was expanding so rapidly that it would assist thirty or more towns and cities in the United States to start an affiliate every year over the next ten years, and that number would continue to increase through the mid-1990s.

True to the philosophy of the grass-roots movement Habitat had become, each affiliate was an independent non-profit organization. A governing board comprised of diverse individuals touched with "infectious Habititis" developed their affiliates to include committees dedicated to local fundraising and awareness, land acquisitions and construction, family selection and nurturing, and many other facets important to growing their affiliate and eliminating poverty housing in their communities.

Naturally, as each community differed from another, some being urban, with virtually unlimited local resources, others being rural, with resource challenges, the structure of each affiliate adapted appropriately in each community. And every affiliate, whether urban or rural, domestic or international, was encouraged and expected, though not required, to contribute financially to build Habitat homes in other locations.

Each new Habitat house became a shining example of what Christian love in action could accomplish. Each house showed how ordinary citizens could work to eradicate poverty within their own neighborhoods and towns. "The statistics and the size of the problem of housing needed for the poor are mind-boggling," Millard would write, "but it is not insoluble. There is a terrible temptation to attend to our own comfort only, and to turn our backs on the needs of others. When we do that, we become part of the problem. Let's find ways to become part of the solution."

## Habitat: A Pilot Effort

But while hundreds of houses for poor families had been built, the value of the projects was infinitely greater than the number of homes completed. And this was, after all, Habitat's mission. It was never to take over or resolve the housing crisis alone, but rather to serve as a beacon of light, as former President Jimmy Carter explained in an interview that appeared in the December 1984 issue of the quarterly newspaper, *Habitat World:*

"There is no way that Habitat can build all the homes that (are) necessary in the world. And what we'll have to do in the relatively near future is to decide not only how Habitat fits within the existing structure of home building, private investors, independent family with the capacity to build, state and federal programs here and in other countries, international organizations like the United Nations and the World Bank, and other benevolent groups, but we'll in addition to that assessment have to decide how Habitat's concept—which I think is unique, and effective, and inspiring—can be used to generate similar efforts throughout the world that won't be directly associated with Habitat at all. My own inclination is that Habitat should not concentrate its efforts in too large a degree in one particular community or even in one particular nation, but that we should implant the Habitat seed in the most needy places that we can identify, and let the Habitat program be, in effect, a pilot effort that could be emulated by others.

"What I'm talking about is—do a limited number of Habitat projects in a particular region and then try to encourage private investors and government officials and others to emulate what we're doing. This is what Habitat wants to do. Plant projects all over the world; sow seeds of hope, encouraging the poor to do all they can to help themselves; and cultivate consciences among the affluent, urging them, privately or corporately, to join less fortunate folks in a spirit of partnership, to solve the problem together."

In 1985, Millard projected that Habitat would work in more than 1,000 U.S. cities and 50 countries by 1995. His predictions were close to the mark. By 1995, Habitat worked in 1,136 cities and 47 countries. That kind of growth did not happen by accident. Millard and Linda and their supporters were so dedicated to Habitat, so intent on raising money and awareness, that they were constantly thinking of new ways to market the organization. One of the most novel techniques unfolded in 1983 on the occasion of Habitat's seventh anniversary.

# — 14 —

# Habitat's Seventh Year Birthday Bash: The Indy 700 Walk

With each passing year, more and more people anxiously anticipated that Habitat would begin in their community. But for every Habitat for Humanity home that was being built or envisioned, money was needed. Indeed, Habitat's biggest challenge was matching leadership capacity with rapid growth and keeping the contributions pouring in. While Habitat for Humanity's renown was growing, Millard knew that more supporters and donors were necessary if additional houses were going to be built.

With raising money for building homes always on his mind, Millard took a fresh look at how Habitat's seven-year anniversary could be fashioned into a fundraiser. It would have to be creative and interesting—not just a mailer to Habitat's faithful contributors. And it should be something that would help dramatize the need for housing and sensitize even more people into helping the poor escape their deplorable housing conditions. Although popular with a small percentage of the U.S. population, Habitat's ministry was still unknown to a large number of people, necessitating the need to get the word out.

A seven-hundred-mile walk, from Americus to Indianapolis, might be just the thing to raise both funds and awareness. The walk could be promoted in the Habitat newsletter, and people could be asked to make pledges toward each mile. Millard would urge others to join the forty-day walk, for either the whole distance or some part of it. They, too, would collect pledges. The goal of the walk would be to raise at least $100,000.

And so, on the third weekend of September 1983, a grand celebration to promote and raise funds for Habitat's seventh birthday was planned in Indianapolis in conjunction with the fall board meeting.

The walk was promoted in an early 1983 issue of the Habitat newsletter, spelling out the threefold purpose:

"First of all, as concerned Christians, we want to dramatize the need of so many people in our world for a simple, decent place in which to live. We want to call attention to the urgency of this problem and to make a bold statement that the problem, as enormous as it is, can be solved. Jesus tells us that with God, all things are possible, and we believe it. However, God has no hands and no feet but ours.

"Second, we hope to raise at least $100,000 by this walk. We are calling on people to make pledges of so much a mile, to be paid before the end of 1983.

"The third purpose of our long trek is simply to say to you that if we can walk from Americus, you should be able to get to Indianapolis somehow! Perhaps you'd like to walk with us. Write if you're interested. You can walk the whole distance, or some part of it."

The public's response was instantaneous: They loved it! Pledges—and gifts—began rolling in, so much so that Habitat reached the halfway mark even before the walk began.

Pledges arrived in checks of $50 all the way up to $20,000. On the night before the walk, former First Lady Rosalynn Carter's secretary informed the Fullers that Rosalynn and her daughter, Amy, would join them for the send-off, walking with them to the edge of town.

Three months prior, Millard started training for his own participation in the walk. Although at first, Linda was not too keen on the idea, she thought it best that she train, too, just in case Millard sprained an ankle or had some other injury that would prevent him from walking temporarily and she would need to take his place. They started walking three miles a day. After about a week, they increased to five miles per day. When muscle soreness let up, they started getting up early to walk five miles before breakfast and another five after dinner. "The training had a lot of benefits," Millard noted. "Linda and I enjoyed the time together—away from the phones and the chance it gave us to visit about things going on with the children and other personal matters."

Two pairs of worn-out shoes later, Linda and Millard were ready. Later, during the walk, when the first 140 miles had seemed like "a piece of cake" to Linda, she decided to walk alongside Millard the whole distance to Indianapolis. Nothing pleased him more than for her to make that commitment.

At 6:00 a.m. on Wednesday, August 3, 1983, the kickoff for what had been charted as a forty-day, seven-hundred-mile walk was held in front of the Habitat headquarters building at the corner of West Church and Dudley. A large crowd had gathered for the brief send-off ceremony, which closed with shouts of "Habitat *Oyée!*"—the cheer the Fullers had brought home from Zaire. (In Zaire, when a large meeting is held, and a person wants to affirm someone, the leader simply yells that person's name, followed by "*Oyée,*" pronounced *oh-yea,* and the crowd echoes, "*Oyée!*")

At 6:30 a.m. the entire assemblage, including former First Lady Rosalynn Carter and her daughter, Amy, fell in behind a banner reading:

## 700-MILE WALK
## AMERICUS TO INDIANAPOLIS
## HABITAT FOR HUMANITY

"It was exciting for us to walk through downtown Americus with a former first lady of the United States and first daughter by our sides," Linda would say later. "That's when I started thinking I'd go ahead and walk all the way to Atlanta."

As the walk started out, the crowd numbers were over two hundred strong. From town to town, the crowd would dwindle, but as they approached another town, more people would be added. While Linda would laugh and chatter to everyone the whole way, Millard's mood was a bit somber. For him, the trek would be bittersweet and crystallize how far not only Habitat had come, but society as well. With these thoughts, he was humbled, even tearful. As the group marched up Dudley Street, past the courthouse, turning right on Lamar Street and heading into downtown Americus singing, "We're Marching to Zion," Millard was reminded of the tremendous significance this hymn held for Linda and him. "It was the song God put in our hearts eighteen years earlier, when we were returning to Alabama on a plane from New York City," Millard said. "We had just decided to change our lives' direction completely, and to follow a path of Christian service."

Millard recalled the last time he and Linda had walked up Lamar Street for another type of demonstration. It was in August 1971, and the black citizens of Americus had become incensed over instances of discrimination and police brutality. Meetings were being held in black churches all over town. Protest walks were being staged around the courthouse. Several people from Koinonia, after investigating the citizens' complaints, had joined their cause, and hundreds of people had marched along this same route singing "We Shall Overcome" and "Ain't Nobody Gonna Turn Us Around."

By 1983, much had changed—for the better. The group

marching shoulder to shoulder was an integrated group—the mayor, the police chief, a former First Lady, and a black city councilman were among them, celebrating Habitat's mission and coming together to help the needy. "My heart was talking to me," Millard would later say, "and my joy and gratitude were overwhelming at times." Linda, too, was seeing and feeling the many exciting things going on with the housing ministry's ability to break down the walls of discrimination. "When so many from all across the country join forces to help build a home for those in need of a decent place to live," she observed, "there is a real chance for brotherhood and sisterhood among all to grow—regardless of one's age, race, religion, or political views."

## Birdsie's Feed Store

Signs of progress emerged at every turn. As the group headed north on Lee Street, Millard saw the building that was once Birdsie's Feed Store. "It had been dynamited in the late 1950s because the store sold some things to Koinonia during the boycott by local merchants," Millard said. "It was never reopened. Now, every other store in town was gladly doing business with the farm." After Birdsie's Feed Store, the group passed a long row of houses built by the Partnership Housing program of Koinonia—each using Kingdom Economics. Twenty-three new homes had been built right around the Staley Middle School by Koinonia and Habitat building crews, replacing the falling-down shacks that had stood there for years. "As my eye scanned these sturdy homes, and as many of the occupants stood in their yards and waved to us, my heart filled up again with emotion," Millard would later write. "I could feel tears coming. This is why we're walking, I thought."

Example after example of a new time—a new era—was around every corner and on every street they passed.

Throughout the long walk to Indianapolis, Millard's drive to get the word out—to bring in donations so this housing ministry could continue—intensified. The walk was proving

Habitat for Humanity could do just that. From town to town, from city to city, the group marched on—and they were joined by many others along the way. From time to time, they received police escorts—once that even included law enforcement officers on horseback. The Habitat group would walk briskly behind the police car or horses, passing out Habitat materials to anyone who seemed interested. All the while, they would shout, "Habitat *Oyée*," and poke Habitat newsletters and fliers into the windows of every car that had a driver with a friendly face, and into the hands of anyone on the sidewalks who looked receptive. "The policemen would sound their sirens every couple of minutes so no one could ignore us," Linda said. "We did get a lot of attention. It was great!"

The group often stayed overnight in the homes of various church families. On Sunday mornings, they would fan out to different churches to worship and to tell the Habitat story in the afternoon. On and on they marched, eighteen to twenty miles per day, stopping to talk, witness, and drum up donations and support for Habitat for Humanity. They even stopped to enjoy an Atlanta Braves baseball game in Atlanta.

When the group arrived in Indianapolis on Monday, September 12, the celebration that followed was spectacular. For three days, Habitat volunteers from thirty-nine states, the District of Columbia, and twelve foreign countries jammed the Roberts Park United Methodist Church. The evening national news covered the event, and viewers saw clips from a slide presentation on homebuilding around the world titled "Celebrate Habitat." It moved many of them to tears. More than the $100,000 goal was raised, a large number of new supporters were enlisted, and many seeds were planted for new Habitat affiliates all along the 700-mile route.

On Saturday, a special "separating out" service honored eight new volunteers who were about to leave for overseas projects. Habitat Board Member David Rowe reminded the exuberant, cheering, and filled-with-love-and-purpose crowd that the joy they were feeling was perhaps the experience of

Linda and Millard end seven-hundred-mile trek from Americus, Ga., to Indianapolis. Zenon Colque Rojas of Peru (standing between Linda and Millard) and Hugh O'Brien of Ireland (not shown) also walked the entire distance, 1983.

Seventh Anniversary Celebration of Habitat for Humanity, Indianapolis, 1983

"Heaven on Earth," and that Habitat was blessed by God since their work, their mission of building homes for those in need, was a demonstration of God's love in action. He would tell the spellbound crowd:

"It is not enough to speculate on social change. There are people who prefer to sit in a lovely office, talking, and planning, and theologizing. On the other extreme, there are terrorist groups who prefer to create mass horror and fear in the hope that some new order will emerge. But between the theory brokers and the terror brokers stand those like Habitat for Humanity, who choose to act, however humbly, who choose to serve, however inadequately, who choose to work, however meagerly . . .

"So we build, and we build, and we build. We build houses; we build communities; we build friendships; we build mailing lists; we build compassion. We build with the spirit of God poured into every foundation, fired into every brick, driven into every board, turned in with every key. We build amid mountains of red tape, and frustration, and culture shock, and language difficulty, and personality conflicts, and financial crisis, and homesickness, and jealousy. But still somehow we squeeze the love of Jesus into every joint.

"Our building is a symbol of how God's love and our love can work together."

The group left Indianapolis fired up with fresh determination. And it was not long after this exciting weekend that Millard began thinking about walking the thousand miles from Americus to Kansas City for Habitat's tenth anniversary in 1986. These walks received widespread news coverage—thanks to Millard's marketing genius—and helped Habitat for Humanity capture people's hearts, inspiring them to respond to the overwhelming need for decent and affordable housing throughout the nation and around the world.

Atlanta Mayor Andrew Young, left, talks during lunchtime visit here with Millard Fuller and Mayor Russell Thomas, Jr

## Atlanta mayor Young visits here at Habitat for Humanity

Andrew Young visits with Millard and Americus Mayor Russell Thomas, Jr., 1984

## Vintage Fuller . . .
## "Jesus Built My House"

I was in Charlotte, North Carolina, speaking in a church. I spoke in an early service and was slated to preach at the second service. There was about an hour between the two services. I asked one of the laymen in the church, "Would you drive me out to Optimist Park? I want to go out and see where we built those fourteen houses in five days sometime back." By that time the Habitat people had built a grand total of fifty-seven houses.

In Charlotte, they've now built almost two hundred houses in Optimist Park and in Belmont, a neighborhood right across the creek. They've transformed these two neighborhoods. I said, "I just want to see it." As we drove into the neighborhood that day, I could see that a tremendous transformation had taken place. There were no more wrecked cars. There were no more boarded-up windows. There were no more weeds growing all over the place and trash scattered all over the streets as there had been in the past. It was a beautiful neighborhood of well-kept, well-manicured lawns and modest but good and solid houses.

We got to the street where we had built the fourteen houses. I told the man who was driving the car, a man named Aubrey, I said, "Aubrey, drive really slowly." It was very emotional for me to see those houses and see how beautiful they were. We got down to the end of the street, turned around, and started coming back up the street. And when we got right in front of the house that Jimmy and Rosalynn Carter had worked on, we stopped because a car in front of us stopped to let someone out. There was a little boy playing in the front yard, a little tyke, maybe five or six years old, and when he saw our car stopped, he, like a kid will do, he comes running out, put his hand on the car, and he said, "Man, y'all got a pretty car!" And I said, "Young man, you've got a pretty house." I said, "What's your name?" He said, "My name is DJ." And I asked him, "DJ, who built your house?" And I thought for sure he was going to say, "Jimmy Carter built my house." But instead, with this big smile on his face, he said, "Jesus built my house."

Witnessing with a hammer, the message gets through. That's what all of us are called to do. To be the hands, the legs, the arms, the feet of Jesus.

—Millard Fuller

Jimmy Carter (left) with house leader, LeRoy Troyer, and another volunteer cutting pieces for steps, Pikeville, Ky., 1997

Former First Lady Rosalynn Carter putting the theology of the hammer to work

Habitat's most famous volunteer, former President Jimmy Carter

First Lady Rosalynn Carter signing a hard hat

# — 15 —

# President Carter
# Becomes Habitat's
# Most Famous Volunteer

Habitat was on the move. In just seven years, from its humble beginnings in 1976, scores of Habitat homes had been built in thirty-two U.S. cities and seven foreign countries. Despite its burgeoning success and the fact that more and more people throughout the nation and the world were seeing how this rapidly expanding ministry was touching thousands of lives each day, only those who worked closely with the organization realized how much "muscle" went into its success. They also knew how many more volunteers and contributions were needed to propel Habitat to greater heights and fulfill the Fullers' cherished dreams that the Habitat housing ministry be in every country on the face of the Earth. This goal was about to get a hand from a former president of the United States. His status, down-home demeanor, and popularity with a large Christian audience would make Jimmy Carter's involvement with Habitat a natural fit—one that would serve both Habitat and President Carter well in the coming years.

Because he generously gave permission to Habitat to use his signature on millions of mailings, even today some people mistakenly believe that Carter started Habitat for Humanity after he left the White House. Often, his letter was the first time people had heard about Habitat, so they naturally associated his name with the organization. In fact, President Carter only learned of Habitat for Humanity in 1980 from Ralph and Jane Gnann, his friends and former neighbors in Plains, Georgia. In September of that year, the Carters invited the Gnanns to spend a couple of days at the White House shortly before the Gnanns left for Zaire to volunteer for two years with Habitat.

## The Carters Become "Very Interested"

When President Carter left the White House in January 1981, he and his wife, Rosalynn, returned to their home in Plains, Georgia. The Carters had been members of Plains Baptist Church prior to their sojourn in Washington, D.C. During their time away, the church had split over the issue of openness to blacks attending worship services. Members who felt that the church should welcome all races had left the congregation and built a smaller church about a mile down the road. Upon their return to Plains, the Carters joined the new Maranatha Baptist congregation, where President Carter began to teach the adult Sunday school class. It was here that he heard more about Habitat's enlarging ministry from Habitat volunteers and staff who came from Americus to attend his class. In turn, the Habitat volunteers reported back to Millard how, during his classes, President Carter shared his passion for woodworking and carpentry: He had even built his own desk after coming home from the White House. The volunteers strongly suggested that Millard make an appointment to talk with President Carter about the idea of getting involved in Habitat's ministry.

So it was that, in 1982, Habitat's board invited President Carter to a board meeting that was held in Americus at the Presbyterian Church. Carter accepted. "Habitat for Humanity," he told them, "is putting theory into practice in providing shelter for the poor." He also shared his feelings about Koinonia and Clarence Jordan: "I am proud to be a neighbor of Koinonia . . . and to have seen, from perhaps too great a distance, the profound impact of Clarence Jordan on this country . . . and to have known this quiet man who demonstrated in his own life an image of Christ with human fallibility, yes, but with the inspiration of Christ. I think I will be a better Christian because of Clarence Jordan, Koinonia, and Habitat. And I hope to grow the rest of my life, along with you."

The board, especially Millard, was thrilled with Carter's words. Clarence Jordan had been the most influential spiritual leader in Millard's life, helping Millard clarify what God's love in action looked like and was meant to be. Habitat for Humanity was, in effect, a housing ministry based on the application of God's love. Building homes for those in need was, as Millard said, "the Theology of the Hammer." So Carter's high regard for Clarence Jordan really touched Millard.

Later that year, Habitat would receive a generous financial contribution from the Carters. By December 1983, the Fullers had expanded the Habitat headquarters in Americus and invited both President and Mrs. Carter to speak at the inauguration of the new offices. The Carters accepted and brought glowing words of affirmation to those in attendance. Convinced that the Carters were deeply interested in Habitat for Humanity, Millard paid a visit to President and Mrs. Carter on January 23, 1984.

"President Carter," he asked, "are you simply interested in Habitat for Humanity, or are you very interested?" Smiling broadly, President Carter looked over at Rosalynn and then quietly replied, "We're very interested."

"Well," Millard responded, "what do we do with that interest?"

Carter told Millard to return to his office and write a letter explaining all the ways in which the Carters could be helpful,

Third Habitat headquarters building, 1983

and then he and Rosalynn would think about the matter and decide what they could do.

Sixteen days later, Millard mailed the following letter to President and Mrs. Carter:

> February 8, 1984
> President and Mrs. Jimmy Carter
> Plains, GA 31780
>
> Dear President and Mrs. Carter,
> First of all, I want to thank both of you profusely for meeting with me at your home, and for giving generously of your time to discuss Habitat for Humanity. Your words of encouragement and affirmation meant a great deal to me personally, and to all of us who work closely with this growing venture. Your assurance of your strong interest in the work causes hope and rejoicing among us.

As you requested, I returned to the office and engaged everyone in prayer and discussion about how you could be most helpful to Habitat for Humanity. You asked us not to be bashful in suggesting possibilities. As you can see from the long list, we have taken you at your word!

1) One of you could serve as a Director or an Advisor of Habitat for Humanity. By separate mail, I am sending you a full list of directors, advisors, and Habitat project representatives. We are authorized by our Articles of Incorporation to have twenty-five directors. We currently have twenty-two directors. New people are elected each year at the fall meeting. Directors meet twice a year, in the spring and fall, always in a different Habitat project location. Advisors meet with the directors once a year, in the fall. Directors are expected to attend meetings. Advisors are urged to attend. Most directors pay their own way, and advisors travel at their own expense. Both advisors and directors are encouraged to help with administrative expenses of Habitat. Most give generously to those expenses.

2) Make media contacts. The Salvation Army, CARE, Red Cross, the Boy Scouts, and similar organizations have immediate name recognition. Habitat for Humanity does not. You went from "Jimmy Who?" to "Jimmy Carter," a worldwide household name, in a short span of time. If you could make contacts with the appropriate media people to encourage them to do something on Habitat for Humanity, that would be most helpful.

3) Put us in contact with key foundation and corporation people who could be helpful. In 1983 we raised about $2,400,000 from all sources for all projects. This money came almost entirely from individuals and churches. Practically nothing was given by corporations and foundations. That ought to change.

We also need equipment—trucks, construction tools, office computers, media equipment—that could either be donated or sold at a reduced price.

4) Write a letter to your personal friends telling them about Habitat for Humanity and your support of it.

5) Write an endorsement letter in a direct mail campaign soliciting support for Habitat.

6) Put us in touch with other well-known persons who might want to be helpful to Habitat.

7) Do a public service announcement for Habitat for use on television and radio.

8) Do a thirty-minute videotape interview with me about Habitat for Humanity. It would then be made available throughout the country for church school classes and discussion groups.

9) As Southern Baptists, you could be specifically helpful in encouraging more support from them by writing letters to key people. As you know, Habitat for Humanity is totally ecumenical. We have a lot of Southern Baptist support, but not nearly in proportion to what other denominations are doing. We want to change that.

10) Let us arrange speaking engagements in a few key areas of the United States. You would attract large crowds, and of course we would actively promote the events, in accordance with appropriate guidelines set in consultation with you.

11) Visit some overseas Habitat projects. You would gain a more in-depth understanding of the work of Habitat in the third world, and at the same time the trip would give Habitat international visibility and credibility.

12) Visit U.S. Habitat projects.

13) Be a volunteer. If you would work on the Americus construction crew for one day, it would set a great example. You, Rosalynn, could help either in the office or on the construction crew—we don't discriminate against women! We would document your volunteer work on film and let your example inspire others.

14) Personally contribute money. You have already done this, and your gifts are deeply appreciated. Your example of regular contributions will mean much more than the actual dollars you may give.

15) Pray. I am a strong believer in the power of prayer. Your regular prayers are as important as anything on this long list.

As I said above, this is a long list, and I know that you may be able to respond positively to only a few of the suggestions. On the other hand, this list may prompt you to think of other ways in which you could be helpful.

Again, I want to thank you for your friendship, encouragement, and support.

Respectfully, Millard Fuller

## The President Straps On a Tool Belt

A few days later, Millard got his answer. "You wrote a good letter," Carter said. "Rosalynn and I have been talking about it, and we think we can help in most of the ways you suggest." In fact, the Carters agreed to do everything on the list! Millard could scarcely believe it. Carter was serious—and wasted no time in calling people he knew to get them interested in Habitat. He agreed to serve on Habitat's board of directors and Rosalynn on the board of advisors "effective immediately." Once the word got out, Millard had no problem recruiting other big names to join the board.

After visiting a struggling Habitat affiliate as part of a trip he made to New York City, President Carter requested that plans for the first Jimmy Carter Work Project be set in motion. This, too, would bring huge visibility to Habitat for Humanity. Within a month of joining the board, President Carter volunteered a day's work with the construction crew in Americus. He proved not only to be a capable recruiter of volunteers, but a very dedicated and skilled worker. "President Carter always arrived ten minutes early for morning devotions," Millard reports, "and then labored diligently all day."

The annual Jimmy Carter Work Project (JCWP) became extremely popular. Volunteers joined the former president and first lady of the United States clad in jeans and tool belts, helping to give low-income families a decent place to live—a place to call home. That first year, there were less than a hundred volunteers. By the second, more than two hundred presented themselves, ready for work. Many people literally planned their vacations to coincide with the Jimmy Carter

President Carter at work on a Habitat house, Chicago, 1986

Work Project, loading up campers, pickup trucks, and suitcases with tools. RV parking space and sleeping accommodations in schools and hotels were arranged for the week. Everyone was there to help build homes and enjoy the camaraderie. Said Linda of this time, "Fun was had by all. The angels had to be singing!"

## Blitz Builds

The public returned time and time again to participate in what became known as Blitz Builds—the putting up of a home or cluster of homes within a five-day week. The Jimmy Carter Work Projects especially drew a huge crowd, and for good reason. Imagine saying to your friends and co-workers, "I just got back from helping to build homes for Habitat for Humanity. It was great fun and the family whose home I was working on actually moved in at the end of the five days of the build. I took tons of pictures, and even got a few shots of President Carter working. Here's one of me with my house team standing by the homeowners and the former president of the United States, and the former first lady, too!"

Such times were exactly what Habitat needed to become a household name. And there were plenty of them. On one occasion in 1985, after an overnight bus ride from Americus to New York City, the Fullers, President Carter, volunteers, and staff were looking for a place to worship on a Sunday morning. It being summer, though, many of the churches had already completed their services, or their services were already underway. The bus stopped at a fire station in Edison, New Jersey, where they inquired whether there was a church nearby that might have an 11:00 a.m. service. They were directed to the small St. Stephen's Evangelical Lutheran Church, but when they arrived, the sign indicated that here, too, the service was already in process.

"What do you want to do?" President Carter asked.

"We don't have time to go anywhere else," Millard responded. "Let's go in. We're in time for the sermon!"

Jimmy Carter working
on a Habitat house

Much to their surprise, they discovered that the morning service had already concluded, and the congregation was in the rectory having a birthday party for a member who now lived in a nursing home. Of course, the entire congregation recognized President Carter, and stood and clapped when they saw him. The Habitat volunteers apologized for barging in on them, sang "Happy Birthday" to the elderly birthday boy, and then asked if they could use the sanctuary for worship. The pastor, E. Walter Cleckley, Jr., astonished that President Carter had come to his church, told them, "Of course, you may use the sanctuary. But if you'd like, we'll be glad to repeat our service for you." And so the service was repeated. Imagine the buzz in that community over the next few months—not to mention new Habitat fans!

President Carter's presence didn't only motivate people to open their hearts, but their wallets as well. At the end of the 1985 Jimmy Carter Work Project, a huge crowd filled St. Bartholomew's Episcopal Church in New York City for the special concluding celebration. Following an evening of music, speeches, and prayers, hard hats were passed down the pews for the offering. The collection was then dumped into wheelbarrows and pushed up the aisles to the front of the sanctuary. In just one evening, over $10,000 was raised!

## Vintage Fuller . . .
## Ten Nails

Habitat is not a doctrinal organization. Doctrine is the province of the church. The Church of God has doctrines. The Presbyterian Church has doctrines. The Methodist Church has doctrines. All churches have doctrines, and that's fine. But in Habitat for Humanity, we bring all of these people with different doctrines together, and we just simply agree on the tool of Jesus, which is a hammer. And we agree that the Gospel compels us to serve with love in our hearts. But we do have one doctrinal point, and that is if you don't have a Habitat bumper sticker on your car, you are living in sin. And we say that because we need a lot of people involved with this ministry to eradicate substandard housing, so we've got to do something to invite strangers in. I travel on planes a lot, and I'm so concerned about not living in sin that I have a bumper sticker on my briefcase! People often see the briefcase and say, "Habitat for Humanity? Let's see now, what do you do?" Then I say, "We build houses for people in need of a decent place to live." And sometimes they say, "Well, gee, I'm not sure I've ever heard of that." And I say, "Well, Jimmy Carter works for us." And a light bulb goes on. "Oh, that's the organization that Jimmy Carter works for. Oh well, then, I know all about Habitat for Humanity." More recently, they've seen my bumper sticker, and they say, "Oh, Habitat for Humanity! That's the outfit whose houses didn't blow away from the hurricane down in Miami! I know about your organization. How can you explain your houses not blowing away?" And I always tell them, "Because we build them on rocks! The Bible says you build your house on a rock and it won't blow away, and that's what we do. Another reason is that our houses are built mostly by volunteers, a lot of people who really don't know what they're doing. So if the rules call for two nails, they put in ten. And then when a hurricane comes along, it doesn't have a chance to destroy a Habitat house!"

—Millard Fuller

## Raising Funds and Awareness

President Carter's creative fundraising efforts benefited Habitat on a number of other occasions, too. When it was brought to President Carter's attention that a company had used his picture in an ad campaign without his knowledge, he called the company's head office and inquired pointedly as to who had given them permission to use his image. When it was discovered that they had neglected to secure permission for the use of his photo, President Carter noted that he wasn't seeking personal remuneration, but he did think it would be a very nice gesture for the company to send a contribution of $10,000 to Habitat for Humanity. Within a few days, Habitat received the check. And when the Ralston Purina Company contacted the Carters requesting permission to feature the Carters' cat, Misty Malarky, in the company's 1986 calendar, the Carters approved on the condition that a gift of $5,000 be made to Habitat for Humanity.

Like Millard, Jimmy Carter was a tireless crusader. For all the invitations to speak to colleges, conventions, and all types of organizations that flooded his office daily, President Carter sometimes accepted the invitations—but only on the condition that a "generous donation" be sent to Habitat for Humanity.

LeRoy Troyer and Jimmy Carter on a Habitat work site, 1989

In the fall of 1984, when the Carters took a personal trip to several South American countries, they made their last stop at the Habitat project in Puno, Peru. Naturally, wherever they went, there was huge media coverage. In a meeting with Peruvian leaders, the Carters discussed the purpose of their visit to the country—and spread the word about Habitat. By the time the Carters had left, the entire nation had heard about Habitat.

By 1986, Habitat for Humanity had become known to millions of people throughout the world. And, in the case of every project, a few people had contacted Habitat headquarters requesting assistance in starting a Habitat affiliate in their own town, state, or nation. New doors opened for raising funds, securing volunteers, and acquiring land, tools, and materials.

President Carter served faithfully on Habitat's board of directors for three years (1985–88), and both President Carter and Rosalynn helped in scores of other ways in the years to come. Through their efforts and publicity, Habitat reached an entirely new level, both nationally and globally.

## President Ford Gets Involved

As a result of the publicity generated by the Carters' involvement, Habitat began to get a lot of mail. Many letters were very positive; most people were impressed with President Carter's integrity and his strong Christian witness. Other letter writers, however, complained that Habitat had become an arm of the Democratic Party, and requested that their names be removed from Habitat's mailing list because of its "open association with former President Carter, a Democrat."

"Habitat," Millard explained, "isn't political, and it's my experience that both [Republicans and Democrats] are needed to help us build homes for the poor." Still, always one to remove barriers to getting on with the work of building homes for those living in poverty, Millard began to look for a

APRIL 1991

# Habitat receives high praise from former President Gerald Ford

Enjoying a light moment with Habitat for Humanity President Millard Fuller during a press conference on February 4 in Indio, California, former President Gerald Ford endorsed Habitat's work. The ex-president was briefed on work Habitat is doing specifically in the Coachella Valley, which includes Indio. "My best contribution is a public en-dorsement," Ford said. "We need to get valley people to understand the program and to endorse it." Ford, who was quoted in The Indio Post as stating that Habitat has the best low-cost housing program he has seen, agreed to serve on the Habitat for Humanity board of advisors. Advisors include former First Lady Rosalynn Carter, Gospel singer Amy Grant, John Bontreger of Signature Inns, Inc., and many others.

Habitat activity in the Coachella Valley area has escalated with the acquisition of two lots, reported Coachella Valley HFH Director Clarence Spier.

(Photograph by Daniel Sims, Desert Sun Community Newspaper Group)

well-known Republican to become involved in Habitat for Humanity. Hopeful that former President Gerald Ford might agree to get involved, Millard paid him a visit. Millard discussed with the former president the dilemma Habitat faced with people thinking the organization had come under the influence of the Democratic Party, and he confessed that he needed a highly visible Republican to be involved and supportive. "You, sir," Millard announced, "are a highly visible Republican! If you would become involved with Habitat, that would be very helpful to counteract this idea that we have become political."

President Ford was immediately and totally positive in his

response. He said that he knew about Habitat and thought it was a very fine program. He would gladly embrace Habitat and be supportive in whatever ways he could, including service on the board of advisors. The Fullers and President Ford then stepped outside to a waiting press conference. President Ford began by stating his support for Habitat for Humanity and announcing his agreement to serve on its board of advisors. "But," he continued, "I can't be another Jimmy Carter. I don't have construction skills. If my wife gives me a nail to put up a picture, I bend it!"

Millard laughed, and then quipped, "Mr. President, Habitat for Humanity can use anyone. Even a totally unskilled person, such as yourself, can serve as a bad example!"

President Ford enjoyed the press conference and involved himself in supporting Habitat and its mission for many years to come. And Millard's strategy to involve a Republican president effectively put an end to the talk about Habitat being a Democratic organization.

But while involving prominent figures so as to draw attention to the cause of poverty housing was urgently needed, nothing excited the Fullers more than recruiting people from all walks of life to join the movement to eliminate substandard housing. "If you can hold a hammer, or send in a dollar to buy one for someone who can," Millard told a crowd of would-be volunteers, "we can use you. And need you."

## Habitat Becomes a Movement

Greatly aided by President Carter's and President Ford's support, Millard Fuller's dream that Habitat for Humanity would be as well recognized as the Boy Scouts of America was coming true. Millions of people throughout the world were hearing about its work and beginning to grasp the idea that poverty housing was something they had a stake in helping to eradicate. And few could take aim at this movement. It wasn't political; it wasn't denominational; it wasn't gender-biased; and it was color-blind. Millard noted, "It's just plain ole fun to

Newt Gingrich and Millard on a
Habitat work site in Pikeville, Ky., 1997

find a black Baptist working with a white Episcopalian and learning that a Presbyterian really can drive a nail. And to get these conservative folks and these liberal folks and the west side of town getting to know the east side of town and folks from the north getting to know folks from the south. Why, I once saw Newt Gingrich maneuvering a piece of drywall into place with the help of Jimmy Carter! Now that's a perfect example of the "Theology of the Hammer" and goes to show you that all things are possible!"

Habitat for Humanity was becoming a household name, and a well-loved one at that. Millard's vision launched and energized the housing movement worldwide. His contagious enthusiasm, prayerful leadership, and inspiring words of encouragement ensured that the idea of Partnership Housing—of putting hands and feet to faith—would continue to grow, expressing itself uniquely in every community it touched.

## Vintage Fuller . . .
## Joanne Waters

I was on the West Coast, in Eureka, California, and the Methodists were holding a conference. They brought about 1,200 Methodists together from northern California and Nevada for their Jubilee '92 Conference. And they decided as a part of that conference, instead of just coming and having sessions, they would work with the local Habitat affiliate and build two houses. And so they raised money, they bought materials, and over four days they built one house for a poor family in the little town of Manila, and they built another house for a woman in McKinleyville. I was there on the last day, and they took me out to the building sites where the houses were nearing completion.

When I came up to the building site in McKinleyville, I saw this woman coming toward me. She was weeping. She came right up to me and grabbed me, and very strongly embraced me and tried to speak. She was never able to say anything. Eventually, she turned and walked away from me. The project director came over and said, "Millard, that's the homeowner. Her name is Joanne Waters, and don't worry about her crying. We've been building this house for four days, and she's been crying for four days. She's a single mother. She has a nine-year-old son and an eleven-year-old son. Her husband abandoned her. She's a waitress in a local restaurant. She doesn't make enough money to afford housing, and so she now lives in a garage. She and her boys are trying to make a life for themselves but things are tough. Seeing her appreciation for this home we are building her has touched my heart! The first day we got the walls up, we put the trusses up, we put the felt on, we got the doors and the windows installed, and at the end of the work day we all went home. And then I remembered that I had left something at the construction site. So I got my flashlight and I went back over there, and when I was walking around inside, I heard a noise. I went into what would be the living room, and there, sitting in the middle of the floor, was Joanne Waters, by herself, in the dark, just silently weeping. For me, it was this magical, wonderful, incredible moment." In building homes for others, I've had thousands of those moments in seeing the gratitude and thankfulness within someone's heart. And so have the thousands of volunteers who come and build homes for those who need them. That experience is truly a feeling of unconditional love. Very pleasing to God.

—Millard Fuller

# — 16 —

# Growing a Movement

With houses going up all over the world, Millard often said, "The sun never sets on Habitat." During the annual Jimmy Carter Work Projects alone, volunteers would build as many as 293 houses in five days. Habitat was truly on the move: The number of building sites around the globe quadrupled, as had its mailing list. A new building was erected at Habitat headquarters to accommodate the ever-growing staff of volunteers.

At times, it seemed to Millard that Habitat had taken on a life of its own, advancing into so many locations so quickly. Everywhere Habitat went communities blossomed, making the face of Habitat ever-changing, dynamic, and powerful. It was a lot to be responsible for. Millard had great confidence in the local leadership of the affiliates and his staff and volunteers in Americus, but being Habitat's champion would require more of him than confidence; time and again, Millard would look back to his upbringing for the tools he needed to lead this movement.

## Responsible Stewardship

The good stewardship Millard learned from his father in his earliest entrepreneurial years would serve him well in this rapidly expanding ministry. His father's reminder to Millard that "a dollar saved is a dollar earned" now meant that every dollar donated to Habitat was used wisely, frugally, and toward the goal of building a house for someone. To that end, Millard ran a bare-bones operation, which was also one of the great selling points he made to potential donors. The organization was staffed largely by volunteers, and administrative costs were extremely low compared with those of similar organizations. In Americus, volunteers received a weekly $50 stipend. It came to be known as their "pig check" because they used it to buy groceries at the local Piggly Wiggly supermarket.

Millard was penny-pinching in granting himself a salary, too. In 1980, his salary was $15,000—not much for a family of six. His salary was supplemented by his part-time law practice. Although Linda dedicated much of her time to Habitat duties, she didn't draw a salary until one day in 1986, when she paid Millard a visit at the office. She told him: "Millard, I know we decided a long time ago to live simply and that you're committed to drawing a small salary from Habitat, but I don't think the Lord wants our children to go without food, and . . . we're at that point."

Millard got the message. "Okay," he said, "we need to put you on the payroll. How much do we need for groceries?"

They agreed to an annual salary for Linda of $8,000. When the Fullers' children started going to college, finances got tight again. Linda's salary doubled to ease the crunch. By 1993, the Fullers' combined salaries were $60,000.

Millard's money management measures were greatly valued and respected. It was well known that every cent Habitat received from donations found its way to building a home for a family in need. Contributions, as well as more volunteers and full-time staff, were always needed. Habitat always had its

Millard receives his first honarary doctorate at Eastern College, St. Davids, Pa., 1985

hand extended to help recruit more sponsors, prepare building sites, acquire building materials, select and work with the families who would be the new homeowners, and get commitments for food and beverages for the volunteer builders. Millard and Linda were always looking for creative ways to raise more money. And always they came up with a plan which others would get behind, and have a lot of fun while doing.

## Aim High—A Thousand-Mile Walk from Americus to Kansas City

With the ever-growing need for contributions, Millard set in motion his most ambitious fundraising agenda yet for Habitat's tenth anniversary celebration. Based on the success of the walk from Americus to Indianapolis, Indiana, in 1983, Millard conceived a thousand-mile walk from Americus, Georgia, to Kansas City, Missouri, where a Habitat board meeting and tenth anniversary celebration would be held. A goal was set to raise $1 million—ten times as much as the Indianapolis seven-hundred-mile walk—as part of an overall $10 million goal for the tenth anniversary. As importantly, hundreds of new supporters could be enlisted and seeds would be planted for new Habitat affiliates all along the route.

Participants were expected from across North America and around the globe. Delegations of Habitat people from Costa Rica, Zaire, Papua New Guinea, Bolivia, India, Uganda, Peru, Germany, and Ireland would attend the celebration, some of whom were recipients of Habitat homes. With the burgeoning crowd expected to participate, the walk had to be well organized. Volunteers planned every single detail, from driving the route to planning each and every break and overnight stop, each one pinpointed on a map. Arrangements for lodging, meals, police escorts, greetings, and proclamations by officials and church leaders were made. Gymnasiums where walkers could unfold their sleeping bags and take showers were secured. Food would be provided, picnic-style, by churches, civic clubs, chambers of commerce, and other groups. Town gatherings were planned and promoted throughout the communities where the walkers would be staying the night.

The dates for the departure and arrival were set. Jimmy and Rosalynn Carter signed on to walk the first ten miles from Americus to Plains, Georgia, and they also agreed to be in Kansas City fifty days later to welcome the walkers and participate in the anniversary celebration. Rosalynn would present a workshop and President Carter would be one of the primary speakers to the hundreds of persons in attendance. The Fuller's son, Chris, had recently graduated from seminary and signed on to help with logistics for the walk.

On the morning of the departure, Millard inspired those assembled with an uplifting pep talk and prayer, followed by rousing shouts of "Habitat *Oyée!*" as the walkers set off on their fifty-day journey. As with the first walk, nothing escaped the walkers' imaginations to create fun in the name of fundraising. For instance, when they found coins and paper currency in parking lots, on sidewalks and highways, they designated one of the walkers as the "keeper" and placed everything they found in a "money jar." When they arrived in

Kansas City, they counted how much money they had found—a total of $149.14. At some point during the celebration, the "money jar" was put up for auction and brought in three times as much as the actual amount in the jar. The same thing happened with a pair of Millard's worn-out shoes: spray-painted gold, they brought in another $500 for the cause!

Walkers arrive in Kansas City at the end of a 1,000-mile walk

## Aim Even Higher—A 1,200-Mile House-Raising Walk from Portland to Atlanta

Almost as soon as the walk to Kansas City was over, Millard started planning another fundraising walk for Habitat's

### Vintage Fuller . . . The Roses

Millard and I were on a thousand-mile walk from Americus, Georgia, to Kansas City, Missouri, to raise awareness of Habitat for Humanity. We were leading a large group of people and had been on the road for thirty days, walking approximately twenty miles per day. It was a long, exhausting, and quite taxing walk. Most evenings were spent in public gatherings as we shared our dream to eradicate substandard housing in a particular town and around the world. So every day was filled with responsibilities, from early morning to late at night. Finally, one night was *our night* . . . no speeches . . . just the two of us at a small restaurant in Hardy, Arkansas, celebrating our twenty-seventh wedding anniversary. As we entered the restaurant and were being shown to our table, I could hardly believe what I saw. In a vase almost as big as the table were a dozen red roses! My heart will never forget that moment—it literally took my breath away! Some of my most precious moments in life have been associated with our Christian housing ministry . . . always getting to feel the joy and satisfaction of helping others have a decent place to live, a home in which to raise their children. This work creates endless memories of love . . . love for those we help find shelter and safety . . . and love for doing so with volunteers who come from far and wide to help others. And I have the privilege of working alongside the man I love . . . my husband, Millard, a creative and loving man who can figure out how to have roses delivered even in a little town in the middle of the world!

—Linda Fuller

twelfth anniversary in 1988. To create more visibility and differentiate this walk from the previous two, Millard thought, *Why not also do what we say we do—build some houses along the way?* Thus, he conceived the 1,200-Mile House-Raising Walk from Portland, Maine, to Atlanta, Georgia, where the twelfth anniversary celebration would be held. The House-Raising Walk was a twelve-week trek, and walkers traversed a hundred miles per week. A number of participants alternated their activities between walking and building, which took a lot of coordination with local Habitat affiliates along the route. That same year, the Jimmy Carter Work Project—split between building houses in Philadelphia and Atlanta—coincided with the walk.

Because of the spectacular amount of activity, Habitat garnered even greater interest from the media than in previous years. People came to Atlanta from Habitat projects all over the world, and a gleeful group of walkers and builders worked on houses with families in need along the way. The press loved it and couldn't stop writing about it.

Habitat was fast becoming an "all-American" thing to do. And, with so many affiliates abroad, it was a fun and feasible way to plan a "working vacation" practically anywhere around the globe.

## Go Where the Energy Is: Campus Chapters

The walks had motivated an unprecedented number of volunteers throughout the country, among them large numbers of youths. This inspired Gary Cook, director of denominational and community relations and assistant to the president at Baylor University in Waco, Texas, to invite Millard to speak at the campus chapel in November 1987. Gary had been interested in Habitat for Humanity for quite some time, and since there was a new Habitat affiliate in Waco, he thought that having Millard visit the campus would be propitious. Gary had been considering starting a Habitat chapter right on the Baylor University campus. The potential was unlimited: If college and university students all over the world could follow Baylor's lead by raising money and building houses, the effect could have a phenomenal impact on Habitat's growth.

More than two thousand students attended Millard's presentation at Baylor and enthusiastically embraced the idea of starting the first campus chapter of Habitat for Humanity. Ward Hayworth, a Baylor student, was named the first chapter president and presided over a campus chapter with two hundred charter members!

The operation at Baylor was the perfect blueprint for chapters at other campuses. David M. Eastis, from San Jose, California, organized a campus chapter department at Habitat headquarters in Americus and started spreading the word about Habitat to colleges and universities all over the world. The Habitat for Humanity Campus Chapters association was formed, with Gary Cook as president. They adopted the motto: "Love should not be just words and talk; it must be true love, which shows itself in action" (1 John 3:18, TEV).

The Campus Chapters continue to be an enormous success. In just fifteen years, more than ten thousand U.S. high-school and college students built Habitat houses during their spring breaks, often miles away from their homes and schools. By 2005, there were more than eight hundred chapters in high schools, colleges, and universities in thirty-seven countries. (In March 2004, Linda and Millard dedicated the 800th campus chapter at the American School of Manila in the Philippines.)

## The Magical Years

These were inspired years for the organization and for those who participated in Habitat's activities. Millard was never shy in his proclamation that the goal through Habitat for Humanity was to completely eliminate poverty housing and homelessness from the face of the Earth. And people were hearing it, and getting it. Thousands upon thousands of houses were being built in communities all over the world. Volunteers were truly making a difference in the lives of impoverished families. And, in the process, their own lives were being touched as well. Building homes alongside family members who would be recipients of the Habitat home, and then to watch as they accepted the keys atop a Bible, thank those who had helped make a home possible, and then turn, walk into their new home, was a powerful experience that people never forgot. And once their service had ended and they returned to their own community, they never stopped talking about it.

Volunteering brought about magic in other forms, too. Love blossomed on work projects and on the walks. Such was the case for Fred Schippert, a retired mathematics professor from Detroit, and Ellen, an architect from Ohio. Fred proposed to Ellen by phone while he was participating in the thousand-mile walk to Kansas City. Ellen flew to join him on the walk, and news of the upcoming nuptials spread. Ellen and Fred selected a church for the ceremony near the rest stop for the following night. Those on the walk delighted in picking wildflowers they would use to decorate the church. During the ceremony, walkers who had come from foreign countries were asked to read certain passages of Scripture in their native tongues. It was a sweet, simple, and very meaningful service.

These were special years for Linda and Millard personally as well. They are both fond of recalling when they spent an evening alone together in 1985 and made another promise to God. They were in New York City for the second JCWP. After dinner, Linda and Millard took a cab to St. Patrick's Cathedral. "It was a clear night with a full moon," Millard recalled. Sitting on the same steps on which they'd cried and held each other twenty years earlier, when life for both of them had been so uncertain, they marveled at how far God had brought them. They vowed then and there that if God willed it, they would return to that special place again in twenty more years.

The year 2005 seemed an eternity away. As it happened, God had other plans. That was a watershed year that would bring the end of a tumultuous and agonizing conflict with Habitat International's board, followed by a challenging new beginning for the Fullers. They would not visit St. Patrick's Cathedral again until June 2007. But the memories of these magical years would warm their hearts and strengthen them for the trials to come.

## Vintage Fuller . . .
## Sho' Nuff Religion

Nobody loves a good worship service more than I do, but we are called to make religion real, to make our faith come alive. Helping others have a decent place to live is one way to do that and it doesn't take too long for others to recognize it too. I remember a time in mid-1987 when Linda and I and about four hundred other volunteers descended upon Charlotte, North Carolina, where we were building fourteen houses in five days. It was the biggest blitz build ever done up to that point. People would say, "You're gonna build fourteen houses in five days?" We said, "Yeah."

"You mean you're gonna start on Monday and by Friday you're gonna have all these houses finished and people can move in?" We said, "Yes. Homes will be built. We're even gonna have the land-scaping done. Families can move in, cook and eat dinner in their homes on Saturday, and have a Sunday dinner after they get back from church. That's what we're gonna do."

They said, "You can't do that."

We said, "Watch." And so we started. And we built those houses. And I'll never forget, it was on a Tuesday, all of those people were out there, a tremendous sea of humanity. By that time they had the walls up and all the trusses and the plywood on. After they put doors and windows in, a guy from the neighborhood walked up and said, "My goodness, that's a lot of folks! Who is paying all of these people building all of these houses?"

I said, "No one's paying these people."

"What?" he said. "Out in this hot weather, they're building all these houses for nothing? Do they even know these people they're building these houses for?"

"No, they don't know 'em, they're all strangers," I said.

"You mean they're out here in this hot weather working for nothing to build houses for folks they don't even know?"

"Yes," I said, "but it's even worse than that."

"What do you mean?"

"These folks paid a lot of money to come here and work for nothing to build houses for folks they don't know."

He said, "Why would folks do something like that?"

"Because," I said, "they want to put their faith into practice. They're helping others who need a hand."

"Man, that's sho' nuff religion," he said. "That's sho' nuff religion."

—Millard Fuller

# — 17 —

# Expanding the Dream

By the late 1980s, Habitat for Humanity had become a household name. More houses were being built; more volunteers were becoming involved; more and more people the world over understood the Theology of the Hammer. Millard explained it this way: "Faith must be incarnated; that is to say, it must become more than a verbal proclamation or an intellectual assent. True faith must be acted out. Within the context of Habitat for Humanity, the Theology of the Hammer dictates that the nail be hit on the head, literally, and repeatedly—until the house is built and the needy family moves in. It means, too, that continuing love and concern must be shown to the family to ensure success as a new homeowner. We can agree on building and renovating simple, decent houses with and for God's people in need. We are called by God to the work of housing the world's poor."

Millard also believed that there were enough resources to take care of all of the needs. "Within the context of housing, within the context of shelter needs, we have enough material and human resources to build at least a simple, decent house for everybody in the world," he said. "There is enough sand, there is enough cement, there is enough wood, there are enough materials of all sorts to build a simple, decent house for everyone. And there certainly is enough money to get the job done. Providing shelter for our poor neighbor is not a problem but an opportunity. God challenges us to be a part of the solution and not the problem."

## Habitat for Humanity: A Part of the International Solution to Poverty Housing

"Our goal in Habitat for Humanity," Millard said, "is to completely eliminate poverty housing and homelessness from the face of the Earth. Our intention is to make substandard housing and homelessness socially, politically, morally, and religiously unacceptable." This message was getting out. In Zaire, where the Fuller family had lived and worked in the mid-1970s, over a thousand houses had been built in thirty locations by 1990. The story was the same in country after country. In the beleaguered nation of Nicaragua, where Habitat has been building houses since 1984, Habitat built five hundred houses after a devastating hurricane. In Australia, projects were starting in Adelaide, Melbourne, Sydney, and Wollongong. Former President Jimmy Carter led over a thousand volunteers in building a hundred houses in a week of intense building in Tijuana, Mexico, in June 1990. In late 1989, Habitat launched projects in what would soon be the former Soviet Union. As the 1990s approached, Habitat prepared to go to England, New Zealand, Zimbabwe, Poland, and China. In Peru alone, a total of forty houses a month were being built in five locations, and by 1992, Habitat was erecting eight houses a day there—nearly three thousand houses a year!

The Theology of the Hammer is not just a matter of glibly talking and a way of pronouncing words and going to church and looking and acting and sounding religious. It is a powerful way of living. It's a powerful way of being concerned about our neighbors who are in need, and in the context of The Fuller Center for Housing and Habitat for Humanity, concerned about our neighbors having a decent place in which to live. For sure it is not about accepting shacks with people living in pitiful conditions.

We must want to love our neighbors as we love ourselves. You got that extra coat? Share it! Got extra food? Share it! Do something. Some months back in Americus, I walked into my office and there was a telephone message for me to call this certain lady in town who was very, very wealthy. I had never, ever in my life received a phone call from this woman. Naturally, I wondered what she wanted with me. I phoned her and told her who I was. As soon as she recognized my name, she said, "Why are you taking so long to build Dorothy's house?" I said, "Dorothy who?" She said, "Dorothy, my maid. You folks over there at Habitat are building Dorothy a house, but it's taking too long." Then I said, "Who is your maid?" She said, "Dorothy." I said, "But I mean what is her whole name?" She said, "Dorothy. I told you my maid. She's worked for me eight years. I don't know why it's taking you so long to get her house built." I said, "But tell me her name." I ran my computer mind through its rounds and I thought right away that I knew of at least three women in town named Dorothy we were building houses for right at that time, so I said, "You've got to tell me her name." The woman did not know her maid's name. She'd been working for her for eight years. So I said, "Where does she live?"

She said, "She lives down the block." I said, "Now I know who you are talking about. The reason that we are not quite going as fast as we all would like is because we don't have enough money to go any faster." I said, "Do you know where we get the money from to build these houses for these low-income families?" She said, "Well, I don't know exactly." I said, "We get the money from concerned men, women, boys, girls, and churches, folks of goodwill who would like to help their neighbors have a better house. If you would contribute, the work would go faster."

Boy, that was the wrong thing to say. She was concerned enough to make a telephone call and criticize us because we weren't going fast enough, but not concerned enough to give any of her own money to help the construction go faster. As I hung up the telephone that day, I realized I had just had a telephone conversation with the rich man in the Bible, except right here in Americus, he's a woman.

—Millard Fuller

Habitat International headquarters in downtown Americus, 1990s

## Habitat Headquarters Covers a Full City Block

Habitat's phenomenal international success was mirrored in North America as well. By 1987, its Americus international headquarters—built almost entirely by volunteers—covered a full city block. Twenty-five houses in the surrounding neighborhood accommodated over 170 volunteers who worked at the headquarters. Habitat had twelve regional centers throughout the United States, and a national center with three regional offices in Canada.

By 1990 major corporations were joining Habitat's corporate sponsorship program. Employees were encouraged to volunteer with Habitat, provide financial support, and raise awareness of Habitat's work. At the same time, their involvement underscored their corporate commitment to their community. Southern Bell Telephone Company was the pioneer of the program. The company provided funding for Southern Bell teams that built houses with local affiliates. Teams made up of Southern Bell employees and retired employees raised money to match what Southern Bell donated. They also gave of their own time to build houses with Habitat affiliates in thirteen states of the United States.

In 1990, the Fieldstone Company in Orange County, California, helped the local Habitat affiliate build forty-eight houses, donating the lots, putting up a $2-million no-interest loan, and providing experts to direct construction. Fieldstone's executives had been inspired to join Habitat when they saw the video, *The Excitement Is Building,* which shows the construction of twenty houses in Atlanta during the Jimmy Carter Work Project. What especially inspired them was the commitment of the John Wieland Company to build six of the twenty houses.

Like the individual volunteers before them, corporations realized how important and effective their contributions were to their communities, their employees, and their reputations. Greater corporate involvement set the stage for even more dramatic growth. Momentum was building in the quest to eliminate poverty housing. The organization seemed positioned to accomplish great things, but the glory days were suddenly interrupted by a power struggle within the ranks of leadership. And Millard was about to get the first of two doses in his tenure of being overthrown.

# — 18 —

# Controversy

One Sunday morning in March 1990, the Fullers' phone rang while they were getting ready to go to church. When Millard answered the phone, Linda could tell by the way he reacted to the caller that he was receiving a grave message. She thought perhaps one of their friends had passed away. Then she heard Millard say, "I can't come to Atlanta if I don't know the reason!" After a few more questions that didn't make any sense to Linda, Millard hung up and related the conversation to her.

A Habitat director had called to ask him to drop whatever he was doing and meet with several board members at a hotel room in Atlanta. Oddly enough, he was instructed not to bring Linda. At first, they would not tell Millard why he was urgently needed in Atlanta for a Sunday morning meeting, but when he insisted he wouldn't come without knowing why, he was told that some women had accused him of inappropriate conduct toward them. Within thirty minutes, both Linda and Millard were in their car headed north.

They entered the designated hotel room and saw several board members and a former chair of the board, David Rowe, then on staff as vice president of overseas programs. No one commented on Linda's unexpected presence. Rowe announced that several women had accused Millard of inappropriate conduct. Millard asked, "What did I do? How many women?" Rowe simply answered, "Several." When Millard asked, "Who are these women?" Rowe said the women had been promised confidentiality. It went back and forth with very little information made available to Millard.

Rowe then suggested that to discourage the women from making more formal allegations or pursuing charges, it would be best for Millard to distance himself from Habitat headquarters. In fact, the board wanted Millard and Linda to move to Atlanta, about 130 miles away from headquarters so that the women "wouldn't fear retaliation." They also instructed Millard to see a professional counselor about his "misconduct." Bewildered, but feeling sure things would calm down and get sorted out, Millard agreed on a compromise to work from his home for the next month while the misunderstanding got resolved.

Within days, Millard learned "several" women (according to Rowe) would in reality be four women, one of whom had complained that Millard told her she had "beautiful eyes." Another said he hugged her after listening to her talk about her husband's drinking. One woman said Millard had introduced her as a "beautiful woman," while the fourth reported that he had sneaked up behind her and covered her eyes for a "game" of guess-who. Millard was dumbfounded that the women had found his spontaneous actions to be offensive, and yet sorry that he had caused distress for the women. Embarrassed and remorseful, Millard would write each one of them a letter indicating how sorry he was to have offended them. He would explain that he meant only to compliment, tease, and/or empathize with them, and that if they had perceived his actions as harassment, that was not his intent.

Millard and Linda then met with Rosalynn and Jimmy

Carter at their home in Plains about the matter, prompting Carter to write the following letter to the board:

———————————

March 26, 1990

To Directors, Habitat for Humanity:
I appreciated your sending me the information about the allegations against Millard Fuller . . . I read the documents with great interest and concern. Subsequently, I have discussed the issues with Millard and Linda, David Rowe, Geoff van Loucks, and LeRoy Troyer.

I feel a responsibility to give you my own thoughts. The events themselves and the subsequent furor are obviously of great significance to the Fullers and to the women involved. It would be a mistake to minimize their personal anguish or emotional reactions. However, as far as Habitat is concerned, a mountain has been made out of a molehill. The reputation and future of Habitat are now at stake, depending on how this emergency is handled. Any enterprising news reporter could make a national scandal out of it, a la Bakker and Swaggart. The draft press statement that I have seen would be a disaster! The question is, what might be done now to protect the interests of everyone and, in particular, Habitat for Humanity.

Millard has acknowledged to me that he has caused the women anguish and distress, and he is eager to apologize and ask their forgiveness. At the same time, he does not deserve to be punished by action of the Board of Directors nor personally humiliated. He should remain deeply involved in Habitat, performing the duties for which he is most uniquely qualified. In my opinion, it is not appropriate nor necessary to force him to undergo "counseling." If he and Linda want this kind of help in order to improve management techniques and to understand proper personnel interrelationships, then that should be their decision. They tell me they want to have this assistance.

I am naturally physical in my own demonstrations of affection and appreciation and, in a few cases, it was obvious that my actions were not welcomed. I remember that, when the JFK library was dedicated in 1979, I went down the stage shaking hands with the men and hugging the women, sometimes giving a kiss on the cheek. Jackie Kennedy Onassis visibly flinched away, in full view of the nation's TV cameras. Earlier, while running for president, I came into the ABC studio in New York and met Barbara Walters (who had been a long-time friend) with a fond embrace. She chastised me, saying that my attitude was sexist. Two years later, when I met her with both hands behind my back, she walked up and gave me a kiss.

Without minimizing in any way the significance of what has happened at Habitat, let me say quite frankly that I have had some similar kinds of relationships with some of my own female employees and associates. If one ever complained officially, there could be an avalanche of similar charges. It would, of course, be very discomforting to have them exposed in headlines. This experience at Habitat will cause me to be more careful with my own conduct.

Millard wishes to respond positively to the women's concerns, and has written all of them a note, as follows:

"The last few weeks have been a traumatic time for Linda and me and, I know, also for you. I realize now that I have caused you distress and embarrassment. For this, I apologize and ask your forgiveness."

If this is adequate for the women, it should be enough to assuage the Directors.

Millard has also decided to request a month's vacation so that he can devote some extra time to his new book and prepare for the proposed change from Executive Director to President as the long range decision of the board of directors is put into effect. Since he and Linda will be on vacation anyway and away from the office, it would be strongly advisable for the record and to answer future inquiries for the board to rescind the order forbidding Millard to go to the headquarters. This would be hard to explain later on. Geoff van Loucks agrees with this.

If all this can be done, perhaps permanent damage can be minimized, both to the people involved and to the reputation and effectiveness of Habitat.

You have my prayers and best wishes, and thanks for your continuing service in one of God's finest organizations.

Sincerely,

*Jimmy Carter*

———————————

Millard was hopeful the women knew he was sincere in his apology, and that they would forgive him. And he was thankful to Carter for his support and understanding, and felt sure Carter's letter would put the board's mind at ease.

He was wrong on both counts. While at first the four women accepted Millard's apologies, the following day they let it be known they had changed their minds. And the board gave Millard an ultimatum: He could either accept being a figurehead—merely raising money and making speeches for Habitat—or he could resign.

Carter was outraged, calling the board's action "quite disturbing," and said his future role with the organization would hinge on the resolution of what he viewed as a "power struggle" that unfairly punished Millard.

Stories began appearing in newspapers, and Habitat was inundated with letters, some directed at the board, all supporting Millard. Editorials in newspapers across the nation glowed with positive statements about the Fullers and their tenure with Habitat. Morris Dees, Millard's friend and former law partner, and co-founder of the much-respected Southern Poverty Law Center, weighed in, saying, "The present accusations are so out of character for Millard as to be humorous if they were not so serious. It was Millard's Christian love that led him to create Habitat."

Because the women had taken back their accepting Millard's apology, the Fullers were suspicious that there was more to this issue than simply his crossing the line of being too familiar in his words and gestures. President Carter would see the true struggle and characterize it as such: "Habitat has been plagued by small-mindedness and ineptitude, and unfortunately Millard and Linda have had to endure this."

Carter sent a statement to the press, explaining, "One of our most exciting and gratifying experiences has been with Habitat for Humanity. We have enjoyed not only its challenges, but also the tremendous growth experienced by the organization. Unfortunately, it is this extraordinary expansion that has caused some very difficult personnel problems, involving the role of Millard and Linda Fuller, Habitat's founders and the inspiration for many of us volunteers. There has been something of a power struggle in the international headquarters that has nothing to do with building homes for poor families around the world. Habitat has a worthy mission to fulfill that transcends the identity of its leaders. We will continue to be supportive of that mission."

Reflecting back on the crisis a decade and a half later, President Carter would note of the incident: "My impression then was that there were ambitious people who wanted to gain control of the organization, even at the expense of the Fullers, Carters, and many others."

The solution to the problem actually became an opportunity for Habitat. Millard had full authority again, and a COO was hired to take care of the day-to-day operations. With the burden of managing daily operations lifted, Millard was free to pursue his vision for the movement.

## Sunny Days Return

With the black cloud lifted, a new burst of energy would run through the organization. In the following months, Habitat for Humanity would open more regional offices around the United States, followed by offices in Costa Rica, Thailand, South Africa, and Hungary. Closer to home, Habitat unveiled a bold plan in 1992 called the Sumter County Initiative. The goal was to eliminate poverty housing from Americus and Sumter County by the year 2000. Millard figured that since the headquarters of Habitat for Humanity was in Americus, and it had as its goal to eliminate poverty housing in the world, then it was of paramount importance to set a goal to achieve this at home. It was a hard sell to the board. The proposal initially met with resistance, but following a passionate speech during which Millard actually jumped up on a table ("There is a fine line that divides faith and foolishness," said Millard. "We need to get as close to the foolishness line as possible without crossing it. Think creatively and boldly! Let's issue the challenge. Set a date! We can do it! With God, all things are not necessarily easy, but they are possible!"), the board approved the proposal.

In September 2000, at the end of a Jimmy Carter Work Project held simultaneously in New York City, Jacksonville, Florida, and Americus and Plains, Georgia, the completion of thirty-five houses fulfilled the ambitious goal of the Sumter County Initiative. One of the houses was designated as the "Victory House," representing triumph over substandard housing. By changing the mind-set of a community and stretching their imagination, what once seemed impossible became a reality. And, inspired by the success of the Sumter County Initiative, many Habitat affiliates began similar projects as part of the 21st Century Challenge.

## Vintage Fuller . . .
## Dead and Buried and Got Dug Up

It was about the sixth or seventh house that we had built at Koinonia, and it was for a man whose name was Willie James Reynolds and his wife, Rose Bell. We have a lot of double names in the South. They had lived in a very pitiful house that was falling down and had no water, no insulation, the roof leaking—a very terrible situation. We built a very modest house for them. It was like a palace compared to where they had been living before. They were so excited about that new, simple, little house that they moved in the very afternoon that we finished it. As I walked up there after the house was finished, they were moving their very, very modest furniture into the house. Little Rose Bell, who was five feet tall, stood in the middle of the floor grinning from ear to ear. She was so happy! I said, "Rose Bell, I've come up here to find out if you got moved in all right."

"Oh yes, Millard, we got moved in just fine."

"And I want to know if there is anything wrong with the house."

"No, Millard, there ain't nothin' wrong with this house."

I said, "You know, like, do the doors and windows open and close like they should? Does the toilet flush properly? How about the sink, have you found a leak in the sink?"

"Millard," she said, "there ain't nothin' wrong with this house. I'm tellin' ya, there ain't nothin' wrong with this house. Bein' in here is like we was dead and buried and got dug up."

I've often thought about what Rose Bell said that day. In various ways all of us should be constantly finding people and situations that are dead, buried, and covered up in order to help bring them to the light because the God that we serve is a God of light, a God of love, and a God of caring.

—Millard Fuller

# — 19 —

# 100,000th House . . . and Picking Up Speed

By 1995, Habitat had built 40,000 houses in forty-three countries. And the pace of building had never been greater—the organization would build its 50,000th house by 1996, the organization's twentieth anniversary. The anniversary celebration was held in Atlanta and included several hundred people participating in a 140-mile nostalgic walk from Americus to Atlanta. They were met there by about 100 cyclists who had biked down to Atlanta from Canada.

Then, in the year 2000, three major events coincided during a single week in September. The annual Jimmy Carter Work Project took place in several locations: Harlem and Queens, New York; Jacksonville, Florida; and Americus and Plains, Georgia. One of ten units being built in Harlem was designated as Habitat for Humanity International's 100,000th house. A major television network news broadcaster, Tom Brokaw, rode his bicycle to the worksite and helped dedicate the house along with New York City Mayor Rudy Giuliani and former Secretary of Housing and Urban Development Jack Kemp. The Fullers were elated to celebrate such a tremendous milestone of providing homes for half a million people!

A few hours following this celebration, the Carters and Fullers flew to Jacksonville, where 103 homes were being built by primarily local volunteers over a two-week period. One of those homes was designated as the 100,001st house built by Habitat . . . the beginning of the next 100,000 houses! The four "celebrities" lent a hand with construction for a few hours before a big rally was held on site with a full caldron of media as there had been that morning in New York City. Then, the four of them flew to Americus and Plains where work had begun the first of that week to build thirty-five houses to be completed on Friday. One of those thirty-five homes was designated as the final house that officially ended poverty housing in Americus and Sumter County. Hundreds of people gathered in the yard of what was termed the "Victory House," and Millard led the crowd in singing "Victory to Jesus."

It was an incredible week! There was more than enough inspiration and encouragement to drive this highly regarded "popular movement" on to the next hundred thousand homes.

## Women Builds: "Women, Put on Your (Nail) Aprons. We Have House Work to Do!"

Millard and Linda continued to cast a wide net to try to educate still more people about the need to eradicate poverty housing. For Linda, this desire to spread the word meant involving more women in building Habitat houses. In July 1991, the first all-women-built house went up in Charlotte, North Carolina. Former First Lady Rosalynn Carter joined an all-women crew to build this first house. Plumbers, electricians, and sheetrock "mudders" were all women. The only

Rosalynn Carter at first Women Build, Charlotte, N.C., 1991

men on site brought meals and refreshments, and, from time to time, a male inspector would appear at various stages of construction. From "Port-a-Jane" potties to T-shirts bearing logos such as "Look, Look, See Jane Build," the turnout of women made the first build an historic and highly visible occasion. Word traveled quickly about the Habitat house that only women had built. The next affiliate to try this idea was Twin Cities Habitat for Humanity in Minneapolis, Minnesota. To recruit a large number of women, they ran an ad in the local newspaper with this appeal: "Women, put on your nail aprons. We have house work to do!" And women from everywhere turned out in response.

Next came an all-women's build in Southern California's Coachella Valley. The goal was to build a house for the Marez family, who had lost their home through a series of catastrophic events. Ray Marez, a maintenance worker for

Women Build, Charlotte, N.C., 1991

Morningside Homeowners Association, was the sole provider for the family. His wife, Ronda, a former bookkeeper, had suffered an aneurysm that paralyzed her left side, leaving her disabled and unemployable. They had three children: Rachel, Matthew, and Michael. Their new home would accommodate Ronda's disability. Linda recruited about forty women from fifteen states, as well as some thirty wives of board members of the National Association of Home Builders. By mid-afternoon of the sixth day, the house was complete, looking every bit like the rendering! The Marez family stood looking at their new property—one that had been no more than an empty lot, a roll of blueprints, and a dream just a week before. The youngest boy summed it up best. "Wow!" he exclaimed. "A house with a yard!"

## Prototype for the "First Ladies' Build"

The Coachella Valley house would serve as a prototype for the "First Ladies' House," which would be built the following spring during a Jimmy Carter Work Project in the Appalachian Mountains for Pam Sykes and her son Jordan in

Pikeville, Kentucky. Standing shoulder to shoulder to build the home for the Sykes family were First Lady Hillary Rodham Clinton, former First Lady Rosalynn Carter, First Lady of Arkansas Janet Huckabee, First Lady of Delaware Martha Carper, First Lady of Oklahoma Cathy Keating, First Lady of Kentucky Judi Patton, First Lady of Kansas Linda Graves, former First Lady of Virginia Jinx Holton, Washington attorney Holly Eaton, along with many other volunteers—all of whom set aside political, career, and personal differences to help Pam and Jordan have a home, a refuge, and a place to be with family and friends. This project, in turn, would serve as the kick-off project for some fifty houses to be built that week, and some ten thousand-plus throughout the year. Indeed, during an eighteen-month period, forty-seven First Ladies and three women governors participated in at least one and as many as twenty Women Builds in their respective states.

The author with First Lady of Oklahoma, Cathy Keating, 1997

Women Builds began to spring up everywhere, and Habitat for Humanity established a Women Build department at Habitat headquarters. As Habitat International's Women

First Women Build in Calgary,
Alberta, Canada, 2002

Linda Fuller (left)
installs siding on a
Calgary house

Build program director Fiona Eastwood said, "I often hear city, state, and national leaders advocate that we need to raise taxes for improving schools so kids will get better test scores. Well, for those kids who don't have a decent home, no amount of raising taxes will matter. But if we provide a mom with a house so she can better tend to the needs of her children and their safety, that, I think, is one of the best ways to improve test scores!"

Habitat's mission, and the gender-specific builds in particular, found a home within the hearts of women across the country. "Habitat for Humanity is always a woman's cause," said Donna Schuller, wife of Pastor Robert Schuller of Crystal Cathedral in Garden Grove, California, who was one of many who convened groups for Women Blitz Builds. "First of all, there is the joy of building a home for a family—all of whom show up on the construction site each and every day," said Donna, "so it's all very personalized. And then there is the camaraderie of women working together and actually building a house from the ground floor up. It's very rewarding." Said former First Lady Cathy Keating, wife of Governor Frank Keating of Oklahoma, "There is great delight in working side by side with so many women in a vast array of professions, from top executives to homemakers. From incarcerated women to presidents' wives. All have such a reverence for what we are doing—building a home for another woman and her family. The satisfaction is immeasurable."

## New Ideas Emerge

While Linda was focused on promoting the Women Build program, Millard was getting more and more invitations to keynote at house dedications, milestone events, commencements, national gatherings, and conventions of all types. Sometimes Linda traveled with Millard, particularly when they would visit multiple Habitat for Humanity worksites in foreign countries. On occasion after occasion, their plane tickets literally took them around the world. At times, they shook hands and dined with presidents, prime ministers, and royalty, while at other times they had opportunities to spend the night in sparsely furnished Habitat homes.

The most rigorous speaking trips for Millard were during Building on Faith Week, slated annually for the third week of September. Habitat affiliates were challenged to engage faith congregations in building houses. The affiliates that built the most houses received a visit from Millard. Some weeks, Millard visited ten or more states—even in foreign nations—in one week. "Speaking for Habitat was similar to a political campaign," Millard said, "just no election!"

## Prison Partnerships

The desire to spread the Habitat gospel extended even into prisons. Millard launched a program called Prison Partnerships that involved inmates in Wisconsin, Texas, Illinois, and Michigan. Inmates built component parts on the prison grounds that would later be assembled into Habitat houses. Says Millard, "This is such a two-way blessing. Inmates are building the cabinets. They're building the trusses. They're building sections of the walls, and they're raising shrubbery, they're raising flowers, they're making the house number signs, doing all kinds of things."

In some cases, certain prisoners were allowed to work on actual Habitat worksites and attend house dedications. They would often weep and share that helping a family to have a good house was the most meaningful thing they had ever done in their lives. In some instances, inmates were able to build up "sweat equity" hours that could be applied in the future if they were ever chosen to be a Habitat family partner.

## The Global Village and Discovery Center

Millard also sought to share the Habitat story by pursuing plans for a Global Village and Discovery Center, a kind of educational tourist attraction that would showcase poverty housing worldwide on four acres near downtown Americus, a few blocks from Habitat's headquarters. The plan was that visitors to the site would stroll along a winding path, past twenty-six houses of the sort that Habitat builds in Africa, Asia, and Latin America. Plaques on each house would tell visitors how much such houses cost, information meant to encourage donations.

The model houses would contrast with a section that portrayed typical housing conditions in the developing world. A theater and a store selling Habitat T-shirts, caps, jackets, books, and similar products were also planned for the site.

The project was successful, paving the road for more lucrative partnerships. "There was a man who was teetering as to whether to enter into a $2 million partnership with Habitat when he went through the Village," Millard told a crowd. "For him, seeing was believing, and he decided to become a partner right on the spot. And a visitor from England was so touched after visiting the Village that she agreed to pay for a house in Africa—an entire house. These sorts of actions go a long way in the quest to eradicate slum housing. Imagine the impact if more people would do that." Millard estimated that some seventy thousand visitors would come annually to the Global Village and Discovery Center.

In addition to educating visitors to Americus about poverty housing around the world, Habitat sent volunteer work teams on Global Village short-term mission trips to various countries for the purpose of opening eyes to the problem of poverty housing. Most trips lasted two weeks. The cost was minimal because lodging was provided, as well as some meals, by the host community. The Global Village participant paid airfare, a certain amount to help the hosting Habitat affiliate purchase building materials, and a modest fee to cover administrative expenses for the Global Village program. In return, not only did Global Village trips build houses, but the participants got the chance to experience a new culture. From Millard's perspective, the trips let participants follow Christ's command to "love your neighbor as you love yourself" and "welcome the stranger."

## A New Home of Their Own

And, after building homes for thousands of people, the Fullers finally built a house of their own! All these years, they had lived in a 1910 two-story house they had purchased in

## Vintage Fuller . . .
### Building a Home: A Universal Language

On Habitat Builds for women, I see a spirit of sisterhood wherever I go. Women are especially eager to break through the barriers that threaten to keep us all from experiencing the comforts and the fullness of life. Building homes for one another is an equalizer. Democrats and Republicans, millionaires and welfare recipients, retired folks and young people, college students and former U.S. presidents, homemakers and first ladies—and even inmates—all come to work alongside a family in need of a home. Everyone parks judgment and their titles at the entrance to the worksite.

I remember a time in Illinois when several inmates from a women's correctional facility had come to help. The heat pump needed to be installed, and nothing more could be done on the house until the heating unit was in place. Arrangements had been made with a heating and air specialist to come that morning, but he failed to show up. The site supervisor, as well as the volunteer builders, were frustrated until one of the inmates said, "I can install it. It was my work 'before'" [she was sentenced to time]. Everyone was dumbfounded—but only for about three seconds. "What are we waiting for, then? Let's get to work!" The woman got the job done by giving directions to her "assistants." When she finally said, "That's it. It's hooked up and ready to go!" everyone clapped, cheered, and hugged their new friend for a job well done. They genuinely admired this woman for being so knowledgeable and skilled at something the rest of them knew nothing about! With her contribution came even more acceptance. For the rest of the day, others readily included her in conversations as the women went busily about their work, asking her how she was doing, inquiring if she had kids, and so on. Remorseful for her crime and devastated at the lives she'd forever changed, she wept while telling her story. But her involvement at the Habitat worksite that day ensured she was now changing lives for the better, including her own. It was a story she could proudly tell her children about someday.

—Linda Fuller

1977 for $12,500, with no air conditioning through the hot Georgia summers. For Christmas 1996, Millard gave Linda a Christmas card inscribed with these words: "Merry Christmas—my gifts to you this Christmas are: a piece/peace of property of your choosing in a beautiful rural setting and a house of your choosing on that property. Love, Millard."

While thrilled, Linda knew there were insufficient funds in their bank account, and they had no other savings that would allow for such expenditures. But she was married to a man who operated on faith, so she put the card in safekeeping in her chest of drawers in case she needed it as a reminder in the future. At least, they could begin building up their savings because they had just completed putting all four children through college.

Within three years from the time Millard gave Linda the card, they found four wooded acres outside of Americus and began building Linda's Christmas house. Moving day was in January 2000—new millennium, new house. "It was such a beautiful experience for us," said Linda of the new home, "For months, Millard and I felt as though we were living in someone else's house; we had to get used to having such a beautiful home in such a lovely setting. But as usual, God had provided, and for it, we are thankful."

## Worldwide Praise

Their zeal to eliminate poverty housing around the globe would win the Fullers wide recognition and numerous awards. Between 1990 and 2004, they would write a dozen books, garner some sixty-plus honorary doctorates, and earn more than a dozen major recognitions and praise from the best of the best. "I don't think it's an exaggeration to say that Millard Fuller has literally revolutionized the concept of philanthropy," said President Bill Clinton upon awarding Millard the Presidential Medal of Freedom, the nation's highest civilian honor to recognize individuals who have made major contributions to the United States and their own communities.

"Twenty years ago he founded Habitat for Humanity to provide decent homes for disadvantaged people. To fund his plan he didn't ask people for their money; instead, he asked for the sweat of their brows. In return he gave them something no tax deduction ever could, tangible proof that they had improved someone else's life with a home."

Habitat—and Millard and Linda—were riding high!

Millard receives Presidential
Medal of Freedom, 1996

To Millard Fuller
with appreciation and thanks
Bill Clinton

# — 20 —

# An Allegation
# and Ensuing Investigation

In early March 2004, Linda and Millard Fuller, along with
former First Lady of Indiana, Judy O'Bannon, traveled
to Asia to visit Habitat's work in six countries: China
(Hong Kong), Singapore, Philippines, Indonesia, East
Timor, and Thailand. During the first leg of their three-
week trip, in Hong Kong, Millard received an urgent phone
message to call Habitat's board chair, Rey Ramsey. As usual,
Millard had a packed itinerary, but as soon as he had a
break, he returned the call. Ramsey wasn't there. For five
days in a row, Millard continued to call, but Ramsey was still
unavailable. Millard was growing concerned; it seemed especially odd that Ramsey would place such an urgent and mys-
terious call and then be unavailable. Finally, on the sixth day,
Millard reached Ramsey.

The news wasn't good. Ramsey had called to inform
Millard that a woman on Habitat's staff had accused him of

Former First Lady of Indiana, Judy O'Bannon, dedicating
a Habitat house with the Fullers in Thailand, 2004

"inappropriate conduct" when she was driving him from the
Habitat headquarters to the Atlanta airport. Millard told the
chairman the allegation was ridiculous; not only could he not
recall the trip in question, but he was most certain he had
never behaved "inappropriately." Though Millard was filled
with questions, Ramsey would say no more, simply that this
woman's complaint had come to the board's attention, but
that Millard need not worry because "the board was taking
care of the matter." Feeling it would be helpful to lay out the
truth and let it speak for itself, Millard suggested that both he
and the accuser take a polygraph test. Millard was certain the
woman would not agree to take the test because she was fab-
ricating her story, and that would end the matter. However,
Ramsey rejected the idea of the lie-detector test (and would,
in fact, ignore the results of a polygraph Millard would pass
several months later) and, instead, dropped a bombshell: The
executive committee had already hired a New York law firm to

investigate the woman's allegation. Millard couldn't believe what he was hearing.

"I'm not afraid of the lie that woman has told about me," Millard remarked to Linda after getting off the phone and briefly explaining the situation to her. "What concerns me most is how the board is overreacting to it."

The more Millard thought about the phone call, the more disturbing he found it. No one had so much as talked with Millard before involving the attorneys; why wouldn't they want to know what he knew about the incident? How could a rumor go from the Habitat for Humanity International legal counsel to a New York law firm in such a short time? And how could all this happen without his knowing? Millard did spend a lot of his time in the field, but he was also highly engaged in Habitat's inner workings. On a regular basis, he made it a priority to meet with various supervisors and department heads. How could something as serious as an allegation that involved him get by him? And why had this woman made this allegation when it couldn't possibly be true? He traveled quite often and usually went to the airport by one of three means of transportation. Most often, Linda and he traveled together, so they drove together. When Millard was making a trip alone, he would go by shuttle or catch a ride with a staff person who was also going to the airport or elsewhere in the Atlanta area. His travel coordinator had standing instructions to find him a ride with a staff person, if possible, to save the $75 cost of a shuttle ride. Over the years, scores of people, both men and women, had driven him to the Atlanta airport.

Bewildered, the Fullers continued with their packed schedule for the remainder of the Asian tour, but they were anxious all the while to get home and sort out whatever was brewing.

When Millard and Linda returned home, there was an urgent message from an investigator who had been hired by the New York law firm saying that Millard was to meet with her the next morning. Jetlagged, he nevertheless showed up at the Windsor Hotel as directed, along with Linda, although she had not been told to come. The investigator indicated that she would interview Millard alone. "Nothing had been said about her interviewing me separately, which I thought was more than strange," Millard would comment. And why wasn't Linda asked to be interviewed? Exactly what was this "investigator" after?

The investigator informed Millard that she had been in Americus for several days interviewing various people, including the accuser and a number of women (at the suggestion of the accuser) who had previously been employees of Habitat for Humanity International. None of the half-dozen women who worked closely with Millard were sought out or questioned. Millard was the last to be interviewed.

Troubling as this was, what Millard found particularly baffling was how the board chairman was handling the entire matter. Initially, it seemed to Millard that the chairman's position, based on his conversations with him, was: "Trust me and the executive committee. We will handle things, and everything will be all right. It's not that big of a deal, so don't worry about it." But from Millard's side of the fence now, they appeared to be treating the accusations more seriously than Ramsey had implied.

Wanting all the information they could get, the Fullers moved their own fact-finding investigations into high gear. They discovered that the accuser had been employed by Habitat for fourteen years. Her colleagues and friends within the organization would tell the Fullers that she was disgruntled in her work, and had been for some time. Her current job required some travel, and with young children at home and now having remarried, travel had become increasingly burdensome. They discovered that the trip to the airport had taken place on February 20, 2003—some thirteen months earlier. Millard's travel coordinator had informed Millard as well as Linda that someone on staff was going to the airport that same day, and would be glad for him to ride with her. When she did not get a quick answer to her offer, she called back to remind the travel coordinator that she was available. The travel coordinator set it up, and mid-morning, the employee picked Millard up at Habitat headquarters for the trip to the airport. She drove directly to the airport, arriving shortly after noon.

The Fullers also learned from several employees that the woman had recently used a harsh hair remover above her lip, burning her skin and leaving a scab. During the drive to the airport, Millard had remarked that she had nice skin and inquired how she had "hurt herself." Apparently, the Fullers learned, this comment was offensive to the woman.

On the day in question, Millard had been flying to Daytona Beach, Florida, and the employee was herself catching a flight to Oklahoma City. When they arrived at the airport, the woman dropped Millard at the curb, asking him if he had time for a sandwich at the food court prior to his flight. Millard said fine, and the woman parked the car, checked in for her flight, and then the two met up at a designated food stand.

Once back at the Habitat offices a few days later, she told co-workers about her trip to the airport with the "CEO" (of Habitat). She reported that during the drive she and Millard had talked about her young children, and about how her first

marriage had ended in divorce. With implications that her former husband may not have been faithful, a discussion ensued regarding adultery in the Old and New Testaments. They also discussed capital punishment—one of Millard's legal passions. The woman told

The Fullers in Uganda to celebrate the milestone 20,000th house built on the African continent. Their daughter Faith traveled with them as their videographer (not shown) along with grandson Benjamin Fuller, 2001.

her co-workers that while she hadn't said anything to Millard at the time, she had been highly offended by this discussion because she felt that moral and ethical issues should not be discussed outside immediate family and, in fact, she considered the word "adultery" a curse word. She also said that Millard had touched her on the arm and neck.

When the Fullers checked to see how Habitat personnel had handled the woman's complaint, they would learn that although the woman's colleagues had suggested she report her complaint in accordance with personnel policy, she did nothing for some six months. She then reported her concern to the head of her department at Habitat. Personnel in the human resources office asked her, in accordance with personnel policy, to submit a written account of what happened. She refused and told Rendell Day, a staff person in human resources, to "forget it." Millard was told nothing about her claims of "inappropriate conduct." Seven more months went by. Then, she reported her complaint to the legal counsel of Habitat, Regina Hopkins, who then reported it to the board chairman. The woman had put nothing in writing, but oddly, despite her reluctance to document her claims, the board's investigative counsel would eventually help pen a ninety-page complaint on her behalf. At this point, Millard did something he had never done in his almost thirty years at the helm of his organization: He hired an attorney. Millard asked his good friend and former law associate, Ken Henson, Jr., of Columbus, Georgia, for legal representation.

Throughout the ordeal, Millard adamantly denied that he had said or done anything inappropriate, and would later say, "If she had been bothered by anything I had said on the ride to the airport that day, why would she ask me to have a sandwich with her before catching our respective flights? She was the one initiating more time together. That doesn't seem like the actions of someone highly offended or upset with someone."

Over the next months, many letters would come forward from Millard's co-workers, saying they had worked closely with him for decades and had never witnessed a trace of impropriety. One of the letters was from Deacon Jim Purks, a fifteen-year veteran of Habitat, who offered an articulate, informed defense of Millard's character, as well as a theory as to why the employee was making accusations. He had known her for many years, and was one of the few staff people invited to her second wedding. "There are many Habitat employees who, over the years, have heard her anger and bitterness against Habitat . . . Venom can build up and fester . . . The preponderance of evidence seems to indicate now that is what happened here . . . Maybe we are to blame. Maybe Habitat, including myself, should have recognized a colleague who was disturbed . . . Maybe we should have reached out to her and tried to counsel her or find counseling for her."

Another letter came from Cheryl Massey, a woman who had worked closely with the woman as well. "I worked for two years in Resource Development with her," Cheryl wrote in a formal letter to the board of directors. "After returning from her trip with Millard, she described to me the events that took place. I have heard both sides of the story, and there is no doubt in my mind that Millard behaved appropriately at all times."

Cheryl later noted: "Millard is innocent of the accusations made, and the fact that the circumstances were so grossly exaggerated by both the accuser and then the board is a crime, really. I talked to Millard's accuser. Today, I'm sure she feels that she was a pawn of the board that had an agenda to move Millard out. I'm betting that after this was all over, she was shell-shocked at all that had transpired and felt used by the board for their own purposes. When the board changed, the culture of the organization changed. Things were never the same after that. It just felt like the magic was gone, and in my opinion, so was the purity under which God had blessed and protected his organization."

Cheryl was not alone in her feelings that the woman's allegation was not the real issue behind the sudden attack on Millard. Millard would also have a conversation with a close friend of his accuser, herself a Habitat employee, who would confirm the perception that the culture at HFHI had changed. She had heard rumors that plans were being laid to move Habitat headquarters to Atlanta and, among other changes, to raise executive salaries. The woman believed, as many Habitat employees did, that Millard would resist these changes and, thus, be an impediment to the board. She surmised that a handful of "corporate" personnel was either cooperating with or being manipulated by the board to remove Millard from Habitat as a result. This young woman would also tell Millard of the hours she'd spent on the phone with the accuser, listening to her cry, describing how the escalation of events surrounding the allegation had "almost destroyed her life." It was her belief that her friend had never intended for things to transpire as they had.

Purks, too, wondered if some members of the executive committee were working against Millard. He wrote, "One perception is inescapable and it is increasingly held by many people: that the allegation of this woman was seized upon as an excuse for a power play and to 'get rid of Millard.'"

Millard was himself arriving at this conclusion. More and more, the board and he were at odds, having trouble overcoming certain philosophical differences. "I'm an expansionist . . . and I don't want to slow down," he would tell a reporter. "We're only in half the countries on Earth. I want to go into the other half." Millard observed that this made some newer board members nervous, who saw their role as trying to more efficiently manage Habitat's explosive growth. "Some of the newer members on the board didn't have experience or know-how in managing a movement," Purks would say. "Organizations are one thing, but a movement is by nature chaotic. Millard was a great manager precisely because he was undaunted by the many moving parts of Habitat's structure as a housing ministry."

And there were other issues. It was no secret that Millard had clashed with the board over the pace of the mission's worldwide growth, but one of the most contentious issues had been his decision to build the Global Village and Discovery Center in Americus. Millard surmised that with the relationship between him and the board growing more strained, the board might be using the employee's complaint as an excuse to build a case against him. "Something's going on," Millard would tell President Carter in an upcoming mediation, "and it's not about any complaint against me, but about something else. We have to learn what that is."

# — 21 —

# April 2004:
# The New York Meetings

Other events furthered Linda's suspicions that a secret agenda was being played out by a few within Habitat's leadership who were using smear tactics to build a case against Millard. One such incident occurred when the board chairman, Rey Ramsey, called an executive committee meeting in New York City for April 1 to talk about the "incident," without first checking with Millard to see if he was available to attend. Expecting Millard to be available without first checking with his travel coordinator wasn't standard protocol. It was no secret that Millard's calendar was fully booked with speaking engagements across the nation, immensely important and time-consuming functions of Millard's fundraising job.

Not surprisingly, Millard had a scheduling conflict with the date set for the New York City meeting. The Fullers were previously committed to be with the president of Dallas Baptist

University to dedicate an eight-foot-high bronze globe at the entrance plaza of the Global Village and Discovery Center. This dedication ceremony and the Fullers' attendance had been scheduled months in advance and was listed on the events calendar that showed Millard's upcoming commitments. The chairman of the executive committee had set up the New York City meeting in direct conflict with Millard's schedule—and supposedly expected Millard to be there.

When Millard informed Ramsey that he couldn't make the meeting in New York, Ramsey refused to reschedule it. He did tell Millard, though, that the executive committee would approve the expense of chartering a private jet to fly Millard from Americus to New York immediately foing the dedication. But to Millard, every dime sent to Habitat had a nail, board, or concrete slab for some yet-to-be-named homeowner written on it. (He went so far as to send personal thank-you notes to many donors spelling out how the money would be used, regardless of how large or small the contribution.) And here was the board chairman telling him to simply hop a private jet and they would approve the expenditure. Millard wanted no part in this extravagant expense, but his attendance at the meeting was important. In order to fulfill their commitments to attend both meetings, the Fullers made arrangements to participate in the New York meeting via conference call. In the phone call, Millard asked the committee to consider possible motives as to why the woman in question—who did not bring the matter up until six months after the alleged incident, and then dropped it for seven months before bringing it up again—had suddenly surfaced. The conference call over, the Fullers felt it had gone well and breathed a sigh of relief. They thought the matter had ended. A few weeks later, however, the chairman called an emergency meeting of the full board to be held on April 29 in New York City. Millard sent the following letter to the board appealing for reason and asking for an end to the "mess."

To: Habitat for Humanity International Board

Date: April 16, 2004

Dear Fellow Board Members,

You have probably received a communication recently accusing me of certain actions against a woman. I cannot address any specifics because I have not seen what has been sent to you.

I do know, in general, about the matter but there has been much secrecy involved and information has been withheld, so I am at a great disadvantage in being able to respond.

I do want you to know that I have not acted improperly with any woman. The accusations against me are totally and completely false.

The complainant did not file any complaint as required by our personnel policies and as required by federal law. And our board chair and our legal department have not followed our own internal written policies.

Linda and I are distressed concerning this situation beyond what words can express. I am being treated unfairly by any standard.

Our chairman assured me that a meeting of the executive committee on April 1 would resolve this matter and lay it to rest. I answered all questions at that time. I was shocked that he mailed out material to you and other board members and called for a full meeting of the board on April 29. Such a meeting is unnecessary and a waste of Habitat's money and your time. We can discuss this matter [at the international board meeting] in Mexico if there is a felt need to do so . . .

I want to assure you that this matter has been blown out of proportion and is an embarrassment to me and, I know, to you. It should be resolved among us without my or Habitat's reputation being damaged because of unfounded and unsubstantiated allegations.

May God guide us out of this mess that was totally unnecessary and uncalled for.

In Christian partnership,
Millard Fuller

---

# The New York April 29 Meeting

Despite Millard's assertion that an additional meeting was unnecessary, the board chairman refused to cancel the emergency meeting. Once at the meeting, Millard and his attorney, Ken Henson, Jr., could see there were problems. "The meeting on April 29 was a travesty," he would write. "Only a few board members were present and while others were participating by phone, not everyone could hear the proceedings. But no one seemed to care. It was as though holding a meeting was important, but what happened there didn't matter all that much. We later learned that the board had essentially been told by the PR firm and the law firm that they had to take some action."

As things got underway, Millard and his attorney were told they had one hour to present "their case." Ken Henson spoke first, laying out the brief but salient points he felt would cause the board to question their own assumptions:

- No charges had been filed; there was but an "allegation." And Millard had denied the allegation.
- Millard had offered to bear witness to his innocence by taking a lie-detector test—his accuser didn't take one.
- According to witnesses, the accuser had been a disgruntled employee for many years. She had threatened, on numerous occasions, to file claims against Habitat and to try and get money out of Habitat. This was not an isolated event, and there were letters supporting this.

- Neither Millard nor his attorneys were ever given an opportunity to even read the full ninety-page report so as to respond to the allegation.
- The investigator's bias was suspect. A fair investigation would include interviewing persons who worked closely with Millard on a daily basis. The accuser "had kept notes and had a memo," but would not let anyone look at them, including the investigator.
- Habitat personnel procedures had not been followed.

When it was Millard's turn to speak, he once again reminded the board that he was innocent of any involvement in the accusations. "I am as innocent as the driven snow," he said.

Their hour up, Millard and his attorney were asked to leave the room so that the board could deliberate.

Sometime after the meeting, a staff member—chagrined at the disrespect shown to the Fullers—gave Millard and Linda some information they would find shocking: The executive committee had held not just one, but a series of secret meetings prior to both April meetings. As a member of the executive committee, Millard should have been informed about any and all such meetings—even if he was the subject of them. Even worse, the Fullers learned that a high-profile public relations firm had been hired by the board and was represented at the meeting that day. It was the firm's opinion that the "problem at hand" could potentially lead to the demise of Habitat's "valuable brand" (estimated at the time as worth $1.8 billion), and that it would be wise to get rid of "the source of the problem." The firm's recommendation: remove the founder and president from the organization.

When former board member Don Mosley (founding member from 1976 to 1983, and again on the board from 1997 to February 2005) was asked to comment for this book about this meeting, he said: "The way it went down was definitely unfair and disrespectful to Millard. I think the board was 'blinded' by their agenda and did not want to add information that might change their foregone conclusion."

## A Misdated Memo Gives It Away

After the meeting with the board, Millard, his attorney, and Linda were met by a small delegation of the board informing them of the executive committee's decision.

Millard was handed a memorandum of their findings—dated, oddly enough, April 26—three days prior to when the meeting was held! Clearly, in one of the private sessions, the executive committee had already decided on the matter! The April 29 meeting had been a mere formality.

Clues that an orchestrated "plan" was in progress were piling up.

To Millard's great dismay, the memorandum from the executive board stated that Millard had "most likely" engaged in inappropriate conduct, even though there was no evidence. The report also made mention of the incident from fourteen years earlier, when Millard had been called on for "expressing affection inappropriately"—a matter wherein President Carter had called the board's action "quite disturbing," and what he viewed as "a power struggle unfairly punishing Millard," and that "a mountain has been made out of a molehill."

The memorandum concluded that a succession plan should be adopted, that Millard should be relieved of his duties as CEO, and that he should be fully removed from Habitat leadership by January 1, 2005. The "decision" had been a foregone conclusion—as the board minutes would show. The Habitat board had already adopted the recommendations of the executive committee.

In reading the paper before him, Millard would learn that board member Nic Retsinas, who would later become chair of the board, had made a motion to retain the services of Paul Leonard as acting chief executive officer "in the event that Millard did not continue with his duties."

Millard was asked to give his response to the memorandum by the following Monday.

# — 22 —

# "On the Edge of a Cliff . . ."

Upon his return to Americus, Millard called his immediate staff into his office and briefed them on the matter. He also held a meeting with the senior vice presidents and told them about the board's decision. Millard also felt the need to brief President Carter, and called him, setting up an appointment.

On May 1, the Fullers met with President Carter at his home. While there, they were surprised to learn that Ramsey had phoned Carter immediately following the April 29 meeting and told him what had transpired, as well as the decision reached by the board.

The Fullers felt their meeting with Carter went well and left feeling hopeful that things would finally get straightened out—especially since Carter said he would send a letter to board chairman Rey Ramsey to set the record straight. Carter's letter read:

May 1, 2004

To Chairman Rey Ramsey,

After my discussion with you this past Thursday, I also had an opportunity to meet with Millard and Linda Fuller, and have given the present matter serious prayer and assessment. The essence of the decision to be made should be what is best for Habitat for Humanity, the thousands of families who are now enjoying and will benefit from its fine services, and what is fair and proper for the Fullers, Habitat's founders and its heart and soul. Since it is obviously important to you, the basic desire of the directors needs to be fulfilled.

As you may know, I was deeply involved in the episode of 1990, and came to realize a few facts. One of them is that Habitat is a tremendous corporate structure involving tens of millions of dollars and an even greater wealth of goodwill and popularity. My impression then was that there were ambitious people who wanted to gain control of the organization, even at the expense of the Fullers, Carters, and many others. I know very few of the current directors and trust that you all are certain that this is not, once again, a factor in the recent proposal made to Millard.

Another fact, fourteen years ago, was that the allegations against Millard were never proven, most of them were superficial at best, but that he may well have been guilty of indiscretions that caused embarrassment or discomfort to some of the women involved. Another fact is that the eventual resolution of the issue was both wise and proper, and has resulted in almost fifteen additional years of unprecedented achievement because of the inspired leadership of the Fullers.

I have considered carefully the information you gave me in our telephone conversation and that was provided by the directors to Millard and his attorney, and it is obvious that there is no proof of impropriety, much less of actual sexual misconduct. It is a case of conflicting reports, the earliest official notice of which was made by the accuser more than a year after the alleged incident. I am convinced that Millard is innocent of any serious impropriety.

Furthermore, the directors' demands are excessively harsh and counterproductive even if there were some truth in the allegations, in that they will bring disgrace to Millard, despite his continuing incredible dedication and service to Habitat, and will seriously undermine support for the organization among us and many other dedicated contributors and volunteers. Observing the dates on the documents I've seen, the directors' basic decision seems to have been made before you called me at noon on April 29.

As everyone knows, I have not had or desired any authority within the Habitat organization since I completed my term as an international director. Since then, Rosalynn and I have served for more than two decades as volunteers, raising funds with mass mailings and leading the highly publicized Jimmy Carter Work Projects. We have maintained this relationship because of our belief in the Habitat program and our love and respect for Millard and Linda.

My strong recommendation to the Fullers and to the directors is that Millard agree to resign as president and CEO at the end of this year or a few days later on his seventieth birthday. He could make this announcement during one of the upcoming meetings of the board of directors. Subsequently, I hope he will agree to continue to promote Habitat, help with its funding, and perhaps be offered proper honors and some appropriate title. The Fullers could then decide whether to accept this offer for further service.

This should be the end of the current altercation, honoring both legal principles and those of our common Christian faith. There is no need to insult and debase the

Fullers with counseling and special training programs and, in the process, bring serious damage to Habitat for Humanity.

Sincerely,
Jimmy Carter
Copy to Habitat Directors
Millard and Linda Fuller

------------

The Fullers were pleased with Carter's letter. He had addressed their concerns and was especially clear about removing the language of "wrongdoing." He had made it clear to the board that he had considered carefully the information and found "no proof of impropriety."

Carter's letter alone was powerful, given his stature and influence in Habitat, but his wasn't the only voice weighing in. In an impassioned two-page letter, Don Mosley tried to get the board to see that the course they were setting may not be the correct one: "We are standing on the edge of a cliff, in danger of making a great mistake," he wrote in a May 2 letter to his fellow board members. "We are being carried along by a process that seems entirely rational on the surface but which may lead us to an act that all of us will ultimately regret. We still have the opportunity to avoid the tragedy, if we have the moral courage to do so. Instead of just continuing lockstep over the edge, we need to set aside the deadline a few hours from now and take a calm, wise, and prayerful look at what we are doing." In closing, he reminded them that fingering Millard would "bring great harm to a wonderful organization that has so much to offer this world." He closed with these words: "My own heart would be one of the first of millions to be broken over such a needless tragedy." Letter upon letter was sent expressing the sentiments of Deacon Jim Purks who at one point in this

Former President George H. W. Bush and the Fullers at the
Points of Light Medallion unveiling ceremony, 2003

ordeal would write: "The entire episode has the signs of overreaction . . . It appears the board members closed the door—
and, I fear, their minds . . . Habitat for Humanity has grown
enormously. It is probably almost frightening for a board to try
to get its 'arms around' such a huge and fast-growing organization and mission . . . The board has . . . expressed its concern
about the management of Habitat, about the failure to bring
along a successor, and about the perception of major decisions
being made unilaterally . . . They are legitimate issues . . . for
honest dialogue and negotiations—not for draconian rush-to-
judgment measures."

The Fullers believed that such persuasive input should
have put an end to the board's insistence on hanging tight to
the "misconduct" allegations. It didn't. And that they continued to be used as a legitimate reason to discredit Habitat's
founder's good name and character was even more disturbing—especially in light of the fact that Ramsey had told
Millard he was not to utter one word to anyone about what
was going on.

The rumor mill went into high gear.

## Gag Order and "House Arrest"

The tension intensified between Millard and the board when the executive committee caught wind that Millard was answering volunteers' and staffers' pleas for an explanation of what was happening. When Ramsey learned that Millard was talking to people, he fired off a letter to Millard, accusing him of violating instructions that he not contact Habitat employees. But the real surprise came when Millard read the lines that he was "relieved of his managerial duties, effectively immediately," and that he was banned from Habitat's offices, including his own.

Millard was astounded.

The founder and president of an organization with an outreach in a hundred countries would work from home. Some months later, in a letter to Carter, Millard would write: "I felt like a school child who had to 'behave' so that my superior would give me a passing grade and I would get to stay on a bit longer."

Millard's "house arrest" caused an even greater uproar among people in the office, not to mention Habitat for Humanity International affiliates the world over. All were left to wonder what was truly going on at Habitat headquarters? What was happening with the founder of their organization?

Millard believed something had to be said. A culture of transparency had always existed at Habitat. How could he suddenly just clam up and say nothing? Was the board implying that he had no right to defend himself against an accusation he knew not to be true? Since the board was refusing to clear his name, should he be barred from doing so himself? Ironically, the woman involved in the allegation would also sign a "confidentiality and non-disparagement" agreement (accompanied by a "severance payment"), which would prevent her from talking as well.

Living under these restrictions was impossible for Millard. Finally, after several days, he was able to convince the board chair and the executive committee, with approval from

President Carter, that he needed to send out some kind of notice explaining why he wasn't in his office. The letter sent to Habitat Partners on May 13 explained that the board and Millard were "working through some issues" and that Millard, at the board's request, would remain out of the office for a few days.

With tensions continuing to escalate, Don Mosley appealed to President Carter to mediate yet again. Carter agreed, and a May 21 date was set.

# — 23 —

# President Carter Mediates

The May 21, 2004, mediation session at Carter's home office was attended by Linda and Millard, and Millard's legal counsel Ken Henson, Jr. Also in attendance were Millard's brother, Doyle Fuller, and his son, Jacob—both of whom were lawyers in Montgomery—and Griffin Bell, Jr., a labor relations lawyer from Atlanta. The board chairman Rey Ramsey, two other members of the executive committee, and their legal counsel rounded out the other team.

Doyle had suggested Millard get in touch with Bell, widely considered to be one of the country's premier experts in labor relations. Millard took the advice and had talked with Bell, who, after carefully reviewing the situation, told Millard that though misconduct allegations must be treated seriously, HFHI's board needn't fear a lawsuit because the allegation couldn't be substantiated. This meant there was no viable legal case. Millard was confident that Bell's legal opinion would get the board's attention and open their eyes to the illegitimacy, if not the wrongfulness, of their claim.

Millard receives the Builder Award
presented by the U.S. Chamber of Commerce, 2004

## Plan B

The mediation began and seemed to being going well. But President Carter would surprise Millard and his group when he introduced a new wrinkle to the issue: The executive committee had told Carter that they believed Millard was a poor leader. When the Fullers asked for clarification, Carter said he had been asked by the executive committee not to reveal the reasons that were given. "This is almost laughable," Linda would say. "I don't know what they could possibly mean by poor leadership; that's really reaching! What's going on here?"

In looking back on that day, the Fullers surmised that the board had developed this new complaint because they were aware of Griffin Bell, Jr.'s legal position. Presented with this legal opinion, the executive committee needed a new justification to move Millard aside—so it was on to "Plan B," claims of poor leadership. The following letter, which the Fullers would receive just prior to the international board meeting in Mexico City, depicts the legal opinion of Griffin Bell, Jr., that influenced those sequestered in separate rooms at the mediation on May 21.

---

Fisher & Phillips LLP
Attorneys at Law
1500 Resurgens Place
945 East Paces Ferry Road
Atlanta, GA 30326

June 7, 2004
Millard Fuller
Americus, GA 31709

Dear Millard,
You asked that I write you a letter setting forth my opinion of the Habitat investigation of the belated complaint by a female employee alleging inappropriate behavior by you some seventeen months ago. As you are aware, my firm is one of the few in America that engages exclusively in the representation of employers in employment matters. We provide advice on and personally direct investigations of alleged acts of sexual harassment on a daily basis.

When a complaint of harassment is received, an employer must investigate the charge immediately and take appropriate action. The employer's duty in investigating is not only to protect the complaining party from further injury, but also to protect the accused employee if the complaint turns out to be false.

Based on my own twenty-five years in employment law, I studied the investigator's report. Several of the procedures utilized were insufficient and prejudiced to you.

Nevertheless, a few facts floated to the surface. This was an employee disgruntled by what she perceived as an adverse employment action, which motivated her to make a half-hearted complaint many months after the alleged incident occurred. She also was an employee who had previous experience with a pregnancy discrimination claim and, therefore, knew her procedural rights and responsibility under the state and federal laws. She nevertheless chose not to avail herself of those laws. The allegedly inappropriate conduct of which she complained absolutely is not sexual harassment under the law. The allegation of touching was not mentioned by her to the first several people to whom she casually communicated her complaints, which undercuts her credibility. There were no witnesses to the incident, which gives rise to the classic "he said, she said" situation. Since the truth of the allegation is not apparent and certainly cannot be proved then the customary solution for an employer is to confront both employees and inform them that while the investigation was inconclusive, that their conduct would be watched and that they should avoid any contact which would place them in a compromising situation again.

That customary resolution was not followed in this case. Instead, while the investigation stated explicitly that the results were inconclusive, the decision was reached nevertheless to punish the accused as if the results were in fact conclusive. This was by the investigator relying on a charge of inappropriate behavior that occurred fifteen years ago. Such an incident is held in all courts of law to be so remote in time as to not be admissible in evidence; that is, not to be considered by a jury or a judge as to the guilt or innocence of the accused.

Finally, there is no chance of a lawsuit being filed by the complaining employee. Indeed there is no indication that she would have filed a lawsuit. She did not have a lawyer, and while she knew her rights under the EEOC laws, she did not file an EEOC complaint. Moreover, filing

a lawsuit under Georgia law is rare because of the difficulty of proof. In short, she would have been out of court,
if indeed she ever had any interest in going to court.
Therefore, there is no rational basis whatsoever for the
employer to take severe adverse action against you based
on an apprehension of a lawsuit being filed.

In conclusion, this is a classic "he said, she said" complaint of inappropriate behavior in which no formal complaint was ever made. The findings of the investigator
were inconclusive and the customary resolution for such
a situation was not utilized. Instead, punishment was
imposed as if there were a conclusive finding of guilt,
apparently being based on charges some fifteen years ago.
The complainant herself showed no interest in filing an
EEOC complaint and the chances of a lawsuit are remote,
if not non-existent. Habitat is a Christian ministry. The
Ninth Commandment is that one shall not bear false witness against his neighbor. Habitat allowed that to happen.
It failed you.

Sincerely,
Griffin B. Bell, Jr.

------------

## Carter's Recommendations

As it turned out, bringing Griffin Bell, Jr. to the mediation
was a smart move, and its influence showed up in the recommendations Carter would write up following the mediation
and give to both sides. The Fullers read Carter's recommendations and were grateful that Carter had seen the truth for what
it was: "Since there can be no definitive proof concerning the

truth of allegations . . . there should be no public condemnation of Millard." Carter would admonish both sides to refrain from disparaging comments and to embrace a resignation date for Millard effective no later than January 2005, allowing him to continue as CEO until that time. The Fullers decided to abide by these compromises and agree to its terms.

The law firm retained by the executive committee proceeded to write up a legal agreement based on President Carter's recommendations. Remarkably, Carter's one-and-a-third pages got translated into a seventeen-page document.

The Fullers found the longer agreement to be onerous. For one, they were still upset about the impossible-to-abide-by gag order—even if it wasn't a formal demand. It meant, in essence, that after all of Millard's attempts—as well as those of his attorney, President Carter, and board members such as John Stack, a Methodist minister from South Africa—he would be prevented from coming to his own defense. Stack (currently vice chair of the board) had written to Millard: "When I reflect on what had happened [at the international board of directors meeting], I was horrified to realize that I had agreed with the view that you were considered guilty, despite a lack of evidence. I immediately e-mailed Rey and the executive committee to rescind my vote. I expressed very clearly that I agreed completely with Don Mosley's suggestion that we ask Jimmy Carter to meet with you, Rey, and the executive board to resolve the matter . . . I will vote to clear your name completely."

For Millard, the agreement the board finally presented him with was unacceptable, because, as he stated, "It's predicated on a complete lie." After much discussion and back-and-forth revisions—and as Millard would later say, "pressuring"—on June 6, just three days prior to the Mexico board meeting and after five revisions, Millard reluctantly signed the agreement. In the days and weeks that followed, Millard increasingly felt as though he had "sold his soul" in the painful injustice forced upon him.

On the day Millard signed the agreement, Rey Ramsey issued a letter to the board: An agreement had been reached with Millard's accuser, including "a severance payment, a confidentiality agreement, a non-disparagement agreement, and a full release."

If Ramsey had wanted Millard's head on a plate, he pretty much got it. Little did anyone, including the affiliates in the field doing the good work of Habitat, know that their founder and inspirational leader was deep in the throes of being removed from the ministry he had founded.

# — 24 —

# The International Board
# Meeting: Mexico City
# (June 10, 2004)

The evening prior to the board meeting in Mexico City, the executive committee requested that Millard meet with them early the next morning. There was no mention of the purpose of the meeting, and Millard was reluctant to attend because he had prepared his speech to the board and wanted to remain calm and not get upset by any unexpected confrontation. But Linda saw this as an opportunity. She suggested to Millard that she request to meet with the executive committee to ask them some pressing questions on her mind. They had refused to hear her at the New York meeting, but this time they agreed to see her.

Now holding court with the executive committee, Linda thanked them for finally meeting with her, but told them she had felt slighted when, at the April 29 meeting in New York, the full board had agreed to hear from her, but instead kept her waiting for three hours—and then refused to let her speak to them. "As Millard's marriage partner for some forty-four years and his partner in co-founding Habitat for Humanity International," she told them, "I consider your actions insulting and disrespectful. First of all, how can you accuse Millard of being a 'poor leader' when he was just named 'CEO of the Year' by the *NonProfit Times?* Why are you in such a rush to get Millard out of Habitat? Why not allow him to remain president and CEO until the millionth person lives in a Habitat house? How can your hearts be so hardened as to not allow this decision that would be good for Habitat, good for the public, and good for Millard?" Silence loomed in the room. Little effort was made to challenge Linda's questions. Rey Ramsey finally broke the silence. "Look, we have to write a statement right now. It's almost time for the board meeting to start. We need to talk to Millard." It was 8:00 a.m. and time to step across the hall to the board room.

## Millard Speaks

The meeting began with a devotional presented by board member John Stack. By 10:30 a.m., it was time for Millard to address the board. He got right down to business. He began by telling the board in his own words that he was not guilty of misconduct and was grieved by the board's overreaction to the allegation. He conveyed his frustration regarding the secret meetings of the executive committee and the way donors' contributions were being squandered on unnecessary meetings and legal fees. He distributed the letter from Griffin Bell, Jr., which outlined findings that were significantly different from those of Habitat's lawyers. Millard challenged the board's newest assertion that he was a poor leader by stating the many tremendous accomplishments made by Habitat during his tenure. He outlined why the agreement he signed on June 6 was a source of conflict for him.

Of particular importance was that he be allowed to continue serving as CEO until late 2005 so that he could still be president when the 200,000th house was dedicated to the millionth person—and he passionately pleaded that he be allowed this courtesy. This, he said, was a milestone, a sign of accomplishment of his steadfast devotion to an organization founded under God's direction and driven by his commitment to working "in partnership with God." That house would be an indication of how far and wide he had served his God, carrying the message to the far corners of the world. Millard assured the board that should he be allowed this request, he would then announce his planned retirement in late 2004 or January 2005. In that way, there would be plenty of time to find another president and CEO and have that person engaged in a smooth transition. In fact, this new CEO could be announced around the time of the 200,000th house event so affiliates could know that he was "phasing out." And then he said, "So that's where I stand. Now, I would like to hear from some of you."

Board member Kathleen Bader took this opportunity to liken Millard to a for-profit corporation CEO. She pointed out: "Seventy years old is time for any CEO to step down. At Dow, execs 'walk' at sixty."

Millard chuckled and said, "I'd offer examples such as Jimmy Carter being head of The Carter Center at age eighty, Dan Rather, Larry King, and others who are still in leadership roles. I don't see my age as a barrier yet."

Larry Pribble offered his belief that Millard had been victimized, but should have done more to prevent his own victimization. "I have a lot of respect for your leadership, and I agree we have all been victims. I have struggled. I am struggling as to whether I want to remain on the international board of directors. There are two things that make me particularly sad. First, that the international board of directors has been negligent in having serious discussions with you before now about succession, and secondly, that you didn't do more to protect the ministry from appearing to be above reproach of having accusations of 'inappropriate misconduct.' Billy Graham has managed that in his organization."

In classic Clarence Jordan form, Millard leaned on Scripture for his response, reminding Larry and the other board members that ministry can often be risky. "Did you remember that Jesus had a woman of bad reputation wash his feet with her hair? Billy Graham would have never allowed such a thing. Jesus did. I think Christians need to be somewhat vulnerable; otherwise we never come in contact with those Christ wants to save. We do, indeed, need to focus on what God wants because that's what is important. Sometimes crises come about, and there are reasons for them. A ministry can grow and blossom out of a crisis if we make the right choices."

Chairman Ramsey then asked Millard if he had one last statement he would like to make. "The agreement that I was more or less forced to sign is in a spirit of fear that doesn't come from God," said Millard. "I'm not the enemy of Habitat. I want the best for Habitat. I want us all to operate in a spirit of love. Linda and I were at the World Economic Forum in January. So many of the social entrepreneurs wanted to know how Habitat for Humanity grew so strong and so fast. Well, it takes a leader full of God's spirit, not a manager, to make this kind of growth happen . . . to raise money and come up with ideas that make it happen. It doesn't just happen by accident."

Millard concluded his remarks by walking over to Habitat's attorney Regina Hopkins, and handing her a signed revocation of his agreement. The Fullers then left the room—and the board deliberated their fate.

# — 25 —

# The Coup d'État

Finally, at 4:00 p.m., five-and-a-half hours after Millard's impassioned speech, the board reached its decision: Millard was to announce his retirement on July 1, 2004, and retire on May 15, 2005. Especially created for Millard, there would be a "symbolic" celebration of the 200,000th house on May 15.

Millard said "no deal."

"We can't dedicate the house in May of next year because those numbers of houses would not have been built by that date," he told them. "That wouldn't be honest, and I won't participate in it." The board deliberated some more and reverted to the proposal made by President Carter on May 21: Millard would announce his retirement by December 1, 2004, to be effective in January 2005. Conveniently, the board did not follow President Carter's direction to correct the finding in April that Millard was "most likely" guilty of wrongdoing. And that was that. The board members, many of whom had once worked side by side with the Fullers driving nails and pouring cement to build houses for the world's poor, now cast their lot with those who wanted to take Habitat corporate, telling the Fullers, basically, they had outlived their usefulness. One board member would later say, "There was a pit in my stomach as I watched the two people I'd admired more than anyone in my life file out of the boardroom. Being a part of this was one of the most shameful moments of my life." But on that day, not one of the board members dared ask for clemency for Habitat's founders and visionary leaders.

Linda and Millard were so distressed by the board's hard line that they left Mexico City immediately and returned home two days before they had planned.

On the agonizing trip home, the couple struggled to give voice to their feelings and what to do next. How did these actions of the board, so ill-conceived and hurtful, fit into the history and future of their lives and Habitat's ministry? They began to talk about what they believed had led to the board's decision for a transition—no matter if it meant, in the words of an observant reporter, "the demise" of the Fullers.

They were now fully convinced that the allegation of misconduct was a smoke screen, an exaggerated excuse the executive committee had tried first as a stand-alone reason for removing Millard, and when that failed, had used as a way to embarrass him into submission. But Millard had proven a tougher nut to crack than they'd imagined, and his wife brought forth a steely resolve of her own. Certainly this had dragged on longer than they'd imagined: Already a succession plan was in place.

The Fullers reviewed the issues that had culminated with the board's final decision. First on the list was that the new business-oriented board of directors wanted to move the headquarters from Americus, Georgia, to Atlanta, to which the Fullers were adamantly opposed. For Millard, being based where the roots of the organization started was important. He said, "There is magic in staying where your roots are, such as Coca-Cola in Atlanta, Wal-Mart in Bentonville, Arkansas, and Whirlpool in Benton Harbor, Michigan. When you pull up roots, it's like a plant; there's a very good likelihood it will wither. Habitat has a historical connection with Koinonia, President Jimmy Carter, the Sumter County Initiative . . . all the deep, rich connections we would lose if they put it (the headquarters) in another city." And Millard also felt, from a donor-stewardship perspective, that the cost of administration in an urban center would drive up the payroll costs. President Carter protested the move strongly through an open letter in the local Americus newspaper, claiming that it was a violation of the agreement Habitat had made with him in exchange for his endorsement of Habitat. The move would have meant great economic hardship for Sumter County, as Habitat had become one of its largest employers. Appeasing Carter's protests, the board decided to stay in Americus for the time being and issued a press release affirming Habitat's respect for its past and its roots. But, as Millard predicted, after several weeks, departments such as administration and finance were moved to Atlanta.

Another painful and more personal factor, they believed, was that their friend and neighbor, Jimmy Carter, was not openly critical of the board's actions—and this had discouraged support from certain board members who might otherwise have voted against the Fullers' removal from Habitat. If President Carter was unwilling to publicly take Millard's side, then surely, some argued, there must be something wrong with Millard's perspective. The Fullers were disappointed, but suspected that Carter was unwilling to become embroiled in a public fight because so much of his post-presidency legacy had been built around the success of Habitat for Humanity.

The Fullers discussed the difference in the way they and the executive committee saw the responsibilities of senior management. By the Fullers' design, Habitat for Humanity affiliates are a network of localized organizations established by a simple "covenant" agreement; they share the same mission, branding, and general program model, but are legally independent of one another and the international headquarters. As a result of a consultant's study, Habitat established regional and area offices in different parts of the United States and abroad, attempting to relocate resources from Americus closer to the affiliates in the field. However, another study in 2004 by the same consultant would bolster the board's decision to begin reining in these same affiliates in the name of safeguarding "the brand." A program called The Standards of Excellence was designed and used to evaluate the existing affiliates and prospective affiliates to ensure that there was consistency in the programs. According to newer members of the board, having little leverage over the affiliates was not the most efficient way to manage things. To the Fullers, variation was a good thing. Affiliates experienced success and benefited greatly from the organizational abilities of localized leadership. Where Millard found energy, creativity, and compassion, the new board members found inconsistency and lack of controlled productivity. The board felt a top-down management style was more appropriate for the organization, but Millard believed in inspired grass-roots servant-leadership. There was little common ground.

Executive salaries were another contentious aspect of the differences in values. The executive committee was discussing raising executive salaries significantly. There was talk that Millard's replacement would be offered a salary three times more than what Millard thought appropriate (which would come to pass).

The Fullers' review of all that had transpired also included the fact that with more focus being placed on the Habitat for Humanity brand, yet another of the Fullers' founding tenets for Habitat was being eroded: The storytelling of the Christian witness was being silenced, and the brand was becoming the unifying force. A brand evaluation done by Interbrand in 2002 concluded that Habitat's brand value was $1.8 billion, placing Habitat in the same league as the coffee retailer Starbucks. This discovery emboldened some of the newer management to want to draw in volunteers and donors by enticing them with Habitat's brand name rather than its Christian housing ministry. Dennis Bender, who served as sen-

ior vice president of communications for Habitat, reflected a
new sentiment: "The question now is how do we leverage
brand value to further our mission and goals? Should we
change our strategies and operations to increase our brand
value?"[2] Millard would counter, "If you listen to people in
truly great organizations talk about their achievements, you
will hear little about earnings per share, much less brand
value. What brand did Jesus use?"

For more than thirty years, Millard preached that volunteers should be rallying around the Theology of the Hammer,
the incarnation of Jesus' universal love and concern for the
poor. From Millard's perspective, "Jesus demands divestiture
of wealth and power, both powerful temptations in brand
value-based marketing, even for a nonprofit ministering to
the poor." To the Fullers, spending money on increasing
brand value did not justify a cookie-cutter approach to community building and was not the way to inspire new volunteers to join forces with their housing ministry. The Fullers
felt strongly that sharing stories based on Christian values that
motivated them to give up their fortune and use their lives to
serve those in need was the surest way to create the desire to
make shelter a matter of conscience and action. Silencing the
storyteller and divorcing the organization from its roots
wasn't the most effective way to advance the cause.

And there was the thorn in their side over the fact that the
new board perceived Habitat's Christian witnessing as a barrier to growth. Some felt this was especially significant in
nations where religions other than Christianity dominate, as
well as with the growing groups of people in the United States
who weren't Christian. The Fullers and others, like board
member John Stack, felt deeply that spiritual emphasis was at
the root of the organizational struggle. "We've overloaded the
board with highly successful businesspeople," concluded
Millard. "Some seem put off by my overt declaration of Jesus."

---

[2] J. Quelch and N. Laidler, "Habitat for Humanity International: Brand Valuation,"
*Harvard Business School Publishing* (2003), Case 503-101, 1–27.

Some newer members on the board echoed findings in the brand valuation study that corporate donations were being made because it was good for the corporation, not because of a Christian mission, and therefore, the "corporate" side of Habitat needed to be played up and its role as a "Christian housing ministry" played down. As former Habitat affiliate executive director Kirk Lyman-Barner reflected, "If the brand becomes the message, it puffs its ego and says, 'Look at what the brand has done.'" He observed that Millard's message had always been, "Look what you and God can do!" Nevertheless, a transition to more secular marketing materials and communications was already in the works. The slogan "Every house is a sermon about God's love" was slated to be pulled from corporate headquarters' signage. The Fullers challenged the board on its desire to turn the emphasis away from its Christian roots, but it refused to be swayed.

With this review, the Fullers came to realize they just might be powerless to slow down the wheels of change that were sweeping over the Christian housing ministry they founded. In spite of their strong misgivings and objections, and in the face of incredible pressure—especially the threat of negative media coverage for Habitat for Humanity and the possibility of immediate firing—on June 14, 2004, Linda and Millard signed their individual agreements again.

## Access Denied

Even greater change was in the air. Within a few days of the arrival of the new managing director, Paul Leonard, Millard was cut off from resources normally available to him. In Millard's estimation, calling himself a CEO was now a farce, a deception to the public. Not only did Millard have no authority, but he couldn't even get basic information. Millard had an assistant ask the legal counsel which board members were up for reelection in November. She was refused the information. Curious about how much money was being spent, Millard asked the finance department to tell him how much had been paid to the law firm in New York. He was told that, on instruction from the chairman, that information couldn't be divulged. Millard did finally manage to find out what the law firm had been paid—$413,000. The number was staggering, and Millard was ashamed such an amount of donor contributions had been wasted in this way. To Millard, such expenditures were a blatant betrayal of stewardship.

Others felt betrayal as well. Three board members, Don Mosely, Paul Ekelschot, and John Stack, spoke out about their fury over the way the Fullers were being treated throughout the course of events to date, and eventually, some members would resign as a result. New board member Bob Edgar, the general secretary of the National Council of Churches of Christ, not wanting to become involved in Habitat's internal struggles, resigned even before attending his first meeting. Mosley would say, "Millard is being accused falsely, and the false allegation is a serious breach against Millard and Habitat; a serious error had been made by the board to fire him. I resigned as a result." Paul Ekelschot would plead for the board's ear: "Let us admit that, after hiring lawyers, consultants, and experts, we did not advance an iota, and accept the fact that instead HFHI is moving in a dangerous direction . . . We have a problem, we partially caused or increased it ourselves, we have to fix it."

On July 26, at Don Mosley's suggestion, Millard voluntarily took a lie-detector test in Atlanta administered by Cy Hardin, a member of the National Polygraph Association and former president of the Georgia Polygraph Association, who had administered in excess of fifty thousand polygraph examinations. Mosley had every reason to believe that Ramsey would honor its results.

All of Millard's answers indicated that he was truthful in denying any wrongdoing with his accuser. The result was reported to the full board in a letter from Mosley. Much to the Fullers' dismay, the exonerating results of a polygraph test didn't change a thing. Millard would learn from former board chairman Edgar Stoesz that Ramsey considered the polygraph test a meaningless exercise. Paul Ekelschot would admonish the board to revisit its attitude and behavior toward Millard:

"What I am suggesting is that:

1. We use the lie detector test as a vehicle to eat our hat.

2. We apologize to Millard and Linda, telling them that after he passed the lie detector test we are convinced that his interpretation of the events is the correct one and that we regret our earlier doubts. Our apology should not be in half but generous.

3. We issue a public statement to staff and volunteers, indicating that we have been informed about certain rumors relating to an incident between Millard Fuller and a female staff member, that we extensively have investigated the rumors, and that we strongly believe that those rumors are incorrect.

4. We allow Millard to be CEO till the moment of the 200,000th house and define his responsibilities towards Paul Leonard. Let us not be afraid about losing face.

"I strongly advise that we organize on short notice a Board meeting to discuss this or any other suggestion that takes HFHI from the dangerous path it is on today."

"This whole thing is heartless," said Deacon Jim Purks. "Millard deserves an apology, the clearing of his name, and the opportunity for an honorable, orderly departure as chief executive officer. He needs to be a participant in the decisions and directions chartered in the coming year before his retirement."

# — 26 —

# Second Mediation:
# President Carter

Trying to get some much-needed time to themselves, Millard and Linda spent a few days in the mountain-lake region of northeast Georgia at the home of some friends. Their times alone together had always been a blessing to the Fullers—time to enjoy each other's company, be with their children and grandchildren, and focus on all that God had brought into their lives. But on this particular getaway, it was difficult not to dwell on the agonizing struggle they were going through. At least these few days would give them time to focus again on their relationship and the strength they'd always found there.

But once back home in Americus, the saga continued. In early August, Linda and Millard were sitting in a pew behind President and Mrs. Carter in church on Sunday morning. President Carter asked how things were going. Millard told him, "Not well." At the end of the service, President Carter handed Linda a note saying that he would be willing to get involved again if the Fullers and the board were willing.

Millard got right on it. He contacted Don Mosley, asking him to set up a meeting. Don contacted the board chairman, and all the arrangements were made to meet with President Carter at The Carter Center on August 23.

President Carter met with both groups individually and together, reviewing the goals of each group. The Fullers wanted Millard's name cleared, and for Millard to remain CEO until the 200,000th house was completed. They also wanted Millard's role to be clarified and to have their freedom of speech restored by a removal of the gag order.

Chairman Ramsey responded that the board had determined that Millard had "most likely" engaged in inappropriate conduct with his accuser, but that nothing negative about the incident would be entered in his personnel file. Ramsey reiterated that the board wanted Millard out of leadership, as agreed, by January 3, 2005, leaving day-to-day duties to the managing director in the meantime. Finally, the agreement that had been drafted by President Carter (his one-and-a-half pages expanded to seventeen pages by the New York law firm) was to be honored—no exceptions. In other words, they were holding firm in their resolve on all the issues.

## Carter:
## Board Must Reverse Its Findings of Guilt

While much discussion ensued between the two groups, Carter was quietly reading the agreement. He suddenly interrupted. Taking off his glasses and tossing them down on the pages of the agreement, he looked sternly over to board chairman Ramsey and said that the board must reverse its finding of guilt in regard to Millard. President Carter continued, "Can we do that?" There was dead silence. Ramsey squirmed, looked around at his colleagues, and said meekly, "Yes, I suppose so."

"I remember distinctly the moment President Carter made his statement," said attorney Henson. "Earlier on in that meeting, I asked each of the representatives of Habitat if he or she personally believed that Millard had done anything wrong in terms of the assertions made by his accuser. Each one of them stated no, they didn't believe anything took place. I asked them if they would have Habitat release a statement to this effect. They stated that they could not do this because of the board action, but were willing to discuss it. Essentially, they were using this as a point of negotiation, i.e., they would issue a statement that Millard did something else. They were holding his name and his reputation hostage. Later, President Carter picked up on this and asked them if they would reverse their findings since they clearly had no proof of wrongdoing on Millard's part."

Carter then said that he would write a preface to the agreements for the purpose of expressing deep appreciation for the years of hard work and faithful service the Fullers had provided to Habitat's ministry. Everyone agreed to this. The Fullers were pleased.

Carter continued, "Furthermore, the board should publicly announce this finding of 'no proof' to the staff and volunteers in Americus and to Habitat offices around the world."

Linda and Millard were once again hopeful because of Carter's stand and pleased that Carter had finally been persuasive in getting the executive committee to admit the truth and let it be known.

Carter left to prepare a statement that would be used to communicate the "no proof" change. The new statement read:

> The board will issue to the Habitat staff a statement saying, "The International Board of Directors of Habitat for Humanity has found no proof of alleged inappropriate sexual conduct by Millard Fuller."
>
> All terms of the agreement reached in Mexico in June will be accepted and honored in good faith.

In order to assuage the harshness of the legalistic language in the agreement, a preface will be added, drafted by President Carter, acknowledging and expressing gratitude for the great contributions of Linda and Millard Fuller.

Provided there is good faith acceptance of all terms of the agreement, Paul Leonard will recommend to the board of directors that Millard Fuller's retirement date be extended until the 200,000th house is completed. Paul and Millard will be free to consult with President Carter whenever necessary.

Everyone agreed to the revised statements, shook hands, and parted company on that positive note. But their conciliatory demeanor would be short-lived.

On the way back to Americus that afternoon, not far from the outskirts of Atlanta, Millard received a call on his cell phone from his attorney, Ken Henson, Jr., reporting that one of the New York lawyers had called to say that the firm didn't like the term "no proof" in Carter's recommendations and wanted to substitute the words "insufficient proof." The attorney said that President Carter had agreed with this change, and now they wanted Millard's permission. Millard discussed it with his attorney. Both agreed that allowing the statement of "insufficient proof" would create some doubt regarding Millard's innocence. "They are not content with 'no proof,'" he told Linda. "They're intent on injecting a shadow of doubt regarding my innocence."

Linda and Millard discussed it and then reluctantly agreed to "insufficient proof" just to keep the peace and move forward. (If Carter wrote a preface, it was never added to the Agreements. And, Carter's recommendation that Millard retire after completion of the 200,000th house was not to be.)

## The Emergency Meeting

The next day, Tuesday, August 24, the full board was convened in emergency session in Atlanta. Millard was excluded from the meeting, but Don Mosley reported the board had agreed to Carter's four recommendations, but insisted that the statement issued to the staff be expanded to say that there had been disagreements between Millard and the board. The "disagreements" would center on two issues: a succession plan for Millard leaving Habitat's leadership and an acknowledgment that there was "insufficient proof" to find that he was guilty of wrongdoing.

A page-long memo was distributed to approximately 1,100 persons—to staff and volunteers in Americus, as well as to regional offices in the United States and to area offices around the world.

With that done, the executive committee turned their attention to quieting the rumors now circulating among the affiliates and the media. The goal was simply to explain that Millard was being replaced, and that Habitat was moving on to a new chapter.

# — 27 —

# The Affiliates Find Their Voice

**M**uch to the dismay of the executive committee, the memo did little to quiet things down. In fact, it did just the opposite. Literally hundreds of phone calls, as well as hundreds upon hundreds of letters and e-mails, deluged board members, Habitat headquarters, and Millard—all wanting more information about the "conflict."

For the most part, these letters and questions went unanswered. Habitat staff were instructed not to say a word about the controversy, and this only added fuel to everyone's curiosity and need for answers. Millard felt compelled to answer people's questions, doing the best he could under such stringent restraints. Ramsey, once again, was furious that Millard was "talking" and accused him of violating the gag order in the June 14 agreement he had signed.

## The Colorado Petition

David Snell, a former staff member of Habitat International, a volunteer officer with the Colorado State Habitat organization, and a close friend of the Fullers, offered his help. Now living in Colorado Springs, Colorado, David met with a number of representatives from Colorado Habitat affiliates. Like so many other affiliates, the Colorado group pledged to be aggressive in working to keep Millard in leadership at Habitat. One after another, the affiliates banded together, and under David's leadership, they drafted a petition.

"As affiliates and supporters of Habitat for Humanity," the petition read, "we are an integral part of the Habitat family. Since we are directly impacted by the actions of the HFHI Board of Directors, we deserve some level of involvement. We feel very strongly that the board has acted UNFAIRLY in regard to forcing retirement on Habitat's founder and leader, Millard Fuller." Among their requests was that Millard be reinstated and, in the least, that a transition plan be developed that treated him fairly. The affiliate directors also felt the executive committee should agree to meet with affiliate representatives to hear their concerns about equitable transition planning. Above all, they wanted the board to give reconciliation with the Fullers a try. Thousands signed the petition.

"We have a right to know what was going on, especially from Millard himself," the petitioners wrote. "Through the years, we have always been able to pick up a phone and get information, and we expect to do that now." The lack of access to information only served to raise concerns among volunteers and donors that something was terribly wrong.

## Revoking the Agreements

The board chairman and executive committee were extremely agitated about the petition and Millard's communications with his friends and supporters, stating that Millard had, once again, "violated the agreement." The Fullers argued they had answered only basic questions about the crisis while on a speaking tour.

Nevertheless, another emergency meeting of the executive

committee was scheduled for October 11 to decide what to do about Millard's egregious behavior.

Once again, after prayerful consideration, Millard and Linda decided to revoke the agreements they'd signed on June 14 following the international board meeting in Mexico City. Provisions had been included in the agreements on how to revoke them, and when the process was complete, Millard sent a letter to the full board explaining his and Linda's reasons for doing so, and appealing for reason and reconciliation.

## An Appeal to Reason

In rapid succession over the next couple of days, Millard had numerous phone conversations with David Snell and other friends who were actively involved in the matter. David was moving ahead with plans to mail petitions to all U.S. and Canadian affiliates. These were to be signed and sent to the board in support of Millard, asking the board to reconsider their actions against him. Volunteers with an independent Habitat group in Colorado addressed, stuffed, and stamped more than two thousand envelopes. The letters were to be mailed during the middle of the week of October 4.

Millard was also in touch with his attorney, Ken Henson, Jr., who sent a letter to Baker & McKenzie, the firm representing Habitat, informing them that if Millard was fired, they were seriously considering the filing of a slander lawsuit against his accuser.

In one last appeal to reason, David Snell called Chairman Ramsey and asked if he would be willing to meet with Millard. If not, the petitions to the affiliates would be mailed immediately. Ramsey agreed to the meeting.

Ramsey met Millard at the Baltimore airport, and after three hours of discussion, they agreed that Millard would serve as "founder and president" of Habitat, and not CEO. Millard flew home, hopeful that reconciliation was possible. In that spirit, he wrote Ramsey a letter expressing his gratitude that

Habitat was willing to protect the integrity of the housing ministry.

Ramsey would initiate a letter of his own. His would be directed as a "joint letter" from himself and Millard addressed to "all HFHI staff, affiliates, national organizations, and campus chapters" and would outline the details of the changes in HFHI's management structure. Unfortunately, this memo would not be reassuring to those who received it. Instead, coming on the heels of newspaper articles and rumors about internal struggles at Habitat, it affirmed that foundational leadership changes were occurring without the knowledge or input of staff and volunteers. For an organization that had always been run openly and transparently from its inception, this was indeed a troubling change.

# — 28 —

# The (Hostile) Takeover
# Is Complete

As if the transition to new management weren't difficult enough, a new round of lawsuits was threatened by Millard's accuser, who claimed she was entitled to more money from Habitat because her name was now in the press. Her settlement had guaranteed that she would remain anonymous. Even though she declined to comment when reached by a reporter from *The NonProfit Times* in 2005, she did say she wasn't making comments "yet."

Still, in light of the fact that Millard's accuser was threatening to sue Habitat for more money, the Fullers suggested that they and the board issue a joint statement to the press with the purpose of showing unity and hopefully staving off a lawsuit. The Fullers dearly wanted to prevent Habitat's precious contributions from being diverted from the housing ministry and into yet more legal fees and a claim for money that the Fullers considered "akin to blackmail." But there would be no cooperation to issue a unified response—and the decision was costly to everyone.

## The "Massage" That Rubbed the Wrong Way

Then, in late December, Nic Retsinas sent out an unauthorized letter, mistakenly entitled, "A Massage from Nic Retsinas," to all Habitat employees worldwide stating that certain "turbulence" had been going on, but that Habitat nevertheless continued to thrive. This communication by Retsinas, an international board of directors vice chair, was unprecedented. Many employees and volunteers were puzzled because they had never heard of Nic Retsinas, and his reference to "turbulence" just fueled their desire to know more. Many people, the Fullers included, found his message highly inappropriate.

This unauthorized memo especially angered Linda. She sent Retsinas a cheeky letter saying she would prefer he'd given everyone a "massage" instead of a "message." In her letter, she articulated what she felt was the board's role in the fiasco, and that the injustice they had perpetrated needed to be corrected. She pointed out that neither Habitat for Humanity's legal counsel nor the executive committee had followed its own personnel policies with regard to the accuser. It was a lengthy letter, ending by her calling for the resignation of the board.

Needless to say, the board was not too pleased about what Linda had to say—especially the part calling for their resignations. In fact, they were so displeased that managing director Paul Leonard wrote Linda asking if she intended to remain an employee of Habitat if the executive committee decided not to follow her advice to resign immediately.

The next six weeks would produce a new round of exchanges between the executive committee and the Fullers, culminating in a January 10 letter to Millard from Rey Ramsey that issued an ultimatum: They were to comply with the conditions laid out in the letter (they were forbidden to speak to anyone about any conflict with the board or to "call into question the actions or authority of the Board or our new CEO"), no exceptions, or, "with regret, yours and Linda's employment will be terminated."

On January 31, 2005, accused of being divisive and disruptive to the organization's work, Millard and Linda Fuller were fired by the executive committee.

The Fullers' staff were told to collect their personal items and leave the building . . . immediately.

## The End of an Era

The founders of Habitat for Humanity had been fired! And around the globe, the headlines rang out:

"Habitat wrongs a good man"

"Habitat founder, wife dismissed!"

"The man who built Habitat for Humanity International from an idealistic dream born in rural Georgia into one of the world's best-known nonprofit organizations was fired Monday afternoon."

But the chaos wasn't limited to the headlines. The Fullers' phones rang off the hook, and news reporters were continually knocking at the door.

Bedlam characterized the makeshift office they had temporarily set up in their home. Word had gotten out, and fast! On the evening news, they were shocked to see a report about a truck belonging to a locksmith company parked beside Habitat for Humanity International headquarters. The company had been called to change the locks on the Fullers' office doors of the organization they had founded, effectively impounding all of the Fullers' correspondence files, computers, databases, special gifts and awards from their many travels around the world, and other personal effects. For the Fullers, the humiliation was almost unbearable, especially when CEO Paul Leonard hired Securitas Security Services to stand guard over headquarters. When an *Americus Times-Recorder* reporter asked Leonard to explain the presence of the guards, he would say, "The intention is to protect employees at headquarters . . . and to monitor the facilities during working hours and to be available in the highly unlikely circumstance that they are needed."

In the immediate weeks after their traumatic departure from Habitat, the Fullers coped from day to day as best they could. Not only had Linda and Millard been locked out of their offices, but their support staff had been told to cease helping the Fullers in any way and to stay home for several days before returning to apply for other positions within the organization.

It was several months before the contents of the Fullers' offices were packed up and delivered. Close to two years later, the Fullers would discover that their office furniture was for sale in the local Habitat ReStore. The Fullers continued to receive their salaries for several months and heard that some sort of "settlement" had been worked out, but they had no idea what it was.

For the first couple of weeks, the hardest part for the Fullers was trying to function at home without any staff. Friends volunteered nearly every day to answer the hundreds of calls, letters, and e-mails that came in from their supporters. Some brought their own computers, printers, and other needed office supplies. They set up new e-mail addresses to respond to the literally hundreds of sympathetic e-mails that came pouring in from around the world expressing disappointment at this turn of events and wondering how the Fullers were faring. People wanted to know what they were going to do next.

In the beginning weeks, Millard and Linda weren't quite sure themselves.

## Down, But Not Out

They talked about what they should do—and then they prayed about it. Their goal before being fired from Habitat for Humanity International was to have the Partnership

Housing model working in every nation on Earth. "We've built in a hundred countries and still have nearly that many to go," Millard would say. "The housing ministry is what we believe God has called us to do. There are 1.5 billion people in the world living in poverty. What are we supposed to do, go fishing? I think not. Linda and I are in good health, and we still have work to do. Jesus didn't say, 'Take up your cross and follow me till you're sixty-five or seventy, then put it down, get yourself an RV, and go on vacation.'" They felt strongly that they still had a mission to fulfill.

After the initial shock wore off, the Fullers were eager to get on with their Kingdom work. Exhausted but not finished, "down but not out," they decided to get on with helping families have decent places to live. "My pity-party lasted two days," Linda says, smiling, recalling those days. "And then, we were back to work!"

"Being fired is akin to a funeral," said Millard. "People started bringing dishes to our house like someone had died. I didn't know what it was like to die . . . I hadn't done that yet. But it's pretty nice to be alive when you get all that food!"

## The Global Leadership Council Weighs In

Through the whole ordeal, Millard had been in constant contact with the unique group of Habitat leaders who were the Global Leadership Council (GLC). This group was comprised mostly of former Habitat board members who continued to attend board meetings and acted in an advisory capacity from time to time. The Global Leadership Council chair, Edgar Stoesz, had represented Linda and Millard at the August 2004 mediation with Carter in Atlanta and the so-called reconciliation meeting on January 20. As a witness to the rapidly disintegrating situation, Stoesz contacted several of the Global Leadership Council members and together they crafted a resolution. Specifically addressing Millard and Linda and the board, the resolution acknowledged "the high regard we have for you both and our indebtedness for your contribution to us personally and to the cause we have been privileged to build together and with God's help, we urge you, repeat your offer of continued involvement based on a mutually agreeable job description."

To the IBOD: ". . .We urge you, we plead with you, find some way to:

- Lift the burden of these accusations, which have been such an offense to both Millard and Linda, and take steps to restore relations.
- Define an appropriate role for them as founders and continuing as mutually agreed."

The hope was that the weight of the resolution and those who authored it would demand the ear of the board of directors in Cape Town.

## The International Board Meeting in Cape Town

As scheduled, the international board of directors gathered in Cape Town, South Africa, on March 5. Absent was Don Mosley, who boycotted the meeting in support of the Fullers and in opposition to the process being used to remove them. Edgar Stoesz traveled to Africa for the meeting, carrying with him the January 28 "Emergency Resolution" passed by the Global Leadership Council.

Although a discussion of Millard and Linda's firing was not on the agenda, Habitat by-laws required that any action against the founder and president be voted upon by the entire board. The Fullers, along with Mosley and Stoesz, were hoping the board would honor its by-laws and take up the issue. Anticipating an audience with the board, Stoesz asked Ramsey if he could present the resolution, but was told "their minds are already made up." Stoesz and the GLC were effectively shunned.

In what seemed to be an inevitable conclusion, the board upheld the executive committee's decision to fire both Millard and Linda, and voted to make it official. The Fullers

Millard at home with reporters after firing, February 2005

received a fax on March 6 stating such. Don Mosley would officially resign five days later.

## Regime Change

It was official. And the new leadership didn't waste a moment to rid the office of evidence that the Fullers had ever been at the helm. Tony Schumate, an employee of Habitat, said he was "embarrassed by the way the board treated Millard and Linda up to their firing," but "even more so after it." He told a reporter that photos of the Fullers had been removed from the walls at Habitat headquarters, and that the website had been changed dramatically. Through photos and text, more attention was directed toward Jimmy Carter than the Fullers. In Carter's explanation about how he became involved with Habitat for Humanity, suddenly there was no mention of Millard "recruiting" him and Rosalynn as there had been before. Instead, the website implied that the Carters just happened to show up at a Habitat building site one day. Next came the removal of Millard's nine books from the shelves of the Global Village and Discovery Center gift shop as well as the online store.

The regime had changed.

# — 29 —

# The Calling Continues

E ven before the dust had settled, Millard was already busy
talking to friends and supporters about forming a new
organization, although he and Linda still hoped for reconciliation with the Habitat International board. But they were
also realistic and knew this was unlikely for the foreseeable
future. David Snell would say of the board, "It is very difficult to
take a position opposed to one taken earlier. It is very difficult .
. . but not impossible." But just in case, Snell and others were
actively pursuing the possibility of reconciliation and organized
a "Reinstate the Fullers" campaign. A petition was circulated
over the Internet and across Sumter County, Georgia. A friend
had T-shirts printed up for several rallies that were held.
Thousands of names were gathered. But the Fullers weren't willing to sit back and wait to see what the campaign would bring.
To the delight of many friends, they soon shifted from
"responding to Habitat mode" to starting their new venture. In
this way, Millard could continue to serve Habitat affiliates
through fundraising and other means of support.

Millard works at home to start a new organization

Within weeks, the new organization would be up and running. Millard and Linda went to see their good friend, John
Wieland, a well-known home builder in Atlanta, seeking help
in finding a building from which to operate. A staunch supporter of Millard's, John told the Fullers to pick out a building, and he would pay for it. And, he added, "Fix it up like you
want, and I'll pay for that, too!" They located a fine, old house
right on the main highway leading into Americus, and it was
completely renovated to become their new headquarters.
When the work was finished, John Wieland gave them an
additional $100,000 to help get the new organization going.

Support for the Fullers and their new organization came
from everywhere. Another good friend, Jackie Goodman,
called to see if the Fullers had enough staff to continue with
their work. When Millard told her they still weren't in a position to hire anyone, she told him she was sending $10,000 so
that Millard and Linda could hire their former assistants,

Sharon Tarver and Cathy Smith, who had quit working for Habitat after the Fullers were fired. "And," Jackie said, "when that money runs out, I'll send more."

Even those with little financial means wanted to be a part of the new venture. Two local pastors donated several hundred dollars, and a local physician came to the Fullers' home with a donation of $5,000. Many more contributions arrived, large and small, each one deeply meaningful and appreciated.

Millard went to see Paul Amos, one of the founders of the well-known AFLAC Company based in Columbus, Georgia, with a request for $500,000. Instead, Amos committed $1 million to be paid over five years, with half going to Columbus Habitat and the other half for the Fullers' new organization to be used where needed most. Long time friends Ted and Vada Stanley of Connecticut committed another $1 million for the first year to help launch the new venture. But not all contributions were financial. Many people showed up at their doorstep simply asking, "What do you need me to do?" It seemed as if everyone was pitching in to get back to the business of providing homes for those in need. Millard had some three decades under his belt of fame, charismatic leadership, and a reputation for seeing that the moment a dollar came through the doors it immediately found its way into the waiting arms of a family in need. So when word got out that Millard had set up shop again, this time under the name Building Habitat Inc., people came calling. They so trusted Millard's moral mandate to help the poor that they didn't bother putting stipulations as where the money would be spent. Actor Paul Newman, who had generously supported Habitat for years, gave a check for $25,000 for the new organization, as did many others.

## Millard Regroups: Building Habitat

Thanks to the generous contributions and sweat equity donated by so many friends and supporters, it was soon time to add structure to their new organization. Ever mindful of

Psalm 127:1a, "Unless the LORD builds the house, its builders labor in vain" (NIV), the Fullers prayerfully etched out a purpose and mission statement to guide their new housing ministry. Attorney Ken Henson, Jr., filed the proper

### Vintage Fuller . . .
### Paul Newman

Paul Newman had been a generous supporter of Habitat for Humanity, giving as much as $475,000 in a single year. I remember one time when we were in Lexington, Kentucky, and Paul Newman came to help build houses. He picked up a hammer and drove some nails. He also did some painting. He's a lousy painter, but he tries! So when his huge check arrived, I called him and said, "Thank you for your check. Where do you want us to spend it?" Paul said, "Well, just use it wherever you need it." I suggested that we send some of it to the Mississippi Delta, and to San Diego, California, and Tijuana, Mexico. Paul Newman lives up near Bridgeport, Connecticut, so I also suggested we give some to Bridgeport, where there was a lot of real poverty. And then I added Mexico, Honduras, Nicaragua, and some other places like that. After hearing my list of suggestions on where to spend this money, he asked, "How come you named some countries outside the United States?" I told him, "Because a lot of poor folks live outside the United States." He said, "Yeah, but all these folks who bought my salad dressing live in the United States. I kind of think we ought to spend the money in the United States. Why do you want us to spend some of the money in some of these other countries?" I said, "I'll tell you two reasons, Mr. Newman. First of all, it's good religion. God loves the whole world. God is not a U.S. citizen; he is a world citizen. God's love extends to the whole world, and I think he wants the money we gather up in life to be shared with all the citizens in the world. The other reason is I've got projects going on in these places and we really could use the money to complete the houses." Paul thought about it a moment and said, "Well, then, I think you've got some mighty fine ideas on where and how to spend that money."

—Millard Fuller

papers with the state of Georgia and the Internal Revenue Service so that Building Habitat could become an official 501(c)(3) not-for-profit organization. This process required, at minimum, a governing board of directors, by-laws, a purpose statement, a financial plan, and a first-year budget. All these things were accomplished in record time, and they were off and running!

In April 2005, David Snell in collaboration with the Fullers issued a public announcement: "After leaving Habitat for Humanity in January of 2005, the Fullers were moved by the appeals of thousands of volunteers, donors, and new homeowners to continue their life's work. In response, the Fullers resolved not to let their departure from Habitat for Humanity International slow progress toward the goal of eliminating poverty housing. They pledged not to allow the end of their tenure at Habitat for Humanity International to result in a single needy family being denied access to a quality home.

"That is why Millard and Linda Fuller have founded a new organization—Building Habitat Inc.—to provide financial support, technical assistance, and spiritual inspiration to local Habitat affiliates and other like-minded organizations engaged in the important work of providing simple, decent housing to God's people in need.

"Building Habitat's mission is not to compete with Habitat for Humanity, but to complement its efforts and support its work. Building Habitat will allow Habitat for Humanity to continue to benefit from Millard Fuller's extraordinary talents in raising funds and generating enthusiasm in the cause he and Linda have given their lives to.

"The funds raised by Building Habitat will be passed directly to Habitat for Humanity affiliates and other housing initiatives to promote their house-building efforts. Millard and Linda will continue to be available to promote the ministry through public appearances and promotional events."

Reactions to this announcement were overwhelmingly enthusiastic, with one exception: Almost instantly, Millard was sued by HFHI regarding the name of the new organization, which was deemed too similar to Habitat for Humanity. Not wanting to spend another cent on unnecessary legal proceedings, Millard agreed to change the organization's name.

---

**Vintage Fuller . . .
You Snakes!**

I had been invited to speak to a group of people who were forming a Habitat project in Portland, Maine. The pastor picked me up and was driving me up to the church where the presentation was to be held. As we approached the church, I noticed the entire parking lot was full of cars. "Look at all of these cars," he commented. "Look at all of the people who have come out to be concerned about building houses for God's people in need!" He was so happy he almost ran into a car! And I got excited, too. That kind of outpouring of interest was incredible. There were no parking places, and it was a Tuesday night. Of course, when we went inside I expected to see people all over the place. But no, there were only about fifteen people in the room! "Is this the entire bunch?" I asked. "What about all of the cars in the parking lot?" And they said, "Oh, there's a Weight Watchers meeting here tonight." Disappointed but amused at the same time, I realized that story makes a great parable. When you have all you want to eat, have built good houses to live in, and all your other possessions have increased, it's easier to focus on one's own needs than it is to be concerned about the needs of others. In a church filled with hundreds of people, only fifteen were interested in housing the poor. Do not become proud and forget those who need a helping hand. You must never think that you made yourself wealthy by your own power and strength. Amos, who lived in a time of great prosperity—much like the age in which we live— warned the people of his day how terrible it would be for them to stretch out on their luxurious couches, feasting on veal and lamb. "I despise your luxurious mansions," John the Baptist said. He even called people who came to be baptized "snakes"! Have you ever been to church and the preacher looked out at you one Sunday and said, "You snakes!" I suspect not, but that's what old John said, "You snakes, you've come here to get baptized, and I know how you are living!" He saw the hypocrisy in the way they were living. You got that extra coat? Share it. Got extra food? Share it!

—Millard Fuller

# — 30 —

# A New Organization:
# The Fuller Center for Housing

Now the Fullers had another challenge—to come up with an alternative name for the organization. Their friends and supporters convinced them that the most logical thing would be to capitalize on the Fuller name. Millard and Linda were known and revered for their dedication to the cause of alleviating poverty housing. Their names were already familiar to those associated with the nonprofit housing world, including churches, individual and corporate donors, volunteers, government officials, and others. And they were known in other circles as well. Over the years, they had both received numerous prestigious awards and keynoted at hundreds of regional, national, and international conferences. With some fifty-plus honorary doctorates, Millard had spoken on university campuses far and wide. Wherever he went, town halls, school gymnasiums, and huge graduation ceremonies were packed with audiences who fell in love with the vision of the movement to end poverty housing around the world. Millard would preach as many as seven sermons in one day to full churches. Books were signed and sold. He was nothing short of a hero to many.

Linda was also a popular speaker wherever she went. She had helped to create the much-respected Women Build program, garnering the love and respect of women around the world. She'd also created a Mental Health Partnership program to combine Habitat's affordable homeownership with support from mental health organizations. Former First Lady Rosalynn Carter and others in the mental health field had given their encouragement and endorsement. Linda was also a favorite at women's prayer groups, Bible studies, and conferences, where she spoke and autographed books.

Still, it took some work for friends to convince Millard and Linda that their name should be included in the name of the new organization. Neither wanted celebrity to be the driving force in the new organization, and they were hesitant to draw attention to themselves in this way. But in the end, their supporters convinced them that the story of their legacy would inspire many more people to join the movement. The Fullers agreed to the new name, The Fuller Center for Housing, and the appropriate documentation was filed. The Fuller Center for Housing was officially christened!

Mail started flooding The Fuller Center for Housing's mailbox even before the ink dried on the new stationery. And there would be no shortage of "machine power" as well. A business office store donated two copy machines and a free maintenance contract, and they told the Fullers that when The Fuller Center outgrew those machines, they would replace them with larger ones. Furniture was also donated from banks or greatly discounted by other businesses. Other basic business needs were supplied as well. A friend who had an Internet connection service offered to supply their Internet service provider hosting free of charge. An artist called up and asked if she could help create the logo. A newsletter and website were set up.

One of the most pivotal needs was for a mailing list, which was crucial for fundraising. Habitat for Humanity's mailing list, which the Fullers had worked so diligently to build for thirty years, had well over 2 million names, but that resource was totally lost to them now. The Fuller Center for Housing's new mailing list would have to be rebuilt from personal friends and people who had been supportive and concerned for the Fullers during their ordeal. New addresses came from the petitions calling for the Fullers' reinstatement, and also from the Habitat Partners United website, where people had left messages of encouragement for the Fullers in their new direction. From rebuilding the mailing list to renovating the headquarters, The Fuller Center was buzzing.

## The Fuller Center for Housing Goes Public with Its Plans

In a gesture embracing the legacy and roots of the Partnership Housing movement, The Fuller Center's first board meeting on April 16, 2005, would be at Koinonia Farm. As Millard and Linda had done years ago, they and a handful of like-minded supporters would begin the meeting with devotions, and get to work creating a mission statement and delineating their goals. They publicly announced their intentions in the following press release:

> Despite being fired by the board of Habitat for Humanity International (HFHI) earlier this year, Millard and Linda's commitment to the ministry they founded remains undiminished. Since their firing, thousands of supporters have come forward, many indicating their reluctance to continue supporting HFHI. But the Fullers want to continue working toward their dream of eliminating poverty housing, and they want to use their talents to continue raising funds, awareness, and enthusiasm. Since they can no longer work from within Habitat for Humanity International, they have decided to work alongside it and are organizing The Fuller Center for

First board meeting of the new organization
at Koinonia, April 16, 2005

Housing as a vehicle for their continued involvement in the
cause of eliminating poverty housing.

Habitat for Humanity is a worldwide network of
autonomous, local affiliates, and it is at the affiliate level that
the work of raising funds, recruiting volunteers, selecting
partner families, and building houses takes place. The Fuller
Center for Housing is a Christian nonprofit created specifically to assist affordable housing providers and Habitat for
Humanity affiliates with fundraising and other support. The
Fuller Center complements and supports Habitat for
Humanity's mission to build homes and build lives, but does
not seek to re-create what already exists.

The Fuller Center does not directly compete with Habitat
for Humanity, but will strengthen Habitat for Humanity's
efforts by ensuring that no gifts are lost and that excitement
continues to grow toward the goal of providing simple,
decent houses for families in need. The Fuller Center will
work as a servant and a companion to HFHI and similar
house-building organizations. The structure is in place

through Habitat's 3,700 worldwide affiliates to do the work of getting houses built. The Fuller Center will provide funds and other support to those affiliates and similar low-income housing groups.

Millard ranks among the finest nonprofit relationship builders in America and has thousands of friends and supporters, many of whom are disillusioned by his firing and no longer are willing to donate to Habitat for Humanity International. The Fuller Center for Housing will provide these donors with the means of continuing to support the mission of eliminating poverty housing without funding the organization that they feel has behaved poorly. Additionally, Millard will be able to continue traveling the world, writing books, speaking on behalf of the ministry, and generating support for the cause. Millard's remarkable fundraising talents, while stifled due to HFHI board decisions, will not be lost to Habitat affiliates.

The Fuller Center for Housing will raise funds to boost grass-roots organizations working to eliminate poverty housing, including affiliates of Habitat for Humanity. HFHI has its own well-organized fundraising program and does not need The Fuller Center's support. The affiliates, on the other hand, are always struggling to raise the money they need to carry out their mission, and they will be among the beneficiaries of The Fuller Center's efforts.

With its board members selected and parameters spelled out, The Fuller Center for Housing got to work.

## Vintage Fuller . . .
## Bob Hope: All Gifts Great and Small

On a build in New York City, there happened to be a person in the group who had a lot of money. She was so impressed with how meaningful it was to help others get decent housing that a few days later, we received a $1 million check from her! A person who had been raised in the very building we were working on saw the news articles and publicity on television, and he was so moved that somebody was fixing up the building that he got out his checkbook and wrote a $1,500 gift to Habitat to Humanity to help restore his childhood home. Another person who had read the articles was so touched by what was happening that he wrote a letter to President Carter. "Dear President Carter, I didn't like a lot of the things you did when you were president, but I sure like what you are doing now. Enclosed is my $10,000 check." That same person has since contributed a little over $7 million to this work. At the conclusion of that same build in New York, we held a rally and took up an offering in wheelbarrows. People put over $10,000 in the wheelbarrows to push this work along.

At a build in Charlotte, North Carolina, Bob Hope came to see us. We gave him a hammer shaped like a golf club and nails shaped like golf tees. We went out to the Charlotte coliseum, and people paid $60,000 to hear him crack jokes about Jimmy Carter. And he didn't charge a penny to do it. He paid his own way to get there and wouldn't accept a penny. He donated everything to Habitat for Humanity. A person who had been on the Charlotte build sent in a $100,000 check because he was so challenged and thrilled by what he had participated in.

Another time, a letter came into the office from a very poor man and woman in Franklin Square, New York. They didn't have any money, but they had brooms. They got fifteen store owners to give a dollar each for them to sweep in front of their stores, and they sent in every penny of the $15 they had earned. They said they wanted to help with this work of getting God's people into a decent place to live. I was as excited about that $15 as I was about the million!

—Millard Fuller

# — 31 —

# The Fuller Center for Housing's First Projects

With thirty years of experience under his belt, Millard set out to enlist the hearts and hands of people far and wide. Looking for an interesting and imaginative vehicle to kick off a Fuller Center for Housing fundraiser, the Fullers organized the "Ride to Provide." This ambitious fundraiser was a motorcycle ride starting at the USC-UCLA game in Los Angeles on the first weekend of December 2005. Motorcyclists from across the nation gathered to put on their leathers (as did the Fullers!) and ride from L.A. across the United States to Shreveport, Louisiana. Accompanying them would be an 18-wheeler that would stop to pick up "Christmas" as they rolled along from city to city. As the caravan of motorcyclists and the truck wheeled into a city, the town would greet them, toys and canned goods in hand, ready to load up for the displaced Hurricane Katrina victims on the Gulf Coast. Memorializing the occasion with the sale of an assortment of items (caps, shirts, cups, etc.) gave a boost to the Fullers' budding new movement. People loved it! The Fuller Center raised money—but, as importantly, they gained supporters. From coast to coast, people got involved. Rounding up food and toys for those in need was a tangible way for them to reach out to the suffering storm victims.

The outpouring of aid and fellowship that came with the Ride to Provide proved to the Fullers that they had started their new housing ministry with God's blessings. Yet, even before the tragedy of Hurricane Katrina, The Fuller Center had been responding to those in immediate need of assistance across the nation and the world.

Millard had learned that an entire village in Nepal had burned to the ground, and he set out to answer their plea for help. Millard and David Snell (The Fuller Center's vice president of programs) took on the challenge issued by the former head of housing for Nepal for a hundred houses to be built at $750 each. The Fuller Center alerted the public, and the money and long-term commitments poured in: "Sign me up for two houses!" "My group wants to sponsor one house." "Our church will sponsor six houses." Even young people caught the excitement. Eleven-year-old Levi Lyman-Barner solicited sponsors to help him raise money for a house by riding his bike seventy-five miles on the mountainous Skyline Drive in Virginia. When all his donations were counted, he had enough to build three houses.

Kimberly and Milton Smith of Make Way Partners, a Christian nonprofit based in Birmingham, Alabama, called to tell the Fullers about their work with a ministry in Romania. Called Casa Cana, it feeds the homeless and offers job- and life-skills training. Make Way Partners asked if The Fuller Center for Housing would provide a grant in the amount of $25,000 to complete transitional housing for destitute people in Bucharest. The grant would help families, reduced to living in the sewers, move into mainstream life, lowering their chances of being lured by sex traffickers. With Fuller Center assistance and volunteer labor, Make Way Partners was able to complete construction of transitional housing for four families in the first year.

The Sumter County Initiative, Millard's inspired dream of eliminating poverty housing in Habitat's hometown, had already greatly reduced the need for new house building in the area, so the Americus-based affiliate, New Horizons Habitat for Humanity, reached out to The Fuller Center to "help solve other housing needs" in neighboring counties. Grants from The Fuller Center allowed New Horizons Habitat to complete construction on its 2005 Christmas house (an annual high-profile build) as well as purchase property for two new homes and start work on a third in Marion County. With funding from The Fuller Center, Lighthouse Mission, which works to help released inmates successfully reenter society and provides transitional housing to its clients, was able to renovate a facility in Macon, Georgia, called the Spring Street After-Care Home, which provides transitional housing to its clients. And some of the first Habitat-style homes built in the late 1960s and 1970s at Koinonia Farm were now in need of repair. Through its Heart to Heart program, the residents at Koinonia assisted homeowners in making those repairs. With grants from The Fuller Center, Koinonia repaired homes in the community, doing everything from replacing roofs to repairing breaker boxes. This work helps extend the lives of the homes so they can continue to be habitable for the families for years to come.

There was no shortage of needs—and The Fuller Center for Housing was poised with funding and volunteers, ready to be of service anywhere in the world.

Within months, Fuller Center for Housing "partners" were forming all over. In the fall of 2005, Angela Koncz and a group of enthusiastic and committed volunteers started Building Suffolk—A Fuller Center Partner (the first Covenant Partner of The Fuller Center for Housing in the United States). The Fuller Center provided a $25,000 grant toward its efforts, and after only three months from the start of its first project,

Millard beside the Points of Light Medallion set in the sidewalk
on the Extra Mile Pathway, Washington, D.C., 2005

Building Suffolk had completed five projects. Among many
more community-building projects undertaken by Building
Suffolk, it announced its first Blitz Build of sixteen homes in
partnership with The Fuller Center for Housing, Operation
Blessing, and Centex Homes for the summer of 2008.

## Shreveport-Bossier Community Renewal—
## Building on Higher Ground

When Hurricanes Katrina and Rita hit the Gulf Coast in
2005, Mack McCarter, a longtime Fuller friend and founder
of Shreveport-Bossier Community Renewal (SBCR), gave
Millard a "Macedonian Call" and told him, "We need help!"
The hurricanes were the most costly and disruptive natural
disasters to ever hit the United States. Up to 1,400 people
died, and more than a million-and-a-half people were dis-

Homeowner from Florida who traveled
to Shreveport to help Hurricane Katrina evacuees

Two busloads of volunteers, recruited by Fuller Center for Housing Board
Member D. J. Bakken of Minnesota, work at first annual
"Linda and Millard Fuller Blitz Build," Shreveport, La., 2006

Walls go up on one of the first "Higher Ground" houses in Shreveport, La., built for a family relocating after Hurricane Katrina, 2005

placed. It was a humanitarian crisis unseen in the nation since the Great Depression. Thousands of people, unable to return to their destroyed homes, had relocated to Shreveport, in northwest Louisiana. Living in Federal Emergency Management Agency (FEMA) trailers, shelters, and temporary apartments, these people were in desperate need of immediate housing.

Mack McCarter was no stranger to fixing what ailed communities. Since SBCR's inception in 1994, under his leadership, thousands of Shreveport volunteers had participated in an incredibly effective community renewal effort. Using a city block by city block effort, and incorporating a "Whole Person" ministry that initiated job training, healthcare, and spiritual wellness, the result was a significant reduction of crime in the neighborhoods where they were working. Mack's new challenge was to address the needs of the hurricane victims who would now be settling in the Allendale neighborhood of Shreveport. Economically distressed, Allendale had hundreds of abandoned and neglected shotgun shacks repossessed by the city of Shreveport after a failed experience with a Housing and Urban Development Section 8 Housing (low-income housing) effort. Shreveport's poor were already hurting, and now the city was experiencing an influx of thousands of homeless families. The challenge was enormous, but Mack envisioned an opportunity for revitalization, and he believed his friend Millard was just the person to spearhead the effort.

To enlist Millard's help in this effort, Mack actually drove the 676 miles to Americus, as weather conditions made it impossible to fly and there was no time to lose. When he arrived at the The Fuller Center door, Millard's response was immediate: The Fuller Center for Housing would do whatever it could.

Shreveport-Bossier Community Renewal hosted Millard and The Fuller Center at its office and invited Shreveport city officials, the local Habitat for Humanity affiliate, Louisiana Senator Mary Landrieu's staff, and a host of other influential stakeholders. With everyone sitting around the same table, the local planning officials and their architects laid out a bold vision of mixed housing and commercial incentives. Millard introduced everyone to one of his favorite hymns, "Higher

Ground," which he said would be the theme song of the effort. Cheerleader as always, he even led them in singing it.

Within a few short weeks, derelict houses were being demolished, water and sewer lines were being replaced, and new houses were going up. Even former Presidents Clinton and Bush got involved, donating enough seed money from the Bush-Clinton Katrina Fund to build two houses.

Millard receives a $100,000 grant for
The Fuller Center from the Bush-Clinton
Katrina Fund, New Orleans, La., 2006

The Fuller Center's response to Mack's vision and plea for help became the Building on Higher Ground Initiative, committed to building some sixty new homes, mostly for hurricane evacuees who chose to stay in Shreveport, Louisiana. As the lots were being cleared and foundations poured, Millard returned to town with busloads of volunteers. On a Sunday morning in December 2005, he preached at Mt. Canaan Baptist Church, situated on top of a hill overlooking the construction site. After his awe-inspiring sermon, "Smelling Good for Jesus," brought down the house, Millard and Linda proceeded to lead a march out the doors of the church and down to the building site, where they would start construction on three houses the next morning. It was a classic case of the Theology of the Hammer—putting action behind the biblical words to "love your neighbor." Group after group arrived to catch the spirit Millard had set and spring into action. Donna Schuller from Crystal Cathedral Ministries in Anaheim, California, led a women's crew to work on a house they sponsored, and other work teams came from the Bel Air Presbyterian Church in Los Angeles. Other churches and organizations, including several Habitat affiliates, came to help put a roof over the heads of those in need of a home.

With ten houses already completed by September 2006, it was time to step up the effort, and the first Millard and Linda Fuller Blitz Build was planned. The media had been alerted, and the next day, when the headlines rang out, Shreveport volunteers turned out, as did helpers from all points of the United States and Canada. Teams of people filed into town: D. J. Bakken brought two busloads of volunteers from Big Lake, Minnesota; Jeff Cardwell of Indianapolis brought another busload of volunteers. The Fuller Center for Housing's new board was in town, and many of them also rolled up their sleeves to work alongside hurricane evacuees in need of decent,

Hurricane Katrina evacuee homeowners, Shreveport, La., December 2005

affordable housing. Each day, several hundred people filed into Our Lady of the Blessed Sacrament Church across the street from the construction site where volunteers were serving breakfast, lunch, and dinner.

Excitement was in the air, and everyone was eager to start putting up the walls on "their" houses. Rain had poured from the skies the day before, making the ground muddy and slippery for the first day of construction, but nothing could dampen the prevailing high spirits of the builders! When Father Andre McGrath, wearing his clerical robe along with a Fuller Center cap, took a harmonica out of his pocket and began playing the "Higher Ground" hymn at devotions the first morning, there wasn't a dry eye to be found.

At the end of the week, the houses were virtually complete,

and dedication services were held in front of each new home. A Bible was presented to every homeowner, and a joyous celebration took place for the homeowners and volunteers. Allendale was being transformed from a crime-riddled slum to a beautiful community of new, decent, affordable housing. Katrina victims who had lost everything they owned in one of Mother Nature's fits of temper moved in to their new homes.

Millard cheers the crowd gathered where construction on three houses will begin the following day, Shreveport, La., December 2005

Linda and Millard march from a church to the construction site

The Fuller's—and their style of doing business—were back!

## "Look What Love Built"

Only two years earlier, it had appeared that the Fullers' mission to provide "a simple, decent place to live" had been derailed, but project after project funded through The Fuller Center for Housing proved that you could take Millard out of Habitat for Humanity, but you couldn't take Habitat's mission out of its founding father, Millard.

The Fullers' untiring efforts to continue to eradicate poverty housing did not go unrecognized—or unrewarded. On October 15, 2005, Millard and Linda were honored in Washington, D.C., by The Extra-Mile Points of Light Foundation. The Extra-Mile Pathway honors heroes of the U.S. voluntary service movement. Founders of various organizations have been honored with twenty medallions along the

Pathway that stretches from The Treasury Building eastward on G Street. Some of the recipients include Edgar J. Helms, founder of Goodwill Industries; Clara Barton, who began the American Red Cross; Martin Luther King, Jr., the leader of the civil rights movement; Susan B. Anthony, an early women's rights activist; and Eunice Kennedy Shriver, honored for her work in founding the Special Olympics.

Not long after the ceremony in Washington, Jamie O'Neal, a popular country music star, penned a song called "Look What Love Built"—tailor-made for the Fullers. Shortly thereafter, an episode of *Unsung Stories* (a series about inspiring people) was aired on CMT, a popular country music television network, about the Fullers' inspiring lives and work.

## Vintage Fuller . . .
## Genesis and Serenity

Oftentimes, when natural disasters and other unforeseen events occur, people's lives get disrupted, as was the case with Hurricanes Katrina and Rita. Therefore, thousands of people came to Shreveport. The citizens of Shreveport could have said, "I'm not going to take any responsibility for those people. I don't know those people. They are not kin to me, and here they are coming into town and creating traffic problems." But the Bible's message is clear: When strangers show up at your gate, you must invite them in. We cannot ignore those people who have already been in Shreveport, but we also cannot make small that which God intended to be large. God is big enough to take care of every problem. And so I ask: Would Shreveport be a better city if everybody in Shreveport had a good place to live? Is it God's work to be concerned about whether folks have a place to live? Absolutely! You've got to be concerned about others, especially children. A mother and her daughters are going to live in one of the new Habitat houses in Shreveport. The youngest daughter's name is Genesis. What a great parable! Genesis means beginning, and here is a new beginning. She is such a beautiful child. Another one of those beautiful little girls is named Serenity. What a great set of names! First, you have a Genesis, and then you come to Serenity because there is a certain peace that comes with doing God's work. What will little Genesis become? What will little Serenity become? We don't know, but we know one thing: If we give them a good place to live, they've got a better chance. And that's God's work because we've invited them in.

—Millard Fuller

Millard Fuller at the Fuller Center Gulf Coast work site, 2007

# Responding to Needs
# at Home and Abroad

A bout the same time the work began in Shreveport, The Fuller Center also started renovating houses for hurricane victims on the Mississippi Gulf Coast by working with the Mennonite Disaster Service (MDS) and the African American Missionary Baptist Churches. They also agreed to renovate houses on the Texas Gulf Coast for families victimized by Hurricane Rita, again with MDS.

A Covenant Partner group, called the Chattahoochee Fuller Center Project (CFCP), formed in the area of Valley and Lanett, Alabama (Millard's hometown), and West Point, Georgia. This unique Covenant Partner has launched itself in what Millard describes as the most exciting and fast-paced take-off he has ever seen. In a mere three months from the initial organizational meeting of the group, they had raised over $400,000 and had plans to build six houses. This momentum out of the gate was unprecedented in the thirty-plus years at

Habitat for Humanity! The first house was sponsored by the trustees of the University of Cincinnati who raised $50,000 for the construction of the inaugural house. Fifteen university students worked on the first house, and several have already returned to the Valley project and others and have made arrangements to return yet again. They were joined in their first week of work—a four-house Blitz Build in March 2007—by seventy-five performers from nineteen countries from the "Up with People" musical touring group. A concert became both a celebration and a fundraiser. J. Smith Lanier & Co. of West Point, Georgia, raised and donated $150,000 as a matching grant which was quickly matched—enough to complete the remaining homes in the six-house project. And, in June of 2007, The Fuller Center for Housing would receive its first tithe from the Chattahoochee Project— $40,000.

The CFCP project was modeled on Millard's inspirational vision that became the Sumter County Initiative, calling for the eradication of poverty housing in its target area. Similar Fuller Center projects would begin in Cusseta, Georgia; Spartanburg, South Carolina; and Bloomington, Illinois.

In May 2007, a seasoned and very successful nonprofit organization serving the Potomac Highlands of West Virginia became a Fuller Center Covenant Partner. Emphasizing affordable housing that is sustainable and built using environmentally friendly and energy-efficient materials, this new partnership will take the lead in demonstrating green building techniques to the other Fuller Center Covenant Partners. This was music to the ears of Fuller Center Board Chairman LeRoy Troyer. The accomplished and award-winning architect Troyer wrote, "I am happy to help. I have years of experience and my staff members have an interest. When and how can we help?" Plans were also in the works to begin Fuller Center projects in Arizona, Indiana, Minnesota, Wisconsin, California, Massachusetts, Oklahoma, Arkansas, Pennsylvania, Ohio, and Florida. It was not a surprise when a staffer from the *Chronicle of Philanthropy* observed that The Fuller

Center for Housing was the fastest growing nonprofit start-up they have ever covered!

Internationally, The Fuller Center was already working in Nepal, El Salvador, Nigeria, and Sri Lanka, with inquiries coming from the Cook Islands, Tanzania, Togo, Jamaica, the Bahamas, Haiti, Republic of Congo, Democratic Republic of Congo, Uganda, India, China, Canada, Panama, the Philippines, and Ghana. Work was ongoing and non-stop. In fact, things were moving so fast that The Fuller Center board decided it was time to host the second annual Linda and Millard Fuller Blitz Build. Continuing the exciting work in Shreveport, the volunteers would build ten new homes in one week and make renovations on ten homes needing desperate repairs during the week of September 16–22, 2007. The number of returning volunteers from the previous Millard and Linda Fuller Blitz Build represents both the passion and commitment of the volunteers who bonded with the community.

Within the first two years of operation, The Fuller Center built dozens of houses overseas and made grants of hundreds of thousands of dollars to Habitat affiliates and other groups. It was fulfilling an unmet need by

Fuller Center work
in Sri Lanka, 2006

Fuller Center houses
in Nigeria, 2007

working with families who couldn't even qualify for the traditional Habitat for Humanity houses. Advancing a theme articulated in his book, *More Than Houses,* Millard said, "We could
reach out to the poorest of the poor through creative collabo-
rations with other organizations. We could think outside the
box and start to consider even those living in a box . . . a population previously considered unreachable for homeownership. They can be reached when organizations are willing to
serve as mentors and advocates offering education, job training, and micro-enterprise development opportunities. We can
now attempt to address some of the root causes of systemic
poverty."

Nigeria is a good example of a creative, collaborative partnership. Near the village of Luvu Madaki, just east of the capital city, Abuja, an eighty-house project boasts new homes

## Vintage Fuller . . .
## No More Buckets

We were dedicating a house on the south shore of Massachusetts that was being renovated for a single mother and three boys. They had nowhere else to go, so the renovation work was going on while they were still in the house. About a hundred people gathered in the street late on a Saturday afternoon. After a lady sang a lovely solo and a brief message was given, the mother was called upon to share her feelings about what was happening. When she stepped up to the microphone, she just began to weep. She couldn't say anything. She had a fourteen-year-old boy named Shawn Gilmore. He was just a little fellow, not very big for fourteen, but when he saw his mother was not able to talk, he took the microphone and said, "I'll speak for our family. I want all of you here today to know what life has been like for us in this house. For months we've had eleven buckets in this house to catch the water. There have been leaks right over our beds, and every time it rained at night, we'd have to get up and stand until the rain stopped. In the winter, we didn't have any insulation in our walls, so we've been so cold that it hurts. What's happening here this week with all of these people coming to put insulation in the walls and to put a new roof on our house is like a miracle. On behalf of our family, I want to thank you for coming out and showing love to us in our time of need." There was not a dry eye on that street when that fourteen-year-old boy stepped back from the microphone.

—Millard Fuller

built of concrete block, which are manufactured on site. Each house has a common room, a kitchen, a bathroom, and a small courtyard. Construction costs are less than $2,500 (U.S.), making them affordable for families who otherwise would have no access to homeownership. The unique incremental housing program of Fuller Center-Nigeria provides for the purchase of these simple dwellings as the first step along the way to permanent homeownership. When the three-year mortgage is paid on a one-room home, the owner may sell it back to Fuller Center-Nigeria and use the proceeds as a down payment on a larger home. In addition, this incremental housing program has a positive impact on the local economy by providing employment for tradesmen and laborers, who manufacture building materials and construct houses. Just as homebuilding is an important economic engine in the American economy, it is expected that Fuller Center-Nigeria will have a positive effect on the Nigerian economy as well.

A collaborative partnership has begun in El Salvador just south of San Salvador. In collaboration with St. Joseph's Home for the Poor, The Fuller Center-El Salvador will construct 100 houses in what will be called *Villa de San Jose*. This project targets single mothers who constitute a significant portion of El Salvador's poor. The Fuller Center-El Salvador and St. Joseph's Home will construct these hundred homes in a planned village which will provide not only quality homes for the women and their children, but job skill-training facilities as well. Two Fuller Center board members Jeff Cardwell and D. J. Bakken, would lead the first crews to work on this project.

## The Mission Goes On

The Fuller Center's inaugural years have been stunningly successful. "As we celebrate what love can do," Millard said, "we feel incredibly blessed and energized. I look forward to the future with tremendous optimism. In fact, I expect The Fuller Center for Housing to eclipse all accomplishments to date." Certainly Millard and Linda have enormous dreams and goals for the future. "As we move forward, we are not ruling out any regions, in the United States or abroad, for being too poor in which to work," says Millard. "In many cases, these are places where we can make the greatest difference. The Fuller Center is effective in our mission to help families with the most urgent needs . . . Innovative design and construction methods are proving that the cost of new houses can actually be lowered. We also recognize that renovations and repairs to substandard housing can be as life-transforming as building from scratch."

The Fuller Center for Housing continues to transform lives through community redevelopment projects like those in Shreveport's Allendale neighborhood. And Millard and Linda Fuller—along with thousands of supporters and volunteers—continue to move forward in their quest to eliminate substandard housing throughout the world. In the process, they continue to show us the model for putting faith to work by helping others have shelter—in Millard's words, "a simple, decent place to live."

## "Here I Am, Lord, Send Me"

The Fullers have no plans to retire. In fact, they are both quick to say that as long as body and mind will allow, they want to continue with their exciting and meaningful work to leave the world a little better than they found it. "We've built our house on love," Millard says, "and the homes we've built for others, every single one of them, have been built on sheer love and goodwill. Such love, such good, passes on from one generation to the next. We hope to build for years to come. We had always wanted to take the housing ministry to the ends of the Earth . . . and there are still at least one billion people in the world living in poverty—30 million in the United States alone. It goes without saying that this is a disgrace for a world with such abundant resources. Linda and I both have good health, and we want to continue making a meaningful contribution as long as we can.

"Just as we felt a sense of urgency in the 1970s to do

our part to help God's people have, at minimum, a simple, decent place to live, we still feel that urgency. And, some thirty years later, we will continue to do our part in helping the world's citizens see that it is morally, politically, and socially unacceptable for humans to live in substandard housing. It is a vision and a calling we believe in wholeheartedly—and will continue to embrace for the rest of our lives. Until then, for as long as we are able, we will each answer, 'Here I am, Lord. Send me.'"

"Millard and Linda Fuller Blitz Build," Shreveport, La., September 2006

# Postscript

### Mack McCarter,
### founder and coordinator,
### Shreveport-Bossier
### Community Renewal

Millard and Linda Fuller are remarkable people, aren't they? Bettie Youngs has done a marvelous job sharing the story and journey of these very special people, whose vision and leadership launched the renowned Habitat for Humanity and The Fuller Center for Housing. As she shared with you, I pleaded with Millard and The Fuller Center for Housing to come to our community after Hurricanes Katrina and Rita devastated the Gulf Coast in

2005, damaging more than two hundred thousand homes and displacing more than one million people in Louisiana alone. We needed a miracle. Shreveport-Bossier Community Renewal (SBCR) joined forces with The Fuller Center for Housing to help families who had evacuated to the Shreveport area and, most significantly, families who were already suffering and living in poverty housing in our community. I proudly introduced Millard to our community as the "man who just got promoted from Habitat for Humanity." Millard inspired, challenged, and energized us with a promise of help from The Fuller Center for Housing and, boy, did they deliver! The partnership we formed is now helping residents in other cities as well. The Fuller Center builds houses; SBCR builds community. Together, we are "Building on Higher Ground" to help those who lack the resources and the relationships that could make homeownership possible on their own.

It is not an exaggeration to say that sharing the insights of Clarence Jordan and Millard Fuller remains critical to our human survival today. A lifetime of ministry taught me this truth, which led to the creation of Shreveport-Bossier Community Renewal in 1994. Cities rest on a foundation of relationships. When relationships disintegrate, a city begins to sink. Greater criminal activity, domestic violence, child neglect, substance abuse, high school dropout rates, and other problems are all symptoms of a society with a fundamental lack of caring relationships.

The Fuller Center for Housing and Shreveport-Bossier Community Renewal partnership works to restore the foundation of a safe and caring community by rebuilding the system of relationships. It's a large task and, indeed, no one individual or organization can tackle it alone. Government can help, but they can't do it all. Big business can help. Their participation is needed and appreciated, but corporate focus has historically lacked the sustainability necessary to solve the problems of the poor. It is wrong to think that the capitalist strategies of corporate America can be a substitute for good old-fashioned grass-roots community organizing and mission work by communities of faith. By working together, we can reverse the process of disintegration that has destroyed every prior civilization in history.

Over and over again, I hear a cry going up. From the wealthy and the poor, from the powerful and the dependent, from the global and the provincial, I hear groans and sighs too deep for words. The world today is crying out for a miracle. I believe with my whole heart that all of us working together in community renewal are a miracle. Day by day, more and more caring partners are joining in this march of living with a dedicated purpose—to stop the disintegration of our cities and grow a new model of community. This is much like starting a new technology—a social technology. It takes real sacrifice, but I know we can succeed with your help.

The vision of Millard Fuller goes beyond building houses for a few. We are building hope for many. Shreveport's Allendale neighborhood—an area of decaying houses, high crime, and little income—was chosen for the launch of the Higher Ground Initiative. With hundreds of volunteers coming from throughout the nation, this once-forgotten neighborhood is now a place of fresh hope and new beginnings that is receiving worldwide attention.

A garden grows where trash and bottles once filled a vacant lot. Children gather on a playground built by a local service club. Residents who were once too frightened to come out of their houses now laugh and eat together at neighborhood block parties.

"Many years ago, this was one of the worst communities in the city. Homicides, crime, gang activity—you name it, and it was here," said Jewel Mariner, one of two SBCR community coordinators in Allendale. She lives in a Friendship House that has become an anchor for the neighborhood. "It's amazing to see the transformation in people's lives and in this neighborhood. People used to just call this The Hill. Now it's New Hope Hill. People in the community now have hope."

By the start of 2007, little more than one year after work started, twenty-three new houses had been built in the community. In the coming months, scores of new homes will be added until the transformation of the Allendale community is complete. Each will have its own unique features, designs, and color schemes. Several of the new homeowners have become SBCR Haven House leaders and now reach out to others in the neighborhood.

"I want to be a light on the hill. I care about my community, and I want us to come together," said Dorothy Wiley, who made a new start in Shreveport after she and her family were trapped in the New Orleans Superdome for four days after Hurricane Katrina destroyed their home. "You build a neighborhood by being a neighbor to everybody. You develop relationships one person at a time."

We are fulfilled only as we serve others. We are complete only as we give ourselves to others. And we are perfected only as we seek to love others. This is our task: to become other-centered rather than self-centered. Corporate brands, religious affiliation, one's pedigree and station in life are all meaningless in the Kingdom of God.

Very rarely does a moment in history become so clear in the present that everyone can stand up at the same time and say, "This is special. History is being made." But this is the significance of Millard and Linda Fuller among us. We share in the historic moment of their lives. They are God's gift to the human race. And planet Earth is forever changed because they came to build.

On behalf of Millard, Linda, Bettie, and the thousands of other compassionate volunteers who have joined us, we welcome you to this wonderful journey we call a movement. We thank you for taking the time to learn more about us. I hope you will join with us on this important journey to build safe and caring communities in cities across the nation, and in every corner on Earth where decent shelter is lacking for God's children in need.

God bless you for joining this great miracle.

P.S. Please donate your prayers, time, and talents to this important movement. Ask your church and civic group, your friends and family, to volunteer. Drop us a note, send us a donation, or sign up as a volunteer at:

The Fuller Center for Housing
701 S. Martin Luther King Blvd.
Americus, GA 31719-2257
www.fullercenter.org

# A Final Word—
## by Kirk Lyman-Barner

Tuesday morning, February 3rd, 2009 began as a typical morning for us in the Americus Fuller Center office. The team was gathered around the conference table for devotions as is the custom every morning at 8:00 a.m. to start the work day. Nothing could have prepared us for the shock that came next when Linda Fuller walked in and said to us slowly, but calmly, "I thought you needed to know that we lost Millard last night."

Each person in the room absorbed the news in a very personal way. One staff member said he felt like he was kicked in the stomach for the next few days. My mind began to race to remember my last conversations with Millard. The previous Friday, Millard was heading out of the office for a vacation weekend with Linda. I said, "If your phone rings, don't answer it Millard." He said, "Kirk if I see it is from you, I'll take the call because I know it will be important." And then he laughed. On Sunday, he called on his way back home and left me a voice message. "Kirk, this is Millard. Linda and I were wondering how Cori and the kids did this weekend at the state Lego League tournament." It was a personal call. He loved our children and they loved him dearly as well.

Almost before Linda had finished giving us the news, the office phones began ringing off the hook with calls from around the world. In a small town like Americus, news travels fast; a Habitat employee had learned that Millard died in the ambulance en route to the Albany hospital some 40 miles away and had dispatched an email announcing his death. People began calling immediately in disbelief—how could the man who seemed perfectly healthy, so full of life, still water skiing and keeping a tireless speaking tour, possibly leave us so suddenly?

Linda reflected, "His death on February 3rd, exactly one month after his 74th birthday, was so unexpected that none of us close to him could believe the news. Even though I was physically with him when God called him home, it is still difficult to fully absorb that this giant of a man, my kind and loving husband and partner in housing ministry, is truly gone."

Millard died of an aneurysm of the main artery leaving his heart. He had been struggling with an exhausting cough during the preceding month, but had no symptoms of anything more serious. Just the day before his death, he had shown his characteristic enthusiasm in a monthly conference call with Fuller Center leaders from all over the country who take an hour each month to share with each other the exciting stories from the work in the field.

Throughout the day on February 3rd, calls and messages poured in from Africa, Europe and Asia, from Fuller Center Covenant Partners and Habitat affiliates worldwide expressing condolences, offering words of encouragement, and sharing their plans to honor Millard's life; moments of silence, candlelight vigils, memorial services and work days held in his honor. One of the earliest calls to Linda Tuesday morning came from President Jimmy Carter and Rosalynn. President Clinton also called that day and Linda received a letter from President George H.W. Bush expressing his sorrow at Millard's passing.

That same evening, Americus First Presbyterian Church, a small congregation that had recently agreed to sponsor a new

Fuller Center house, hosted a visitation for the Fuller family. Hundreds of people who traveled from all over the country were joined by neighbors in Sumter County to pay respects to the family in this small Americus church.

On Wednesday, Millard was buried as he wished—reminiscent of the burial 40 years earlier of his mentor, Clarence Jordan, on Picnic Hill at Koinonia Farm. Without being embalmed, his body was placed in a simple wood casket. Some 20 volunteers gathered in the cold to dig the grave, shoveling quickly in the daylight before the red Georgia clay grew harder. It was truly sacred work to those of us who helped.

Nearly 600 people came in from around the country literally overnight to attend the burial. Fuller Center board members, television crews, and local friends joined people who journeyed from as far away as California and Canada to follow the casket through the pecan orchard, up a dirt road to the short, simple and holy celebration. Koinonia's Amanda Moore reported, "A circle several layers deep surrounded the family and others in the seats. As the service began, Linda placed a rose and a hammer on Millard's casket. During the brief, simple service, their daughter Georgia and granddaughter Sophie sang "Happy Birthday to You," reminiscent of Clarence's funeral 40 years before. Chris Fuller shared a humorously imagined reunion of Millard and Clarence in heaven, figuring that all of heaven's residents had mansions, so they might as well come up with a scheme to build houses for people in hell! Millard's friend, Judge George Peagler, gave a brief eulogy and concluded the service by inviting everyone to pick up a shovel on Millard's behalf just one more time—to replace the earth onto his casket. It was the first of many moments that would offer closure to those who would feel Millard's absence so keenly in the days and weeks to follow.

Following the funeral, Fuller Center board members gathered with Linda in Millard's home office and unanimously elected David Snell to succeed Millard as President and CEO of the Fuller Center. The incredibly talented and articulate man who served as the Fuller Center's Vice President of Programs had been Millard's right-hand man for many years and was responsible for overseeing the development of one of the fastest starts for any non-profit organization in history. In just four years, the Fuller Center had expanded to 50 communities in the United States and in 14 additional countries around the world.

David's work involved frequent travel. On behalf of the Fuller Center, his passport holds stamps from Katmandu, Nepal; Colombo, Sri Lanka; Abuja, Yerevan, Armenia; Nigeria; Beijing, China; Pyongyang, North Korea; San Luis Talpa, El Salvador; Bolomba, in the Democratic Republic of Congo (formerly the Belgian Congo) and Congo Brazzaville (Republic of Congo). And yet the stamps don't tell the whole story of his efforts. Many times he journeyed hundreds of miles, by bus, by Jeep, by small plane or fast boat, from landing points in the jungle, over mountains and through deserts to respond to an invitation to share about The Fuller Center and to help start new projects.

One of the most joyous reports David gave to Millard was by cell phone on July 7, 2007, while he was standing in the middle of the village called Bokotola in the city of Mbandaka in the Democratic Republic of Congo. It was here in 1973, when the country was called Zaire, where Millard and Linda Fuller arrived to begin what was to become history's greatest effort to eliminate poverty housing. It was here before Habitat for Humanity had even been formed that Millard and Linda built the first houses internationally, which still stand in tribute to their vision. As David held his cell phone up in the air, Millard wept as he heard the shouted greetings from the original homeowners and their descendants who remembered him 35 years later.

In the weeks that followed Millard's burial, hundreds of people sent messages to David, Linda and the staff encouraging the Fuller Center to carry on Millard's dream. Linda lost count of the number of newspaper stories after they reached

700. She wrote, "Millard's death spurred a number of work days and houses to be built or dedicated in his memory, which makes me proud of how much he was loved and respected. Houses will be built, renovated and dedicated in cities such as Atlanta, Columbus, Americus, Ft. Myers, Pensacola, and South Daytona Beach Florida as well as Baltimore to name a few. Each house honors Millard's legacy as a "living memorial." Families living in decent affordable houses in beautiful and caring communities, all to God's glory, are just what Millard would have wanted."

David Snell is repeatedly asked "Will The Fuller Center continue without Millard?" and his answer is always, "Unequivocally, YES!" The Fuller Center has commitments to groups and the families they serve. The Board and staff have committed to honor Millard's memory and they are encouraged by the tremendous outpouring of support from friends and followers around the world who want the ministry to grow and prosper. He often adds, "Besides, movements don't stop."

David reflected on his first day as President to a newspaper reporter, "Nobody can fill the shoes of Millard Fuller. It will take many people taking on the many roles he played for this organization."

## Planning the Next Moves

Professional football coaches often prepare for an upcoming game by scripting the first few plays and then making adjustments as necessary throughout the game. Similarly, the Fuller Center board and staff and the Fuller family made some quick decisions to script the next few months of activity.

First, the Millard Fuller Memorial Celebration would be held in Atlanta. Faith Fuller secured Dr. Martin Luther King's church as the site, on March 14th, exactly 40 days after Millard had died. The date was selected around the church's schedule, but the biblical significance and symbolism of the 40 days was not lost on Ryan Iafigliola, Director of Special

Programs, who shared his observation one morning while leading devotions. Some significant biblical trials—the flood and the temptations of Jesus in the wilderness—lasted forty days. The Fuller Center was similarly being tossed in confusion, tested to help redefine the focus of the movement, and called upon to keep its biblical foundation the cornerstone of its work.

The next big event would be a world-wide 100-house build week to be called "The First Annual Millard Fuller Legacy Build." It was scheduled during the week of August 30th through September 4th. This was the week that Millard and Linda would have celebrated their 50th wedding anniversary. President Carter confirmed that he and Rosalynn would attend the opening ceremonial events. Glen Barton, The Fuller Center's Director of US Field Operations, surveyed the Covenant Partners. More than 100 house dedications were planned by Fuller Center teams, including a 10 house project in El Salvador. Habitat affiliates also started sending word that they wanted to do something in Millard's honor that week.

Faith Fuller agreed to move from part-time videographer for the Fuller Center to take on the role as Director of Communications. Faith's award winning PBS documentary "Briars in the Cotton Patch" had chronicled the history of Koinonia Farm. Now her first-hand perspective coupled with her experience as a reporter and producer would continue to help share the legacy of her father and the affordable housing movement.

The Fuller Center Board of Directors also began making plans. They kicked off a "Millions for Millard" campaign calling, on one million volunteers to raise one million dollars to begin building homes that would house the next million people.

## Memorial Celebration

The Memorial Celebration in Atlanta was an amazing event. For many of us, it was the first chance we'd had to truly grieve our mentor, leader and friend. Close to 2000 people traveled to attend and thousands more watched via live webcast on the Fuller Center website. Some watched from home, some watched at their offices and many churches showed the live webcast so that people could watch in community. Those in attendance represented the millions touched by Millard's theology. They were rich and poor, black and white, male and female, young and old, rural and urban, and from the United States and almost every continent around the globe.

As the celebration began, the senior pastor of Ebenezer Baptist warmly welcomed the audience, noting that this historical building was a fitting location for the event because Millard had helped so many people live out and realize Martin Luther King's dream. President Carter spoke quietly, with an obviously saddened spirit, sharing how Millard had changed both the lives of him and Rosalynn as well as everyone in the audience. He remembered with a smile how Millard talked him into volunteering with Habitat, the birth of the now famous Jimmy Carter Work Projects. He described the recent bike ride he and Rosalynn made out to Koinonia. During his first moments at Millard's grave, President Carter was struck by how humble the gravesite was for a man who changed the world. He shared with the audience that he solemnly thanked Millard for changing his life and for showing what a Christian could do to put faith into practice. He smiled and said he didn't think it was too presumptuous to say that he spoke those words on behalf of a million people.

Jamie O'Neal performed a song she wrote about Millard and Linda called "Look What Love Built" and Habitat homeowner Hattie Pitts spoke about how her house changed her life. Judah Slavkovsky described what it was like as a child growing up in a Habitat house, how Millard had mentored him and been his role model and that he was just about to graduate from Harvard Medical School as a doctor. Judah was dedicating his life to service providing healthcare to the poor because of Millard. The standing ovation that followed was as much for Millard's impact on the world as for Judah and his accomplishments.

The Fuller children shared memories and life lessons they had learned from their father. Of course the old hymn "Higher Ground" was sung joyfully by anyone who could still muster a voice through the intense emotion. Linda was joined on the steps of the pulpit by children dressed in clothing from many of the countries in which Millard's ministry had taken root. She gathered them around her and told a story about Millard and a little girl who wanted to give all she had to help him in his ministry.

Dr. Tony Campolo delivered an inspiring eulogy with characteristic humor, reflecting on Millard's role as a kingdom-seeker and challenging the audience to continue to support The Fuller Center. Dr. Campolo said that Millard understood that what people do changes them. He demonstrated this concept with the story of Millard welcoming to Americus a man from Ireland whom Tony was counseling. He explained the man was in fear of losing his life for renouncing his life as an IRA terrorist. Millard gave the man a job with Habitat in Americus and the man went on to become an Anglican priest, eventually returning to Ireland to work for peace. Another awe-inspiring tale of Millard's life's impact—and another standing ovation.

Perhaps the most moving speaker of the event was a surprise to most everyone who attended. It was Millard's younger half-brother, J. Doyle Fuller. There was not a dry eye in the church as Doyle told the audience through freely-flowing tears that Millard was his hero long before he ever picked up a hammer. Doyle was born with a physical defect that necessitated a body cast for the first three years of his life. His earliest memory of Millard, and the first time he thought of Millard as his hero, was when Millard would scoop Doyle up in his arms and carry him, body cast and all, up the hill from the house to their father's grocery store. Millard was his hero when he saw him go on to high school and then become a college pitcher and get a tryout for a major league baseball team. He was his hero when he became a lawyer and went into business with Morris Dees and they became "RICH!" but then said he thought Millard was "NUTS!" when he and Linda gave it all away. When Millard and Linda came back from Africa saying they were going to spend the rest of their lives working towards the elimination of poverty housing around the world, Doyle thought his hero had finally lost his mind. Then he realized that if anyone in this world could do it, it would be Millard. He concluded with the lessons he learned from Millard whom he remembers and misses every day: First, you can be a hero by bending over and picking up a crippled child. You don't have to be perfect to do perfect things. You don't have to be Superman to be a super-man. And finally, you don't have to have angel's wings to go where angels go.

At then, at the end of the celebration, the audience marched out with a local band leading the way to a Greater Atlanta Fuller Center house dedication for a family whose home was damaged one year ago to the day by a series of tornadoes that came through Atlanta—a perfect end to the celebration. The house's address was 74, one more than Millard's age, as if to symbolize that the movement he started cannot die.

An amazing amount of progress has been made since the first publication of this book, formerly called *The House That Love Built*, authored by Bettie B. Youngs. What began in 2005 as a platform to allow Millard to continue to speak and raise funds on behalf of Habitat for Humanity affiliates after his termination by the Habitat for Humanity Board of Directors, grew into a full blown construction organization and movement of its own. The recovery effort in Shreveport, Louisiana after hurricanes Katrina and Rita and the invitation to build in Nepal resulted in invitations and exploratory committee efforts in over 100 communities across the United States. In just 4 years under Millard's leadership the Fuller Center created programs for international work teams through the Global Builders program. The Student Builders and Faith Builders programs were developed and spearheaded by Ryan Iafigliola. The First Annual Earth Day Build held in the Potomac Highlands of West Virginia demonstrated once again that with good research and planning, houses built by volunteers can be affordable and energy efficient. And Ryan's Bicycle Adventure team road from San Diego to Savannah during the summer of 2008, raising over $130,000 along the way. Millard's new repair ministry targeting seniors and disabled homeowners which he called "The Greater Blessing Program" had captured the imagination of people all over the nation inspiring small churches and large to rethink the possibility of taking on repair projects in their communities and depressed neighborhoods. But the board and staff knew that for Millard, Fuller Centers starting in 50 communities and 14 countries was just a beginning.

## Congressional Honors

Both branches of the United States Congress introduced resolutions during the week of June 8, 2009, in honor of Millard Fuller, the founder of The Fuller Center for Housing. This is a significant honor and a unique recognition given only to the most distinguished American citizens.

More than 8,000 people from 44 countries signed petitions to get these resolutions before Congress. The House of Representatives resolution (HRES 385 EH) introduced by Georgia Representative Sanford Bishop (Democrat) and 70 other co-sponsors states (in part): "Celebrating the life of Millard Fuller, a life which provides all the evidence one needs to believe in the power of the human spirit to inspire hope and lift the burdens of poverty and despair from the shoulders of one's fellow man." The Senate resolution introduced by Alabama Senator Richard Shelby (Republican) states (in part):

> "Whereas Millard Fuller provided 3 decades of leadership and service to Habitat for Humanity and The Fuller Center for Housing, committing his life to philanthropy and service to others while raising global concern for homelessness and poverty.

"It is resolved that the Senate:

(1) Celebrates the life and achievements of Millard Fuller;
(2) Acknowledges the millions of people he and his organizations have served and the inspiration he has given to so many; and,
(3) Encourages all the people of the United States to recognize and pay tribute to Millard Fuller's life by following the example of service that he set."

During the hearing, some of the Congressmen spoke passionately about the numbers of volunteers who were inspired by Millard, including former President Carter. Some mentioned how Millard forsook his wealth in favor of service to the poor. Others spoke about what it is like seeing a family receive the keys to their new home and the over one and a half million people living in new homes because of Millard's passion and vision.

Rep. Emanuel Cleaver of the 5th District, Kansas City, MO, said, "Millard Fuller turned a simple idea into a global housing juggernaut. Millard Fuller acted out his beliefs. Today, in our society there is a lot of talk about religion. And when all is said and done, too often more is said than done. But in the case of Millard Fuller, he acted on his faith. In my religious tradition, we believe that there can be no measurable faith without works. We say, 'Faith without works is dead.' We have reason to stand up and celebrate Millard Fuller as a man who truly put his faith into action."

## Faithful to the End

Millard's last speaking engagement was on Sunday, January 25, 2009 at the Silver Spring Presbyterian Church which was celebrating its 275th anniversary. He preached twice and answered questions between the services. He was so excited to share the stories of David Snell's world travels, about a recent Millard and Linda Fuller build that was held in El Salvador,

The Earth Day Build in West Virginia and the upcoming second annual Bike Adventure ride during which cyclists would
travel from Michigan to Florida spreading the word, raising
funds and building more houses.

His final sermon concluded with the story of the first
house, built for Bo and Emma Johnson some 40 years ago.
Millard died with the beginning in his heart because he knew
the potential that first story still had to change hearts and
because he truly believed in the biblical mandate which
Clarence Jordan called "incarnational evangelism." He was
filled with hope for humanity.

Millard was, without a doubt, one the world's most prolific
letter writers. His final letter, penned instead of his customary
dictation, on Sunday night February 1st, was for the upcoming newsletter and he titled it "First Things First."

## A FINAL MESSAGE FROM MILLARD FULLER: FIRST THINGS FIRST

*Seek first the Kingdom of God, and His righteousness; and all
these things shall be added unto you.* —Matthew 6:33

At The Fuller Center headquarters in Americus, Georgia, we
start every day with devotions. We do not have devotions every once
and a while, but literally every day, Monday through Friday. Various
members of our staff take turns being responsible for devotions and
we often have local pastors or lay people come in to lead us. From
time to time, visitors from others cities will lead devotions. One
such visitor was our nearby neighbor from Plains, former President
Carter.

We start devotions promptly at 8 o'clock and end no later
than 8:30, the start of our regular work day.

There is a prayer to start off our time together, followed by
the message of the day. Then, there is a time of announcements
sharing grief or joy and prayer requests for individuals or situations.
We also simply have listening time, to "hear from heaven."

I believe that a Christian ministry should have its priorities in
order if the work is to be pleasing to God. Seeking the Kingdom
first, it seems to me, is getting it in the right order.

My spiritual mentor was Clarence Jordan who started
Koinonia Farm, the spiritual home of The Fuller Center. Clarence
said that God has His plans for the earth and He wants us, His peo-

ple, to carry them out. To know God's plans we must seek Him and do so on a regular basis. Too many people, Clarence taught, go off on their own, making their own plans and then ask God to bless them. That is getting it backward! We must seek to know God's plan and then become a part of that.

So, we have devotions. We seek to know the Lord and His plans for us, every day, every week, every year. We also start our work day at various Fuller Center builds with devotions. Again, it is a matter of putting first things first.

Seeking the Kingdom First is what we desire at The Fuller Center. Your involvement in the journey with us is a blessing and profoundly appreciated.

We fervently believe that God desires for all people, all families, to have a decent place to live in our land and around the world. When devotions are dismissed, we go to work on accomplishing that goal. Your help is what makes it all possible. God bless each and every one for your prayers, encouragement and for your financial support.

Millard Fuller, 2009

The life of Millard Fuller was an amazing journey. The charismatic and confident storyteller was convinced that if his followers could spread the word, raise money and launch new partnerships, the Kingdom of God could and would be built on Earth, just as the scriptures promise. The very act of building on faith would indeed motivate more and more people to be inspired to mobilize and use God's bountiful resources to work toward the day when every child in every nation would grow up in a safe house in a decent community. On July 1, 2013, The Fuller Center celebrated the 40th anniversary of the day Millard and Linda and their three children arrived in Mbandaka in the Democratic Republic of the Congo (formerly Zaire). Their experiment with Clarence Jordan's notion of a "Fund for Humanity" launched a movement and revolutionized how mission work is done by churches around the globe.

But Millard never saw it as *his* ministry. It was God's work. Throughout his life, Millard was continuously known for tapping people on the shoulder and telling them "God is calling you to help your neighbors in need."

If this story inspired you and you want to learn more or start a housing program in your community visit www.FullerCenterforHousing.org, or call The Fuller Center for Housing at 229-924-2900.

**—Kirk Lyman Barner**

# — Appendix A —

# Millard and Linda Fuller Timeline

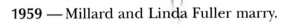

**1959** — Millard and Linda Fuller marry.

**1960** — First child born in Fort Sill, Oklahoma—a boy, Christopher Dean.

**1962** — Second child born in Montgomery, Alabama—a girl, Estin Kimberly.

**1964** — Millard and Linda become millionaires from business ventures with Morris Dees (who afterward co-founded Southern Poverty Law Center).

**1965** — Millard and Linda Fuller turn away from their millionaire lifestyle and rededicate their lives to serving God. They make their first visit to Koinonia Farm, just outside Americus, Georgia.

**1966** — Millard begins two years of fundraising with Tougaloo College, Jackson, Mississippi.

**1967** — Third child born in Glen Ridge, New Jersey—a girl, Linda Faith.

**1968** — The Fullers move to Koinonia to work with Clarence and Florence Jordan and begin work on a new project—Koinonia Partnership Housing. The Fund for Humanity is created.

**1969** — Millard conducts funeral for his spiritual mentor, Clarence Jordan, at Koinonia Farm. The first Partnership house is completed. Bo and Emma Johnson are the new homeowners.

**1971** — Fourth child born at Koinonia—a girl, Georgia Ailene.

**1973** — The Fullers move to Zaire (now Democratic Republic of Congo), taking the principles of Partnership Housing to Africa.

**1976** — After three years in Africa, the Fuller family returns to Koinonia. Habitat for Humanity International (HFHI) is formed. The first office is in an old converted chicken barn at Koinonia.

**1977** — Millard's first book, *Bokotola,* is published, telling about early years of the Fullers' marriage, business success, giving away fortune to seek Christian service, starting Partnership Housing ministry at Koinonia Christian Community, and Fullers' work of successfully carrying the idea to the middle of Africa in 1973 on a plot of land called Bokotola.

The Fullers move ten miles from Koinonia to near downtown Americus, Georgia, so Millard can support his family by practicing law. One room of Fuller's law office is used for a part-time typist for HFH correspondence.

**1978** — House building started in Zaire continues to expand; citizens in San Antonio, Texas, form the first official U.S. Habitat affiliate.

**1979** — HFHI headquarters moves from Millard Fuller's law office to a renovated house next door. Jim and Janette Prickett move from Indiana to Georgia to become administrator and bookkeeper.

The first Habitat house in Americus is built. The first Habitat affiliate in Latin America—Guatemala—is approved.

**1980** — *Love in the Mortar Joints*, Millard's second book, covering early development of HFH, is published.

**1981** — HFHI's fifth year—A total of fourteen U.S. affiliates and seven international affiliates; 342 Habitat houses completed.

**1983** — *Habitat World* is introduced, replacing *Habitat Happenings* as HFHI's news publication.

HFHI celebrates its seventh anniversary with a seven-hundred-mile walk led by Linda and Millard Fuller from Americus to Indianapolis. Hundreds come to Indianapolis from around the United States and overseas for a three-day celebration. From the walk, an extra $100,000 is raised to meet increasing budget needs.

HFHI declares the third Sunday in September as the first International Day of Prayer and Action for Human Habitat.

**1984** — Former U.S. President Jimmy Carter and his wife Rosalynn become Habitat volunteers. The first Jimmy Carter Work Project (JCWP) is held in New York City on the lower East Side.

There are approximately fifty HFH affiliates worldwide.

**1985** — The second annual JCWP takes place, again in New York City, to complete nineteen units in a restored six-story building.

**1986** — HFHI celebrates its tenth anniversary with a thousand-mile walk from Americus to Kansas City, again led by Linda and Millard Fuller.

Millard Fuller's third book, *No More Shacks!*, is published. The first Habitat affiliate in Canada is approved.

**1987** — HFHI headquarters moves to 121 Habitat Street in Americus (named the Clarence Jordan Center on

the thirtieth anniversary of his death in 1999).

HFHI's Campus Chapters program begins. The first Chapter is at Baylor University, Waco, Texas.

The Appropriate Technology department and Covenant Church program are started.

Habitat is formed in the country of Australia.

**1988** — A 1,200-mile House-Raising Walk from Portland, Maine, to Atlanta commemorates HFHI's twelfth anniversary.

The JCWP spans two cities—Philadelphia and Atlanta.

HFHI's Global Village program (short-term mission work teams) and Corporate Partners department are established.

Marriage of Kim Fuller to Jim Isakson, September 17.

1989 — Hurricane Hugo strikes South Carolina—all Habitat houses in the state survive.

Marriage of Chris Fuller to Dianne Reel, March 25.

1990 — The first cross-border JCWP is held in Tijuana, Mexico, and San Diego, California.

Abilene, Texas, becomes Habitat's 500th U.S. affiliate.

Millard and Linda Fuller's book, *The Excitement Is Building*, is published.

Bo and Emma Johnson, the first housing partners at Koinonia, pay off their mortgage.

The first overseas Campus Chapter is formed at the University of Technology in Lae, Papua New Guinea.

1991 — Habitat's 10,000th house is built. Ernestine Higgins in Atlanta, Georgia, is the proud homeowner.

HFHI's fifteenth anniversary is held in Columbus, Ohio, hosted by former Ohio governor and HFHI board member Dick Celeste.

Charlotte, North Carolina—first Habitat house built entirely by women.

Birth of first grandchild, Benjamin, to Chris and Dianne in July.

1992 — Hurricane Andrew strikes south Florida—all twenty-seven Habitat houses in the Miami, Florida, area survive.

The first Native American affiliate is approved. There is a desperate need for decent housing throughout America's Indian reservations, and HFHI's Native Peoples Initiative is partnering with multiple tribes.

The Sumter County Initiative begins with the goal to eliminate poverty housing in Americus and Sumter County, Georgia, by the year 2000.

Presidential and vice presidential candidates Bill Clinton and Al Gore help build a Habitat house in Atlanta, Georgia.

Nashville, Tennessee, builds a Habitat house in six hours.

1993 — The Entebbe Initiative is approved at HFHI board meeting held in Uganda, putting more responsibility for Habitat building outside the United States into the hands of National Partners.

HFHI completes its 20,000th house worldwide during a twenty-house Blitz Build in Americus, Georgia. The 20/20,000 Project kicks off the Sumter County Initiative.

The 1,000th Habitat house in India is completed.

*From Our House to Yours*, HFHI's first of three in the "Partners in the Kitchen" cookbook series, edited by Linda Fuller.

1994 — A devastating earthquake shakes Los Angeles, California, and floods hit Georgia—all Habitat houses in both areas survive.

Birth of grandson, Zachary, to Kim and Jim in May.

The 1,000th U.S. affiliate—Nelson County HFH, Roseland, Virginia—is approved.

HFHI completes its 30,000th house worldwide with the 30/30,000 Blitz Build in Americus, Georgia. The first JCWP on an American Indian reservation is held in Eagle Butte, South Dakota.

HFHI is named the seventeenth largest homebuilder in the United States.

Pensacola, Florida, breaks the record for the fastest-built Habitat house, finishing in five hours, fifty-seven minutes, and thirteen seconds.

*The Theology of the Hammer*, Millard Fuller's book outlining the biblical basis for HFH, is published.

1995 — Building on Faith Week joins the annual Day of Prayer and Action for Human Habitat as annual September observances.

Dedication of HFHI's 40,000th house in Twin Cities area of Minneapolis, Minnesota.

HFHI's second cookbook, *Home Sweet Habitat*, two children's books, and Millard Fuller's sixth book, *A Simple, Decent Place to Live*, are published.

JCWP held in Los Angeles in Watts area (twenty-one houses in five days)—a number of Hollywood stars participate.

Birth of grandson, Joshua, to Chris and Dianne in November.

1996 — Millard Fuller receives Presidential Medal of

Freedom, highest civilian honor in the United States, presented by President Bill Clinton.

HFHI dedicates its 50,000th house worldwide in Pensacola, Florida, during the 1996 Building on Faith Week.

Habitat's 50,001st house is celebrated in Mexico City, as well as the 6,500th Habitat house built in Mexico.

Five hundred JCWP participants gather in Vác, Hungary, to build ten houses. HFHI begins building in Romania, its fiftieth nation.

Three Habitat publications win awards in the 1996 Gold Circle Awards competition sponsored by the American Society for Association Executives.

 Judging by popular support, HFH is ranked in the top dozen favorite charities in the United States, according to a November article in *The NonProfit Times.*

India's first affiliate, HFH Khammam, celebrates its twelfth anniversary and dedicates its 1,000th house.

1997 — Leaders of the U.S. Congress kick off National Homeownership Week by beginning work with Habitat on "The Houses That Congress Built."

Habitat celebrates ten years of formal partnership with students through its Campus Chapters and Youth Programs department.

Marriage of Georgia Fuller to Manfred Luedi, May 17.

Oprah Winfrey challenges her TV viewers to "build an Oprah house" and presents HFHI board chairman Wayne Walker with a check for $55,000. Two years later, the program has nearly met its goal of two hundred homes nationwide.

Robert Fulghum, author of *All I Really Need to Know I Learned in Kindergarten,* donates the royalties from his book *True Love* to HFHI.

Third in cookbook series, *Simple Decent Cooking.*

Birth of grandson, Alexander, to Kim and Jim in July.

**1998** — Habitat for Humanity ranks as the fifteenth largest homebuilder in the United States, according to a ranking done by *Professional Builder* magazine.

Eighty affiliates in thirty-three states celebrate their tenth anniversaries.

Birth of granddaughter, Sophie, to Georgia and Manfred in June.

HFHI's 500th Campus Chapter, St. Norbert College in DePere, Wisconsin, dedicates the 100th house built in 1998 by college and high school students.

Maxwell House concludes a two-year partnership with HFHI in which the company donated $2 million in matching funds to promote the building of a hundred Habitat houses in a hundred weeks with a hundred Habitat affiliates in the United States.

Building on Faith Week—Three hundred-plus houses built in two hundred locations.

Seventy-two hundred students participate in Collegiate Challenge Spring Break house building with HFH affiliates, raising $550,000.

Pensacola HFH builds three houses in one day.

Nashville HFH breaks record again of fastest-built HFH house in the United States—four hours, thirty-nine minutes.

JCWP held in Houston, Texas—A hundred houses in five days.

1999 — More than 15,000 houses built this year, bringing total to 80,000 houses worldwide; 5,000 built in Guatemala alone.

JCWP '99, in the Philippines, is the largest ever, with 14,000 volunteers from thirty-two countries participating. The goal for the six sites was 293 houses in five days; the volunteers evidently took the theme "Let's Build Together" seriously and completed nearly all of them.

Millard Fuller receives the National Jefferson Award from the American Institute for Public Service in the category of Greatest Public Service Benefiting the Disadvantaged.

The house-building record is broken yet again, this time by a construction crew in New Zealand. The Manakau HFH had appliances installed, sod laid, and an inspector satisfied in three hours, forty-four minutes, and fifty-nine seconds.

A new program, the 21st Century Challenge, encourages communities to set a date by which they will eliminate poverty housing locally.

HFHI relocates its Latin America/Caribbean office from Americus to San Jose, Costa Rica, in an effort to decentralize and move services closer to the field.

Building on Faith Week—Five hundred-plus homes (up two hundred from previous year).

**2000** — An HFH affiliate in Gisborne, New Zealand, dedicates five houses one minute after midnight on January 1, 2000, as part of the city's "Gisborne 2000" millennium celebration. Gisborne is the first city in the world to see the first light of the new millennium.

Birth of granddaughter, Jasmine, to Georgia and Manfred in May.

Decentralization of HFHI management continues as the Asia/Pacific department moves to Bangkok, Thailand, and Africa/Middle East moves to Pretoria, South Africa.

The JCWP 2000 takes place in three locations across the U.S. In New York City, twenty houses are built, including Habitat's 100,000th house. In Jacksonville, Florida, 103 houses go up, and thirty-five houses are constructed in Sumter County, Georgia, completing the Sumter County Initiative.

Seventh book, *More Than Houses,* authored by Millard Fuller.

Whirlpool Corporation commits $25 million for five years to put a stove and a refrigerator in every home built in North America.

Programs of HFHI: Women Build, Prison Partnership, Mental Health Partnership, Campus Chapters and Youth Programs, Corporate Partners, RV Care-A-Vanners, Global Village, and Covenant Church.

**2001** — Twenty-fifth anniversary of HFHI held in Indianapolis called "25 & Building."

HFHI is now in eighty-three nations totaling a milestone of two thousand affiliates worldwide.

Linda and Millard Fuller in Brazil to celebrate 35,000th house built in Latin America/Caribbean; Fullers in Uganda to celebrate 20,000th house built on African continent.

Forty thousand homes built in the United States.

Linda Fuller leads "Women Building a Legacy" launch—two hundred women, including fifteen from Northern Ireland, building five houses in one week in Denver, Colorado, celebrating the tremendous success of "First Ladies Builds" (participation of every First Lady of all fifty U.S. states)—more than four hundred HFH houses built in all by women or women-led builds.

Ten thousand students from the United States; twenty thousand in other countries participating in Spring Break Collegiate Challenge.

JCWP, South Korea—136 houses.

*Down Home Humor*—Funny stories about Habitat edited by Linda Fuller.

2002 — Fuller's eighth book—First volume of *Building Materials for Life*, a collection of forty inspiring essays based on Millard's life and faith experiences.

Birth of grandson, Destin, to Georgia and Manfred in December.

JCWP—Durban, South Africa—A hundred homes in five days as part of a thousand homes built all over Africa in three months.

2,332 HFH affiliates worldwide building in more than three thousand towns and villages.

Eighty-seven nations.

Three hundred Prison Partnerships.

Shelby County, Alabama, HFH breaks record for fastest-built house in the United States— three hours, twenty-six minutes, thirty-four seconds.

Jacksonville, Florida, HFH affili- ate is the first in the United States to achieve a thou- sand houses.

21st Century Challenge—Thirty-seven certified com- munities.

2004 — Global Village and Discovery Center opens in Americus, Georgia.

HFH University established to engage and equip leaders in HFH around the world with e-courses and other educational opportunities related to eradicat- ing poverty housing.

150,000th house milestone.

JCWP—Three 21st Century Challenge cities: LaGrange and Valdosta, Georgia, Anniston, Alabama.

Ninety-two nations.

*Briars in the Cotton Patch* documentary on the Koinonia story released—produced by Faith Fuller.

2004 — *Building Materials for Life, Volume II* published.

Millard Fuller falsely accused of misconduct—HFHI board of directors agrees with President Carter's con- clusion of "no proof" regarding allegation but takes steps to remove Millard from leadership at HFHI.

**2005** — Fullers fired by executive committee of HFHI board.

The founding of Building Habitat—a lawsuit forces name change to The Fuller Center for Housing.

Birth of ninth grandchild, a boy, Sean, to Georgia and Manfred in March.

HFHI board confirms action of the executive committee to fire Fullers.

First Fuller Center board meeting held at Koinonia and headquarters in Americus inaugurated.

Building on Higher Ground Initiative launched in Shreveport, Louisiana; Heart to Heart program partnership with Koinonia.

The Fuller Center starts building a hundred houses in Nepal.

200,000th house built by HFHI worldwide celebrated in Knoxville, Tennessee.

*Woman to Woman Wisdom: Inspiration for Real Life* with Bettie Youngs, co-authored by Linda Fuller and Donna Schuller, published by Thomas Nelson.

FCH website launched—www.fullercenter.org.

FCH adds first domestic Covenant Partner, Building Suffolk, in Virginia. Nepal becomes first Covenant Partner overseas.

**2006** —Twenty-three houses completed with Higher Ground Initiative in Shreveport as well as a number of homes renovated on the Gulf Coast.

Marriage of Faith Fuller to Scott Umstattd, May 6.

First Millard and Linda Fuller Blitz Build held in Allendale neighborhood of Shreveport, Louisiana.

FCH work starts in Nigeria and Sri Lanka.

2007 — Kickoff for Chattahoochee Fuller Center Project initiative with goal to eliminate poverty housing in Valley and Lanett, Alabama, and West Point, Georgia (estimated 500 houses).

The hardback edition of *The House that Love Built: The Story of Millard and Linda Fuller, Founders of Habitat for Humanity and The Fuller Center for Housing* authored by Bettie B. Youngs was published with Hampton Road Publishers.

FCH adds Covenant Partners in Alabama, Georgia, Illinois, South Carolina, Australia, the Cook Islands, and El Salvador and receives partnership inquiries from Arizona, Indiana, Minnesota, Ohio, Arkansas, Massachusetts, California, Oklahoma, Pennsylvania, Florida, Wisconsin, Canada, China, Democratic Republic of the Congo, Republic of the Congo, Togo, Ghana, India, Haiti, Jamaica, Bahamas, Panama, Philippines, Tanzania, and Uganda.

*Building Materials for Life, Volume III* published.

Linda and Millard Fuller celebrate forty-eighth wedding anniversary.

Second annual Linda and Millard Fuller Blitz Build in Shreveport, Louisiana.

2008 —First Fuller Center Bicycle Adventure covers 3,300 miles from San Diego, CA to Savannah, GA.

2009 —Millard Fuller dies unexpectedly on February 3, 2009. Buried in an unmarked grave at Koinonia Farm near Clarence Jordan's grave. March 15,

Millard Fuller Memorial Celebration held at New Ebenezer Baptist Church in Atlanta, Georgia. FCH Board officially affirms David Snell as new President of FCH. August 30th, Inaugural Millard Fuller Legacy Build held in Lanett, Alabama with a celebration led by President Carter and Morris Dees as keynote speakers.

**2010** —FCH has more than 50 US Covenant Partners.

**2011** —Fuller Center co-founder Linda Fuller marries Paul Degelmann in Americus, GA.

**2012** —FCH President announces the launch of a "Save A House/Make A Home" initiative to address the US foreclosure crisis.

**2013** —FCH Global Builders program hits 1,000-participant milestone during work trip to rebuild earthquake ravaged Haiti.

**2013** —FCH announces a 40 Years in Africa celebration recognizing the anniversary of the arrival of the Fullers in Mbandaka, DRC (formerly Zaire).

# Appendix B

# Awards and Biographical Information

## MILLARD DEAN FULLER

### BUSINESS AND PROFESSIONAL

The Fuller Center for Housing, Inc., Founder and President—2005–2009

Habitat for Humanity International, Inc., Founder—1976–2005

Fuller and McFarland Attorneys at Law, Partner—1977–90

Missionary, Mbandaka, Zaire, Housing Development—1973–76

Koinonia Partners, Inc., Director—1968–72

Tougaloo College, Tougaloo, Mississippi, Development Director—1966–68

Fuller & Dees Marketing Group, Inc., President and Co-Founder—1960–65

Dees and Fuller Attorneys at Law, Partner—1960–65

# BOOKS

*Building Materials for Life*, Volume III, Smyth & Helwys Publishing, Inc., 2007

*Building Materials for Life*, Volume II, Smyth & Helwys Publishing, Inc., 2004

*Building Materials for Life*, Volume I, Smyth & Helwys Publishing, Inc., 2002

*More Than Houses*, Word, Inc., 2000

*A Simple, Decent Place to Live*, Word, Inc., 1995

*The Theology of the Hammer*, Smyth & Helwys Publishing, Inc., 1994

*The Excitement Is Building*, Word, Inc., co-authored by Linda Fuller, 1990

*No More Shacks!* Word, Inc., 1986

*Love in the Mortar Joints*, New Century Publishers, Inc., 1980

*Bokotola*, New Century Publishers, Inc., 1977

# AWARDS AND PUBLIC RECOGNITIONS

2007  Shining World Leadership Award (co-recipient, Linda Fuller). The Supreme Master Ching Hai International Association

2006  Honorary Secretary of State of Indiana; Servant's Heart Award; People Helping People Network

2005  The Extra Mile—Points of Light Volunteer Pathway dedicated in Washington, D.C., honoring Millard and Linda Fuller with a Medallion along with nineteen other founders of U.S. organizations and movements

2004  The 2004 Builder Award, Kenan Institute of Private

Enterprise; The World Methodist Peace Award by
World Methodist Council

2003   *The NonProfit Times* Executive of the Year; T.B. Maston
Christian Ethics Award

2002   The Niebuhr Medal, Elmhurst College; 21st Century
Leadership Award (co-recipient, Linda Fuller), Georgia
Southwestern University; Georgian of the Year Award,
Georgia Association of Broadcasters; Overcoming
Obstacles Achievement Award; Points of Light
Commemorative Medallion (co-recipient, Linda Fuller);
Auburn University Lifetime Achievement Award

2001   Magnolia Award for Excellence in Housing, Georgia
Department of Community Affairs; World Spirit Service
Award, The World Holy Spirit Movement of Seoul,
Korea; Brooks Hayes Memorial Christian Citizenship
Award, Second Baptist Church of Little Rock; First
Annual Housing Champion Award, Georgia
Department of Community Affairs; 2001 Albert
Schweitzer Award of Excellence, Chapman University;
Lenore and George W. Romney Citizen Volunteer
Award, Points of Light Foundation; President's Cabinet
Distinguished Achievement Award, University of
Alabama; Mark O. Hatfield Leadership Award (co-
recipient, Linda Fuller), Council for Christian Colleges
and Universities; 100 Most Influential Georgians of the
Year and Millennium, *Georgia Trend* magazine

2000   International Quality of Life Award, College of Human
Sciences, Auburn University; 2000 Frank Annunzio
Award, Christopher Columbus Fellowship Foundation;
Brotherhood/Sisterhood Award (co-recipient, Linda
Fuller), National Conference for Community and Justice

1999   100 Most Influential People in Home Building in the
United States, *Builder* magazine; 1999 Jefferson
Award, American Institute for Public Service; 20

Georgians Who Influenced the 20th Century, *Atlanta Journal–Constitution* newspaper

1998 Master Builder Award, Carpenters Company of Philadelphia

1997 Norman Vincent Peale Award; John W. Gardner Leadership Award

1996 Presidential Medal of Freedom, U.S. President Clinton; National Housing Hall of Fame, National Association of Home Builders; Faithful Servant Award, National Association of Evangelicals; Ballington and Maud Booth Founders Award, Volunteers of America

1995 Builder of the Year, *Professional Builder* magazine

1994 Harry S. Truman Public Service Award (co-recipient, Linda Fuller), City of Independence, Missouri

1992 Martin Luther King, Jr., Humanitarian Award, Georgia State Holiday Commission

1991 Amicus Certus Award, Lutheran Social Services of Illinois

1990 Joseph C. Wilson Award, Rochester Association for the United Nations; Temple Award for Creative Altruism, Institute of Noetic Sciences

1989 Caring Award, Caring Institute; Common Cause Public Service Achievement Award; International Humanity Service Award, American Overseas Association (American Red Cross)

1988 Distinguished Christian Service in Social Welfare Award, North American Association of Christians in Social Work

1987 Martin Luther King, Jr., Humanitarian Award, Martin Luther King, Jr., Center for Non-Violent Social Action

1986  Clarence Jordan Exemplary Christian Service Award,
Southern Baptist Theological Seminary

# HONORARY DOCTORAL DEGREES

2004  Pfeiffer University, NC; Florida Southern College, FL;
Coe College, IA; Virginia Wesleyan College, VA;
Maryville College, TN; University of Alabama, AL

2003  University of Portland, OR; Saint Mary-of-the-Woods
College, IN

2002  Wofford College, SC; San Francisco State University,
CA; Colorado Christian University, CO; Defiance
College, OH; Shorter College, GA

2001  Birmingham-Southern College, AL; Roberts Wesleyan
College, NY; College of St. Rose, NY

2000  Hoseo University, Korea; Rhode Island College, RI;
Morehouse College, GA; Willamette University, OR

1999  University of Alberta, Canada; Santa Clara University,
CA; Sterling College, KS; Keene State College, NH;
State University of West Georgia, GA

1998  St. Norbert College, WI; Northeastern University, MA;
Dartmouth College, NH; Middlebury College, VT;
California Lutheran University, CA; Alderson-
Broaddus College, WV; Huntingdon College, AL

1997  Westminster College, MO

1996  Nova Southeastern University, FL

1995  Elon College, NC; Bluffton College, OH; Presbyterian
College, SC

1994  University of North Alabama, AL; Providence College,
RI; Dallas Baptist University, TX

1992  Lynchburg College, VA; Technical University of Nova
Scotia, Canada; North Park College, IL

1990   Westminster College, PA; Wake Forest University, NC; Whitworth College, WA; Mercer University, GA

1989   Susquehanna University, PA; College of Wooster, OH

1988   DePauw University, IN

1987   Ottawa University, KS

1985   Eastern College, PA

## ORGANIZATIONS

Albert Schweitzer Fellowship of America, Advisory Committee member; founded in 1940 to support Dr. Schweitzer's hospital in Africa

National Council of Churches advisory board

Georgia Bar Association, inactive member

Alabama Bar Association, inactive member

## EDUCATION

University of Alabama, Tuscaloosa, Alabama—1960, LLB, School of Law

Auburn University, Auburn, Alabama—1957, BS, Economics

## PERSONAL

DOB: January 3, 1935

Spouse: Linda Caldwell of Tuscaloosa, Alabama

Children: Christopher Dean Fuller (1960), Estin Kimberly (Fuller) Isakson (1962), Linda Faith (Fuller) Umstattd (1967), and Georgia Ailene (Fuller) Luedi (1971)

# LINDA CALDWELL FULLER

## BUSINESS AND PROFESSIONAL

The Fuller Center for Housing, Co-Founder, 2005 to present

Habitat for Humanity International, Co-Founder, 1976–2005

Missionary, Mbandaka, Zaire, Housing Development, 1973–76

Koinonia Christian Community, Americus, Georgia, 1968–72

## BOOKS

*Woman to Woman Wisdom: Inspiration for Real Life*, Thomas Nelson Publishers, co-authored with Bettie Youngs and Donna Schuller, August 2005

*Down Home Humor*, HFHI Creative Services, Editor, 2001

Partners in the Kitchen cookbook series, Favorite Recipes Press, Editor, 1993, 1995, 1997

*The Excitement Is Building*, Word, Inc., co-authored with Millard Fuller, 1990

## AWARDS and RECOGNITIONS

2005 The Extra Mile—Points of Light Volunteer Pathway dedicated in Washington, D.C., honoring Millard and Linda Fuller with a Medallion along with nineteen other founders of well-known volunteer organizations and movements

2004 A Place to Call Home Award by The Zarrow Families and the Mental Health Association in Tulsa

2003 Consumer of the Year Award by The Georgia Mental Health Consumer Network

2002 Points of Light Commemorative Medallion (corecipient, Millard Fuller)

2001 Brooks Hays Memorial Christian Citizenship Award (co-recipient with Millard Fuller) by Second Baptist Church, Little Rock, Arkansas; Mark O. Hatfield Leadership Award by Council for Christian Colleges and Universities

2000 Brotherhood/Sisterhood Award (co-recipient, Millard Fuller) by the National Conference for Community and Justice

1999 Award for Volunteerism and Philanthropy by Council of Independent Colleges

1998 Golden Plate Award by the American Academy of Achievement

1996 Ballington and Maud Booth Founders Award by Volunteers of America (Centennial Year)

1994 Harry S. Truman Public Service Award by City of Independence, Missouri; Huntingdon College Alumni Achievement Award

1993 "Gracious Ladies of Georgia" Award

1990 Temple Award for Creative Altruism by The Institute of Noetic Sciences; Berea College Service Award

## ORGANIZATIONS

Maranatha Baptist Church, Plains, Georgia, Member

Miracle of Nazareth International Foundation, Trustee

Simple Living TV Series, National Advisory Board

Peer Centers of Georgia, Inc., Co-Founder and President

Sumter County Criminal Justice/Law Enforcement/Mental Health Task Force, Founder and Chair

Visions for Sumter, Executive and Collaborative Boards, 1992–Present

Migrant and Seasonal Housing, Inc., Founder (inactive)

# HONORARY DOCTORATE DEGREES

2003  St. Mary-of-the-Woods, IN

2001  The College of Saint Rose, NY

1999  Sterling College, KS

1998  California Lutheran University, CA, Northeastern University, MA

1995  Presbyterian College, SC

1994  Huntingdon College, AL

1993  Dallas Baptist University, TX

# EDUCATION

French Language Study, Paris, France, 1973

BS, Elementary Education, Huntingdon College, Montgomery, Alabama, 1966

# PERSONAL

DOB: February 17, 1941

Spouse: Millard Dean Fuller of Lanett, Alabama

Four Children: Christopher Dean Fuller (1960), Estin Kimberly (Fuller) Isakson (1962), Linda Faith (Fuller) Umstattd (1967), and Georgia Ailene (Fuller) Luedi (1971)

# — Appendix C —

# Supporting Documents

May 2, 2004

Dear Rey, Nic, Jim, and the rest of my fellow IBOD members,

We are standing on the edge of a cliff, in danger of making a great mistake. We are being carried along by a process that seems entirely rational on the surface but which may lead us to an act that all of us will ultimately regret.

We still have the opportunity to avoid the tragedy, if we have the moral courage to do so. Instead of just continuing lockstep over the edge, we need to set aside the 10:00 AM EDT (US) deadline a few hours from now and take a calm, wise, and prayerful look at what we are doing.

There is really only one major disagreement between what the EC has proposed and what Millard has responded, but it is major, and there is an alternative.

As Jimmy Carter argued in his letter a few hours ago, to require Millard to "go to special counseling and train-ing" under these circumstances is "to insult and debase the Fullers." I understand fully why Millard cannot agree to that and why he is deeply hurt that he has been judged guilty of an act against [Millard's accuser] despite his pleas of innocence. It seems almost incredible that a man could have been for years such an inspiration to all of us as a Christian leader—and even chosen as the "2003 Executive of the Year" by the *NonProfit Times* just five months ago—and then be treated like this by the IBOD so soon thereafter, because of a shaky accusation which he absolutely denies and for which we have no proof.

This is not only a course of action certain to hurt Habitat's reputation more than it "helps" it, but it leaves Millard no alternative but to defend himself every time the topic comes up in the future—as every last one of us would do!

Here is an alternative:

First, the statement by the EC on April 26 needs to stick to what it can, indeed, say with fairness and with assurance, namely, that the EC "is unable to determine . . ."—without going on to the "Nonetheless, . . ." statement that is (as I argued in my earlier letter to the IBOD) based almost totally on faulty, incomplete history. I should think it would be significant in some people's minds, at least, that the two of us who were involved most deeply in the most serious of the accusations (the 1990 incidents) and have contacted the IBOD about them, Jimmy Carter and I, both insist that they are being used in a way that is exaggerated and inappropriate. That is especially true in light of the past fifteen years of "inspired leadership," as Jimmy Carter says. To use all that faulty extrapolation from a sketchy understanding of the past adds nothing to the truth about the present matter, but it does create an environment where the truth is certain to be distorted. Is there no room at all in this organization for the Christian practice of forgiveness for past mistakes?

Second, the statement has been made by some that Habitat for Humanity somehow has become a hostile work environment, one in which, presumably, not only

Millard but other supervisors and co-workers are perceived to be a threat. If that is true, it is something which we on the IBOD are responsible to address.

Rather than insisting that Millard himself is "the problem" and either forcing him to resign in disgrace or to undergo special humiliating treatment that clearly would be designed more to cover our own liability than truly to "change" a 69-year-old man just about to retire anyway—rather than this, we should commission a fair and thorough investigation of the accusation which is really against all of us, that we have a hostile work environment. In any large work force, of course, there will be some malcontents, but professional surveyors will know how to evaluate and weight those.

Millard has assured me just this morning that he would welcome such a survey. He further assured me that if, in fact, the professional conclusion turned out to be that we do have a "hostile environment," he would be the first to step forward for the recommended training program, as part of a larger institutional effort.

That would fully satisfy any possible legal requirements. At the same time it would remove the appearance of Millard's having been found guilty of the particular action of which he insists he is innocent. It would help set the stage for a healthier environment in the years ahead, long after Millard has left the scene.

Millard says that he would withdraw his letter of April 30 and cooperate fully in such a course of action, because it holds the promise of constructive improvement of Habitat. He would then be able also to cooperate fully in making an orderly, positive transition to a new CEO over the next few months.

The alternative, it seems to me, only achieves humiliation and bitterness—and it will bring great harm to a wonderful organization that has so much to offer this world. My own heart would be one of the first of millions to be broken over such a needless tragedy.

Rey, Nic, Jim—I'm not in a position to make this into a formal proposal before the full IBOD. You are. I hope it seems as fair to all of you as it does to me. It offers us a less destructive way out of this mess, a way that is more responsible, not less.

I pray that you will take it in the spirit in which it is offered.

Don Mosley

May 11, 2004

Millard Fuller
Habitat for Humanity International, Inc.

Dear Millard:

On March 22nd and April 23rd, acting on behalf of the Executive Committee, I instructed you in writing that you were not to discuss the charges against you with any Habitat for Humanity International employees. This was confirmed with your attorney last Thursday in a telephone conversation, and again on Friday to your attorney in writing.

In addition, in an e-mail sent last Friday (May 6), President Carter admonished you and the Board of Habitat not to make their respective cases or communicate the details of their respective arguments to third parties. We were assured as recently as yesterday morning, by both your attorneys, that such communications had ceased. However, I have been informed that you have continued to contact employees, as recently as yesterday afternoon.

In light of the Executive Committee's instructions and your continued violation of them, the officers feel that they have no alternative but to take appropriate action to protect the organization and the employees of Habitat, including you.

Therefore, the officers have decided that while you will remain the President and CEO, you are relieved of your managerial duties, effective immediately, through and at least until May 21st, the date of the mediation with President Carter. You can continue with your speaking engagements, but while you are in Americus, you are instructed to work from your home. You are also reminded of the Executive Committee's continuing directive that you and your agents, attorneys, investigators, or anyone else acting on your behalf refrain from communicating with current or former employees, as well as any third parties, regarding this matter.

You will continue to receive your normal pay and benefits; you will suffer no adverse economic consequences. We do not intend to make public announcements regarding this matter, and we ask that you do not do so as well. Despite this action, we remain hopeful that the upcoming May 21 meeting between you, us, and President Carter will allow us all to reach resolution.

Sincerely,

Rey Ramsey

Cc: J. Doyle Fuller, Esq., Nabil Abadir, Barbara Alexander, Jim Copeland, Chantal Hudicourt-Ewald, Carol Johnson, Larry Prible, Nic Retsinas, Ron Terwilliger, Chuck Thiemann

May 13, 2004

Dear Habitat Partners,

As some of you know by now, there has been tension and misunderstanding in Habitat circles over the past several weeks. The International Board and I are working through some issues that we hope to resolve in the near future. Please know that I deeply appreciate the expressions of concern and support from many of you during the past few days, but I have a request to make.

I am asking that no Habitat employee or other friends contact me about this matter during the coming days. I will not be contacting any of you. To reduce even the appearance of inappropriate contacts, the officers of the Board have asked me not to come to the office for the next few days. I have agreed to gladly abide by their request. Of course, David Williams and other Senior VPs will be able to contact me at any time as necessary. The more each of us can calm down and focus on our jobs, the sooner we will get this problem behind us.

Finally, I want all of you to know that I thank God for the wonderful work we have been given to do together. Hopefully, we will get past this difficulty as soon as possible and be able to turn our full attention to the far greater problems that poor people are enduring all over the world. Please pray that Linda and I and everyone else involved will have the wisdom to do whatever is most pleasing to God in the days ahead.

In the search for truth,

Millard Fuller

May 21, 2004

From Jimmy Carter
To Rey Ramsey
   Millard Fuller

Subject: Recommendations to resolve the Habitat dispute

I have assessed carefully the presentations of both sides, both this morning and during previous discussions and exchanges of memoranda. My hope is that the following proposal will be adequately balanced to secure final acceptance, however reluctant either side may be on some specific points.

1. Since there can be no definitive proof concerning the truth of allegations made by the female employee, there should be no public condemnation of Millard Fuller and no official deleterious entries by the Board of Directors in his personnel record.

2. Recognizing that the Board of Directors has undisputed legal authority to dismiss Millard Fuller without any proof of impropriety or malfeasance, my recommendation is that Millard agree to announce his retirement at some time prior to December 1, 2004, to be effective no later than his 70th birthday in January 2005. In the meantime he is to retain the title of CEO but relinquish day-to-day management responsibilities of Habitat affairs.

3. Both sides agree not to comment on the present dispute in any way that would disparage the other side, or any other person. The only exception to any comment might be a jointly approved public statement to be issued to inquisitive news media if this proves to be necessary and possible to draft. I would be willing to assist with this if requested.

4. Subsequent to Millard's retirement, he would continue to support and assist Habitat in every way he desires and on his own schedule. One of his natural

responsibilities would be to prepare for the commemoration of the 200,000th home to be built and dedicated, which is expected to occur in October 2005.

5. As long as he wishes to serve Habitat in this way, Millard is to be furnished an office, a secretary, and normal logistical support.

6. For the rest of their lives, Millard and Linda Fuller are to be paid an annual stipend equivalent to the salaries that they now receive. In addition, Habitat will assure that they have adequate health insurance coverage.

7. A more legal agreement encompassing these recommendations would be prepared by lawyers on both sides. If there are questions, I will be available this afternoon to provide answers, but I am not inclined to modify my basic recommendations.

Sincerely,

Jimmy Carter

From: John Stack
Sent: Monday, May 17, 2004 5:39 AM

To: Millard Fuller
Subject: Re: Thank you for your e-mail

Dear Millard,
    It has taken me a while to get back to you because I have been away at our annual Church Synod, and at our HFHSA Board Meeting. At our Board Meeting I showed the videotape of your encouraging address. All of us, Staff and Board members, were deeply inspired by your words of challenge and encouragement. Millard, you are

a unique gift to us in the field. Thank you. As I expressed to you in my e-mail after the Board Meeting in New York, I was overwhelmed by the American legal system, which seemed to me to place too much emphasis on the events in 1990/91, and being overwhelmed, I went with the Board's decision.

When I got home and was able to reflect on what had happened, I was horrified to realize that I had agreed with the view that you were considered guilty, despite a lack of any real evidence. I immediately e-mailed Rey and the EC and systematically set out why I was rescinding my vote at the IBOD. I expressed very clearly that I agreed completely with Don Mosley's suggestion that we ask Jimmy Carter to meet with you, Rey, and the EC in an effort to resolve the matter. I also said that I did not believe you were guilty of the accusations as they were based on hearsay and built on what had happened in 1990/91. I still stand by these views. I am not convinced by the evidence presented that you can be considered guilty. Should the Board discuss the matter further, after the EC's meeting with yourself and Jimmy Carter, whether by telephone conference or at our June Board Meeting, I will vote to clear your name completely.

As I expressed in my previous two e-mails to you, I believe there is a spiritual dynamic to what has happened. Millard, you started Habitat for Humanity as a ministry inspired by the Holy Spirit, and it continues to be an affront to Satan because it is about building and not destroying. Millard, I would encourage you to look beyond the personalities involved and see a direct attack by Satan, "the father of all lies." As you prepare for your meeting with President Carter, Rey, and the EC, I commend to you the words of Paul in Eph. 3:16–20 (personalized). "Millard, I ask God from the wealth of His glory to give you power through His Spirit to be strong in your inner self, and I pray that Christ will (continue to) make His home in your heart through faith. I pray that you may have your roots and foundation in love, so that you, together with all God's people (and the IBOD), may have the power to understand how broad and long, how high and deep, is Christ's love. Yes, may you come to know His love—although it can never be fully known—and so be completely filled with the very nature of God. To Him who by means of His power working in us is able to do so much more than we can ever ask for, or even think of: to God be the glory . . ." I will be praying for you as you meet.

With deep respect and admiration,

John Stack

To: Nabil Abadir; Barbara Alexander; Kathleen Bader; David Hicks; Roger Haughton; Richard Roberts; Jim Copeland; Nic Retsinas; Ron Terwilliger; Carol Johnson; Juel Smith; Mauricio Solis; Symon Msefula; Bob Willumstad; John Stack; Don Mosley; Paul Ekelschot; Billy McGivern; Fernando Zobel Ayala; Larry Prible; Jack Kemp; Tony Lanigan; Janet Huckabee; Chuck Thiemann
Cc: Rey Ramsey
Sent: Monday, June 07, 2004 3:03 PM

Subject: A MESSAGE FROM REY RAMSEY—
AGREEMENT REACHED

Greetings: I am pleased to report that we have reached an agreement with Millard Fuller regarding his retirement from Habitat. Millard signed the agreement last night. We have not yet reached an agreement with Linda, but continue to speak to her attorney. Millard's agreement follows in all material respects the proposal put forward by President Carter. Millard will announce his retirement on or before December 1, 2004, with an effective date of January 3, 2005. We will be working with Millard on a mutual response to the inquiries made by the *Atlanta Journal Constitution*. Following the Mexico Board meeting, we will begin to work on all matters associated with Millard's transition and succession.

I am also pleased to report that we have reached an agreement with [Millard's accuser], the employee who made the complaint. The agreement includes a severance payment, a confidentiality agreement, a non-disparagement agreement, and a full release.

Although these matters are now resolved via signed agreements, I remind each of you that we are prohibited from commenting publicly (even to most employees within HFHI). Our agreement with Millard contains mutual confidentiality and non-disparagement obligations. For this reason, please refrain from public or internal discussion of these matters, and if you are contacted by any members of the media, please refer them to Chris Clarke at ext. xxxx.

I would like to thank all of those who helped bring this matter to a successful conclusion. I look forward to seeing you all in Mexico City.

Kind regards,

Rey

Millard's speech to the IBOD, Mexico City, June 10, 2004

*When I was growing up, I had a chance to witness a lot of dog fights . . . perhaps you remember, too, that when a dog knew he was beat, he would roll over on his back and expose his neck. I am doing the same thing before you today. My neck is exposed to you. I signed an agreement, but it was one of the hardest things I have ever done in my life. I felt like a prostitute selling her soul.*

*I have deep appreciation for Don Mosley, whom Linda and I have worked with for many years starting back in the early '70s at Koinonia. Then, when we were missionaries in Africa wanting to build the first houses in Mbandaka, Zaire, Don came out to survey the land. Now, just recently, we dedicated the 30,000th Habitat house built in Africa, but it was Don who helped us get started with the first ones. Don has felt pain, as I have, about this situation. He encouraged me to swallow my pride and sign the agreement. Ken Henson, Jr., my lawyer, also urged me to sign. Ken has been incredibly supportive and involved in HFH, donating hundreds of thousands of dollars of his personal money, and spent ten years as an unpaid executive director of HFH in Columbus, Georgia, working out of his law office. And I thought Jimmy Carter would have wanted me to sign, too, even though I had not talked to him before signing. Then, after signing, I called and told him I had signed even though I had great apprehension about signing. Jimmy Carter surprised me by saying he didn't want me to sign unless I really wanted to sign. That it would not affect his friendship with me. He also said that he had promised Rey Ramsey that he would honor his commitment to do JCWPs [Jimmy Carter Work Projects] 2004 and 2005. However, he made no commitment beyond JCWP 2005 in Michigan. I don't know about you, but I think it is important for Jimmy and Rosalynn Carter to continue with Habitat after 2005.*

*I appreciate this opportunity to talk with you. We all realize that the agenda of this board meeting is getting totally destroyed because of taking time for this situation. And I am thankful there are no restrictions on my time to talk with you.*

*Healing can take place in openness. I'm not a perfect individual without sin, but forgiveness and truth can heal. Linda and I have been married for almost forty-five years. I have made a lot of mistakes during my lifetime, but not on February 20, 2003. I'm as innocent as the driven snow in regard to that situation. For the Chair of IBOD [international board of directors] to hire a New York City law firm to do an investigation without first talking with me, Linda, and my co-workers and even fail to follow our own HR rules and regulations and finally to take a female employee's word over mine is very hurtful.*

*Linda and I first learned about the accusations and hiring a NYC law firm when we were halfway around the world on a vigorous three-week tour of our work in Asia. I told Linda then that I was not worried about what the female employee was accusing me of because I know I haven't done the slightest thing wrong. What I was worried about was the board overreacting. Our welcome home on March 19, exhausted from twenty-two hours of travel, was learning that an investigator was waiting for me at the Windsor Hotel to question me. It was Linda's idea to go with me even though she was not invited.*

*Then, a meeting was called for me to meet the Executive Committee and Regina Hopkins in NYC on April 1 in the offices of the law firm at a time when I could not attend due to a regimen of shots (which had to be refrigerated) that I had scheduled to take over the next two weeks when I would be home. Also, I had a conflict with a globe being dedicated at the Global Village site. So, it was arranged for me to be there by way of a phone conference. Linda and I thought the matter was over because I thoroughly answered every question.*

*After that, I found out there were other secret meetings going on. Then, much to my dismay, a special meeting of IBOD was called in NYC for April 29. Linda and I were already scheduled to be in NYC for other appointments for three days. My lawyer, Ken Henson, Jr., joined us for the meeting with IBOD on the 29th. Some of you were present by way of conference call, but I understand you could not hear clearly all of what was said in the room. Ken and I spoke about an hour at the beginning and then were dismissed with the understanding that Linda would be allowed to speak later when she arrived following an appointment. Linda arrived at noon and waited for three hours, but was never called. Finally, Ken Henson, Linda, and I were called to meet with Rey Ramsey, Ron Terwilliger, and Janet Huckabee in a private room of the hotel. I was presented with a memo that had been prepared three days previously, dated April 26, and not a word had been changed. I felt like I was being dismissed and was very angry that a special meeting had been called at a huge expense to HFHI and that all they did was rubber stamp what had already been decided and written up by Executive Committee without one word being changed, including the date!*

*I went back to Americus to start trying to find out about my accuser since the chair and others on Executive Committee had refused repeatedly to furnish me with the same ninety-page report and other documents that had been given to other IBOD members. I talked to several people in a very discreet way. Immediately, Rey Ramsey banned me from coming to my office. That raised a lot of questions and made Linda and my staff very distressed that the chair would do such a thing. Word started spreading throughout HFHI senior leadership and other employees as well as around town. I started getting calls and e-mails from HFH affiliates, Europe, and other parts of the world. Then, it started filtering out to the press.*

*I don't think it is in the best interest of HFHI to ban employees from the office. In 1966, Linda and I visited Chief Albert Lithuli, who was banned and under house arrest in South Africa for his outspokenness regarding the evils of the apartheid system of government. Let us at HFHI deal with people in a civilized and a Christian manner. I honored being banned from the office even though I didn't agree with it.*

*I want to pass around something I want us to read. It's a letter from Griffin Bell, Jr. His father, Griffin Bell, Sr., was Attorney General under President Carter. Griffin Bell, Jr., was at the mediation with Jimmy Carter. At my request, he wrote this letter. Mr. Bell is a dedicated Christian, a Sunday school teacher, and I want to read the letter with you.*

*As you can see, the New York City law firm gave a different opinion from Griffin Bell.*

*I pleaded with the chairman to use biblical procedures on this matter. I think when something starts wrong, it can never end up right. We are all "victims" in this matter, board members as well as me. We got off on the wrong foot from the very beginning.*

*If you think I have been negligent in sexual harassment training, you need to know that several years ago IBOD decided that managing HFHI wasn't the best use of my time. Rey Ramsey himself led the effort to appoint a COO, and he agreed it should be David Williams. At the board's request, I was happy to turn a lot of responsibility over to David. I agreed with the board's action that it was best for me to step down from day-to-day management and be on the road and raise money and support. It's true that I haven't been involved in sexual harassment training because that wasn't for me to decide. If the COO and HR Director found it was needed, I would have supported it, but this never came up because it hasn't been a problem that I am aware of.*

*At mediation, Jimmy Carter was told by Rey Ramsey and others with him that I have faults as a leader. Our group asked for specifics of how I failed as a leader, and President Carter told us that he promised Rey's group that he wouldn't tell, and I still haven't been told by Rey or anyone else. I ask you, is that fair? Why am I a poor leader?*

*I feel a passion for this ministry. I push, but I think that is why we are an outstanding housing ministry rather than a mediocre one. In all humility, I want to remind you of the following:*

- *I led the charge to raise the money to build the new Rylander headquarters,*

- *Came up with the idea of Sumter County Initiative that has now blossomed into the 21st Century Challenge,*

- *Initiated Habitat University,*

- *Set the goal and raised millions for More Than Houses $500 million/5-year capital campaign,*

- *Set the goal to build the 200,000th Habitat house for the millionth person,*

- *Came up with the next goal of the Quantum Leap,*

- *And, of course, one of our best advocacy and fundraising tools for the future, the Global Village and Discovery Center.*

*Most all of the above items have been opposed at the beginning but now much accepted and even praised by IBOD.*

*HFHI needs a leader. We may need more managers. However, if IBOD replaces me with a manager, HFH will just become a bureaucratic housing "business" and cease to be a cutting-edge ministry.*

*Now, having said that . . . I want to talk about the agreement I was asked to sign and did sign. If you have read it, you can readily see that this legal document is based on fear. It makes it sound as though I am the enemy of HFHI, that Millard Fuller is a potentially dangerous character and Habitat needs to be protected from me.*

*Here is what I find about the agreement to be onerous:*

*A Managing Director must be hired to keep Millard from taking some "stupid" action or making some unwise decision. I think this is an insult to David Williams. I would hate to see D. Williams hurt in this process. D.W. isn't perfect, but by the fruits you will know them. There is no organization that has grown as fast and has the reputation that HFH has. You have absolute power to fire me. HFHI is more than IBOD. If some action is taken by this board that is not*

*pleasing to our affiliates in Africa, Asia, U.S., donors, etc.,*
*there will be major consequences.*

*I have trouble saying things that are untrue. If a reporter*
*asks if I voluntarily retired, I would have to say no. What I*
*would really like to do is . . . I have given my life for this*
*ministry for years. I want to humbly ask if I can stay the*
*leader of HFHI until after the 200,000th house. I want to*
*announce my retirement on my seventieth birthday, January*
*3, 2005, or even later this year. If you will allow this, then I*
*can feel good about it, and it will be a win-win instead of a*
*lose-lose. I want to continue working with Dave Williams*
*and Tony DiSpigno. I want to leave HFHI strong with me*
*feeling good about it and you feeling good about it. Nobody*
*likes to be forced. I'm pleading for mercy. I'm a supplicant*
*for favor. I'm at your mercy.*

*Regarding the provision for secrecy in the agreement, I'm*
*a talker, and I can't keep secrets. I don't deal with secrecy*
*very well. And all of you need to be able to talk without feel-*
*ing you have to keep secrets. I want to do everything in my*
*power to help this ministry. I will not harm anyone around*
*this table or harm HFH in any way.*

## From Don Moseley

Sent to full IBOD, Jimmy Carter, Paul Leonard, and Regina
Hopkins at 10:42 PM Monday night, July 26, 2004, under the title
"Very Good News":

Dear Habitat IBOD members,

At his own initiative, Millard Fuller took a lie detector
test this morning in Atlanta. The test was administered by
Cy Hardin, a man who has been giving such tests for over
25 years. Mr. Hardin was highly recommended by
Attorney Griffin Bell, Jr., himself an expert in employment

and harassment matters. A confidential report will be available soon to IBOD members upon request, including all the questions asked and Millard's answers.

The test results on every question indicate that Millard has been telling us the truth. I believe the implications of this new evidence are enormous and should be regarded as very good news for all of us in Habitat. After all, how could anyone prefer that Millard be found guilty of the charges that he acted inappropriately toward an employee?

We are all aware that lie detector tests are not absolutely foolproof. However, they are reliable enough as indicators that thousands are administered each year. It is significant that Millard himself has insisted from the beginning that he would be glad to submit himself to such a test. He would have been foolish even to suggest that if he had been guilty of the accusations made against him.

Every fair person on the IBOD—and I hope that is every last one of us—must admit that this changes the balance of things as they have been developing over the past several months. What may have appeared as obstinacy and "incredible negotiation skills" for the past four months now can be better understood as Millard's justifiable (sometimes almost desperate) attempt to defend a lifetime of Christian service and to help set the stage for a graceful transition to new Habitat leadership, rather than being terminated under a cloud while thousands of people speculate about what he might have done. No, he hasn't always been calm and diplomatic in the process, but under the circumstances . . .

It remains true that we cannot know with absolute certainty what happened in that car in February last year. But we have reached a point where the burden of proof that Millard committed some reprehensible act that day, lies overwhelmingly on the other side.

We have reached the point where Millard and Linda need and deserve some individual communications of love and support. Given the lack of clear personal mes-

sages, they have had reason to believe that almost everyone on the IBOD thinks Millard was, in fact, guilty
of some kind of serious misbehavior in that car early last
year. That has been a crushing blow to their spirits.

We have reached the point where we need to take
positive steps to help Millard Fuller, Paul Leonard, and
the other senior staff restore the morale of the Habitat
family and prepare the way for a good transition in due
time to a new CEO. (One of the most constructive steps
we could take in that regard is to agree to honor
Millard's lifetime goal of leading this organization a few
more months to the 200,000th house. I think we should
have the humility to reconsider that matter and to come
to NYC in November ready to make it official.)

We have reached the point when reasonable people
should ask us (as many already are!) what terrible thing
could have happened that justifies undermining
Millard's ability to continue for a few more months as
an inspiring leader and effective fundraiser. (Two examples of such leadership, among hundreds that could be
given: Millard spoke to a thousand people at the
Presbyterian General Assembly in Virginia four weeks
ago. They gave him a standing ovation when he was
introduced and another when he finished speaking.
Then he spoke yesterday to a thousand Methodists at
their Lake Junaluska Conference Center in North
Carolina. Again, the response was enthusiastic. The
Presbyterians and the Methodists are among our most
generous supporters. Would they continue to be so supportive if we were to proceed as though he was guilty
and they learned the truth about it?) We are running a
great risk—for what purpose?

Finally, I think we have reached the point where we
should be asking ourselves, "If this is not about an incident of serious sexual harassment—which seems less and
less likely to have happened at all—then what is it
about?" If we set aside the alleged harassment issue for a

minute, is there some other problem so important that
Millard should, for instance, be forced to resign in January
rather than November of 2005? If so, I, as one responsible
member of this IBOD and a person concerned about justice and basic honesty, must have a clear explanation.
What is it, and why is it so serious that we would put the
whole Habitat family through this ordeal?

If I am the only person on the IBOD with these questions, I need to hear that from all of you too. Fear con-
trols all of us to some extent (and I believe that is one
reason we may rush to the hired protection of lawyers
prematurely); I admit that I am concerned about being
regarded as a confused jerk by a group of outstanding
people like all of you. But I have prayed and struggled
with this thing many hours, trying to understand what I
should do as a follower of Jesus Christ. I cannot be a
silent participant in something that seems not only unjust
but very foolish in pragmatic terms because of the likelihood of an angry reaction from many Habitat supporters
and co-workers. I believe it is time to reaffirm Millard
and Linda unequivocally for a final year of joyful service
through Habitat. If the "emperor is naked," perhaps one
of us has to risk being foolish by calling attention to that
fact. On the other hand, if I am missing some key point
in this—perhaps blinded by my long friendship with
Millard and Linda and the fact that I have invested much
of my adult life in Habitat's work—then I need to hear
your wisdom. If we cannot have an open dialogue about
this within the circle of this IBOD, then my greater fear is
for the future of Habitat for Humanity International.

Don

P.S. I am also sending this letter to President Carter, to
Paul Leonard, and to Regina Hopkins, each of whom has
played a key role and/or has ongoing responsibilities to
help us resolve this matter quickly and fairly.

Dec. 5, 2004

by Allen G. Breed Associated Press Writer

AMERICUS, Ga. (AP)—In a characteristic act of frugality, Habitat for Humanity founder Millard Fuller hitched a ride to the Atlanta airport with a female staff member to save the organization a $75 shuttle ride.

That ride ended up costing him—and Habitat—a great deal more.

Allegations of "inappropriate conduct" during that drive last year led to Fuller's temporary banishment from the headquarters of the Christian home-building organization he and his wife, Linda, founded 28 years ago. Fuller says the board of directors was on the verge of firing him before he asked former President Jimmy Carter, Habitat's most visible volunteer, to intervene.

While the board eventually found there was "insufficient evidence" to substantiate the charges, Fuller says he agreed to step aside as chief executive officer to avoid an "unseemly" internal battle. In a compromise, he retained the largely ceremonial title of "founder and president."

With his 70th birthday approaching in January, Fuller knew the time was coming when he would have to make way for new leadership.

But Linda Fuller worries that the attempt to oust her husband is a symptom of a "culture change" in Habitat from a hopeful religious mission to a bottom-line bureaucracy.

On a recent fall morning in Americus, Millard Fuller strolls down Church Street dressed in his trademark plaid shirt. The trip takes ages, because every few feet, he stoops to pick up litter.

"I can't stand trash," he says, bending his 6-foot-4 body to scoop up a crushed soda can. "I'll tell you a little secret. There's a connection between trash and poverty housing . . . Poverty housing is just an extension of a mentality that will allow trash on a street."

Picking up trash is just an extension of Fuller's brand of "practical Christianity"—teaching by example.

The son of a widower farmer in the cotton-mill town of Lanett, Ala., Fuller earned his first profit at age 6 by selling a pig he'd raised. While studying law at the University of Alabama, he married Linda and formed a direct-marketing company with a classmate that made them millionaires before they were 30.

But when Fuller's capitalist drive threatened to kill their marriage, the couple decided to sell everything and devote themselves to the Christian values they grew up with. Their search for a mission led them to Koinonia, an interracial agricultural collective outside the southwest Georgia cotton and peanut center of Americus. It was there that the Fullers and others developed the concept of no-interest housing—and of having the poor invest "sweat equity" into building their own homes—that would eventually become Habitat for Humanity International.

Since 1976, Habitat has blossomed into a worldwide network of 3,300 affiliates that have built 175,000 houses in 100 countries. Preaching the "theology of the hammer," Fuller has built an army of tens of thousands of volunteers that includes former U.S. presidents, Hollywood celebrities and Fortune 500 CEOs.

Along the way, the founder has clashed with his board over the pace of the mission's worldwide growth and his decision to build a "global village" attraction in Americus with a mock Third World slum and examples of Habitat houses.

Such conflicts usually ended with Fuller getting his way and remaining firmly in control. Not this time.

Earlier this year, the Fullers were traveling in Hong Kong when he got a call from board Chairman Rey Ramsey. He told Fuller that a 15-year Habitat employee had accused him of inappropriate behavior during a drive to the Atlanta airport 13 months earlier. Habitat would not divulge details of the allegations, but Fuller told The Associated Press recently that ████████ accused him of touching her on the neck, shoulder and thigh, and of telling her she had "smooth skin."

Habitat hired a New York law firm to look into the allegations and ordered Fuller to stay away from the office until the investigation was completed.

"I said, 'Just wait until we get home and come down to the office, and you and me and the woman will sit down and . . . it'll be settled in 15 minutes,'" Fuller recalls.

But this was not the first time Fuller had been accused of being too familiar with female staff.

In 1990, several women at the headquarters accused the founder of sexual harassment—a kiss on the cheek, a hug, a compliment about pretty blue eyes. Fuller was prepared to step down until Carter threatened to withdraw his support from Habitat.

Fuller says he grew up in a touchy-feely country culture and freely admits he did those things.

"There was a dispute on interpreting the facts," he says of the earlier case. But this time, "there's not even the TINIEST element of truth in it."

"One of the Ten Commandments is, 'Thou shalt not bear false witness,'" Fuller says. "This is false witness."

████, the 35-year-old wife of a minister, has since left Habitat. Reached at her home in ████████ ████, she declined to comment, citing a legal agreement to remain silent. "There's a lot of information that needs to come forward," she says, "but I can't be the one who can do it."

Asked if Fuller's characterization of the allegations was accurate, Ramsey would say only that it was "in the ballpark."

Mrs. Fuller says the board was "that close to firing Millard" in April before Carter, the couple's longtime friend, came in to mediate. Carter declined to comment on his role. The Fullers signed an agreement to exchange their silence on the matter for their salaries for life. But Mrs. Fuller found the terms unbearable.

"I was very close friends with a lot of the people who worked at Habitat, and it was just tearing me up to be near them and not being able to talk to them or say anything about it," she says, her blue eyes misting with tears.

In August, Habitat announced that a search committee was being formed to look for a successor to Fuller. In early October, the Fullers backed out of their silence agreement and were preparing a mass mailing to affiliates about the situation when Ramsey asked for a meeting.

After the three-hour talk, which Ramsey described as powerful and prayerful, he released a statement saying: "Millard decided to relinquish the position of CEO and the board is accepting his decision."

Although Fuller says there was "some element of thrust" in his decision to step aside, he concedes the change "could be actually a good thing."

Linda Fuller, who doesn't believe [the] allegations, is less conciliatory. "They had an agenda," she says.

In the end, Fuller says he and the board were having trouble overcoming certain "philosophical differences." Sipping sweet tea in the grand dining room of a 19th century hotel across from the headquarters, Fuller says the biggest difference is that many on the board want Habitat to "put the brakes on."

"I'm an expansionist . . . and I don't want to slow down," he says. "We're only in half the countries on Earth. I want to go into the other half."

Newly named interim CEO Paul Leonard—a Presbyterian minister and former executive with housing giant Centex—says it's more complex than that. He says the board was simply trying to more efficiently manage Habitat's explosive growth.

"Millard often refers to Habitat for Humanity as a movement," he says. "But if you've been around movements, they, by nature, are chaotic."

He suggests there are ways of streamlining the organization to build more houses for the money, and a financial review last year uncovered a "material weakness in our accounting." "It's not a huge thing," he says, but "we're being required by the outside world to be sure that we have our house totally in order."

Leonard says it takes more than just a charismatic leader to run an organization the size of Habitat.

"You have to have the enthusiasm that a Millard Fuller brings," he says. "But right alongside of it you have to be organizing and putting in place the people that you need to carry things forward."

It is that last part that most worries the Fullers.

One of Habitat's founding principles was that neither Fuller nor his staff would "get rich off the poor."

For years, the Fullers and their four children lived in a house with no air conditioning, and Linda Fuller made all the family's clothes. During the first 14 years of the ministry, Fuller's salary was just $15,000; his wife worked 10 years for free.

Today, his $79,000 salary is among the lowest of any nonprofit executive in the country. In a Nov. 5 letter to members of the search committee, of which Carter is honorary chairman, Fuller expressed his concerns that the board would hire a high-paid bean counter instead of someone with a "strong Christian commitment."

"The danger, I fear, is that Habitat for Humanity will become a bureaucracy," he wrote. "If we lose the 'movement mentality' we will not go out of existence, but we will stagnate and become just another nonprofit doing good work across the country and around the world."

Walking through the headquarters, Fuller receives warm greetings from some, stony silence from others. He walks tall, regardless.

As long as he is able, and the board allows it, Fuller intends to continue acting as an ambassador for Habitat. He hopes to be on hand next year when Habitat reaches one of its founding goals—housing its 1 millionth person.

In a nearby atrium of the headquarters lobby hangs a plaque with a quotation from 1 Corinthians 3:10.

"As a wise master builder I have laid a foundation . . ." it reads. Though not shown, the remainder of that verse is, "and another builds on it."

Fuller believes he and his wife helped lay a firm foundation. Now he must have faith in those who will build on it.

"I've always felt that this is God's work," he says. "And it's always been bigger than me, from day one."

From: Paul Ekelschot
To: IBOD Members
Sent: Thursday, August 12, 2004 5:57AM

Subject: RE: Don's letter and Regina's update

Dear fellow Board members,

Last week I sent you a message indicating my concerns with the ongoing situation. Since then I received a positive answer on my suggestions by three Board members, but no reaction on it by the Executive Committee. Instead I received a copy of the letter by Rey to Millard and an update by Regina about the events.

Concerning the update I have two comments. First (section C, subsequent events); we can continue to lament on how Millard Fuller is conducting himself, but did we really expect something different? Would anybody of us, who feels his lifework and reputation is threatened, act differently? I certainly would not.

Second, the extensive explanation of the legal position of a polygraph may be correct, but it is completely missing the point. As I suggested earlier, let us not try to lean on legal arguments alone as it does not bring us any further.

The text on the lie detector is completely missing the point because when this thing comes in the newspapers people will not say, "Board came to this decision because there were legal doubts about the value of a lie detection test" . . . No, they will say; "Board sacked Millard Fuller even after a lie detection test proved he was innocent . . ." Let us sit back for a moment, think about what we did and why, and admit that the Board's position is very weak.

Let us admit that, after hiring lawyers, consultants, and experts we did not advance an iota, and accept the fact that instead HFHI is moving in a dangerous direction.

I am afraid that Rey's letter of August 10 will not change anything. There is too much in it indicating what Millard must do and a repetition of earlier decisions. What is missing in it is a reference that maybe the EC and the Board were wrong in believing ▮▮▮▮▮▮▮ rather than Millard Fuller. We have a problem, we partially caused or increased it ourselves, we have to fix it. Now. What I am suggesting is that;

- we use the lie detector test as a vehicle to eat our hat.
- we apologize towards Millard and Linda, telling them that after he passed the lie detector test we are convinced that his interpretation of the events is the correct one and that we regret our earlier doubts. Our apology should not be in half but generous.
- we issue a public statement to staff and volunteers, indicating that we have been informed about certain

rumors relating to an incident between Millard
Fuller and a female staff member, that we extensively have investigated the rumors, and that we
strongly believe that those rumors are incorrect.
- we allow Millard to be CEO till the moment of the
200,000th house and define his responsibilities
towards Paul Leonard. Let us not be afraid about
losing face.

I strongly advise that we organize on short notice a
Board meeting to discuss this or any other suggestion that
takes HFHI from the dangerous path it is on today.

Greetings,
Paul Ekelschot


TO: The Habitat for Humanity International Board of
     Directors
FROM: Millard Fuller
DATE: October 4, 2004
SUBJECT: Revocation of Retirement Agreements

Today, Linda and I revoked the Retirement
Agreements that we signed on June 14, 2004.
As you know, neither of us has ever felt good about
those agreements. We only signed because of enormous
pressure put on us to do so and because we did not want
to do harm to the Habitat ministry.
As a matter of integrity, though, we have now revoked
the agreements. The two principal reasons for doing so are
1) the agreements are based on the lie that I did something
improper on a trip to Atlanta on February 20, 2003, and 2)
the agreements are based on the lie that Linda and I are,
somehow, enemies of Habitat for Humanity and you, the
Board, must "protect" Habitat from us.

We felt that you were "buying us off" with a generous retirement plan. Again, as a matter of integrity, we cannot accept either the money or the agreement because both are motivated, not by appreciation, but by a desire to silence us. Linda and I have honestly tried to reconcile our consciences with the agreements so that we could avoid any more conflict with you. Also, we have deeply appreciated the great efforts made by President Carter and Don Mosley to resolve the dispute between us. Linda and I both have enormous respect for President Carter and for Don and, for that reason, we have diligently tried to come to peace with the agreements.

Unfortunately, we have no peace about the matter. We simply cannot live with ourselves while the onerous agreements remain in effect. Furthermore, your lawyers and the board chairman have been complaining, on a regular basis, about us violating the agreements. And, as you know, we have been complaining about you violating the agreement by secretly arranging for Paul Leonard to come to Americus with the mandate from HFHI BOD to "take over." All such complaining can now cease with the agreements revoked.

My hope is that reason will somehow come to the fore in light of this new situation and that a representative group from the board can meet with Linda and me and work out a good solution to this sad episode. Linda and I are not unreasonable. We want what is best for this God-ordained work. I plead with you, again on bended knee, as I did in Mexico City in June, to listen to us and listen to God and to our beloved partners in this ministry around the world. If we will humble ourselves before God and each other, we can solve this impasse.

There is a proverb from Africa which states, "When the elephants fight, it is the grass that gets trampled." We need to quit fighting and start reasoning together so that this ministry does not suffer.

Can we reason together? Think about it. Please put

away pride and animosity. Linda and I are not your enemies and we are not the enemy of Habitat for Humanity.

What is the real reason for wanting me out of leadership of this ministry? I think you know in your hearts that
I am not guilty of wrongdoing. The chairman and his delegation admitted that in the session with President Carter
on August 23 and so did the full board on the following
day. President Carter said you had no proof of my guilt.
Your lawyers changed it to "insufficient proof." In any
event, that issue now seems to be behind us. So, what is
it? I believe I deserve an answer. And, you owe an
answer to the whole Habitat family around the world.

You have said that I am a poor leader. By what defini-
tion? What has been accomplished under my leadership?
Have the results been good or bad? Was the Habitat ministry in disarray when this matter erupted in March? You
know that Habitat is in good shape. We are raising
money in line with projections. We are on target with
our goals, both in raising money and in house building.
Paul Leonard was not needed at headquarters. He is a
fine man, but he is not needed. David Williams is doing
a good job as chief operating officer.

The chairman and executive committee acted precipi-
tously and unwisely based on an assumption about a
false accusation. The result is the huge mess we now find
ourselves in.

Five years ago, you asked me to give up day-to-day
management. I gladly agreed to do so believing, as you
did, that it would be a better use of my time and talents to
call on donors, fulfill speaking engagements, write books
and, in other ways, promote and expand the Habitat ministry. I have done that to the best of my ability.

Just since this controversy started in March 2004, I
have raised $1.5 million from three people, plus a lot
more in smaller sums. This past week, I traveled and
spoke seventeen times in four states to groups representing thirty-six affiliates and totaling about five thousand

people. This is my life's work. It has always been my dedicated determination to do everything I could to promote and advance the ministry. Even so, I am not the most important issue. God called Linda and me to this mission and God has likewise called thousands of others to it. God is at the center of both the work and of this issue. And, all of the people in the Habitat ministry, especially at the affiliate level, are so vitally important.

You, as international board members, are very important but you are not the sum total of this ministry. There are more than 30,000 other board members of local Habitat affiliates. What do they think? How will they respond to your actions? You need to think about that.

I am willing, as I have said all along, to step down from leadership and to assume another role in the Habitat ministry, but I don't think it is right for you to force me out for false reasons. And, I don't think it is in the best interest of anyone for me to be pushed out in a way that leaves a bitter taste in my mouth and which raises suspicion and animosity in the hearts and minds of Habitat people around the world.

I certainly don't want to demean or insult you in any way. So, please, I implore you, let us reason together so we can stop this senseless battle.

I urge you to pray earnestly and to think for yourself—each one of you. It appears to me that there has been too much of a "group think" going on. Ask God to guide you. I do earnestly pray for you as I pray for Linda and me. I ask you to also pray for Linda and me and for the whole Habitat ministry.

We are at a crucial juncture. Will truth, love, and light be the guide or will we succumb to more lies, fear, and darkness?

God help us all and have mercy on us.

Sincerely,

Millard D. Fuller

## From the *NonProfit Times*
January 1, 2005
*Fuller Forced Out at Habitat for Humanity*
*By Jeff Jones*

Staff allegations, dispute with board are cited as reasons

Last fall, Millard Fuller, founder and president of Habitat for Humanity International, said he had no plans to resign as leader of the international movement he started.

Roughly one year later Fuller has been forced out of his job by the board of directors of the Christian home-building ministry. The announcement that Fuller was stepping down came near the end of a tumultuous year for Fuller and the Americus, Ga.-based organization that he co-founded in 1976 with his wife, Linda.

The year included allegations against Fuller by a female employee of inappropriate behavior and a struggle concerning the organization's future.

The shakeout, now apparently complete, could affect Habitat for years. It is developing a five-year strategic plan that will likely call for an acceleration of home building and increase of operating reserves, officials said.

Habitat created a search committee to find Fuller's replacement, comprised of current and former board members, representatives of Habitat affiliates, and honorary chair, former President Jimmy Carter.

Habitat Board Chairman Rey Ramsey and Fuller said the right things about reaching agreement and were scheduled to appear at an awards ceremony together as this article went to press.

But, getting to this point hasn't been easy. This past March, Fuller learned from Ramsey that a woman had accused him of touching her neck, shoulder and thigh, and "saying some words she didn't like" during a ride to the Atlanta airport in February 2003, according to Fuller. Others told Fuller the woman had accused him of saying the word "adultery, which she considers a curse word," and telling her she had "smooth skin," Fuller said.

Fuller often travels to and from airports by catching rides with Habitat employees or friends to save money.

Reached by *The NonProfit Times*, the alleged victim declined to comment, adding she was not making comments "yet." As a policy, *The NonProfit Times* does not identify persons who allege inappropriate, sexually based incidents. The woman had been with Habitat for "14 or 15" years and left in June 2004, according to Ramsey.

Fuller, who faced sexual harassment allegations by several women in 1990, which were settled internally, denied anything happened in this allegation.

"It was a totally non-event trip," Fuller said. "Even if that had happened, while it's not good conduct, it's not egregious, criminal activity."

Fuller has said in previous interviews with *The NonProfit Times* that he comes from a family of "huggers" and "very affectionate people."

"I used to go to family reunions and my daddy would go around kissing all the women," Fuller said in 2003, while talking about the sexual harassment allegations of more than a decade ago.

He said he was "blown away" then by the fact that the women were offended by him giving them hugs or telling one she had beautiful eyes.

"What I learned out of that was that I have to be very, very careful about relationships especially with people of the other sex," Fuller said.

A source familiar with Habitat said, "A lot of people are un-surprised by the (latest) allegations."

The allegations surfaced "almost by accident" when the alleged victim talked to someone in personnel in early 2004 and mentioned that the alleged incident had something to do with her leaving, Ramsey said. At that point, calls were made to the organization's general counsel and then Ramsey. The board hired a New York law firm to independently investigate the incident. Fuller said that he voiced disagreement with that move.

Fuller said he initially suggested that he meet with the woman and Ramsey to talk about the incident, and that he would take a lie detector test, if necessary. Ramsey, a former practicing attorney, said he and board officers decided that the law required that they not self-investigate.

"I stand by the process" of the investigation, Ramsey said. "It's a very standard and accepted practice what we did."

The board initially found he was guilty in April, Fuller said, and then former President Carter got involved. The board members reversed themselves and said they found "insufficient proof" regarding the allegations, according to Fuller.

Ramsey said the board made findings and compromised on some of the language to reach an agreement. He stressed that the board didn't publish the results of the findings and that President Carter's role has been misrepresented.

"He wasn't brought in to beat the board down," Ramsey said. "The first person who spoke to President Carter was me. I asked him to get involved. He willingly got involved" and agreed to play a mediation role.

Deanna Congileo, Carter's press secretary, declined to go into details. "President Carter continues to support the mission and fine work of Habitat for Humanity," Congileo wrote in an e-mail to *The NonProfit Times*.

Regardless, Fuller and his wife "reluctantly" signed an agreement, giving them salaries for life in exchange for their silence on the issue, Fuller said. Fuller earned a base salary of $79,500, according to Habitat's latest available Form 990.

"There's nothing more unseemly than an internal fight in a nonprofit," Fuller said. "We were trying to avoid that."

The Fullers changed their minds and decided to void the agreement Oct. 4 and exercised a revocation provision, according to Fuller.

"My wife was just totally upset about it because it felt like they were trying to buy our silence," Fuller said. "I believe in openness. Everything was a secret. I didn't like it, and my wife didn't like it."

Fuller and Ramsey reached a second agreement Oct. 7. It was a handshake understanding reached after a three-hour talk, according to both men.

**Philosophy Differences**

The allegations were only one part of a year of discord within Habitat.

Fuller and board members engaged in a struggle over the organization's operating philosophy and future. Fuller expressed hope that the organization would continue to expand worldwide, keep its Christian focus, and pay a new CEO modestly.

"Some on the board think we're going too fast and they want to slow down," Fuller said. "That is contrary to the way I've always operated . . . I have faced this problem from the beginning of this work, of people always hanging on my coattails trying to hold me back."

Ramsey acknowledged there had been disagreements "on the approach to different things but not on the what" of building many houses at a fast rate.

He balked at the idea of a power struggle, pointing out that all the board members are volunteers.

Ramsey added that the organization is developing a five-year strategy that will likely call for building more homes during this five-year period than the previous plan.

The previous plan had a goal of building Habitat's 200,000th house, which is scheduled to happen this year (2005), Interim CEO Paul Leonard said.

The plan required Habitat to build an additional 100,000 homes between 2000-2005 and raise an additional $500 million through a capital campaign, on top of the $2.5 billion from affiliates, normal direct mail fundraising, and work with corporations, according to Leonard. The campaign total is now roughly $415 million, Leonard said.

"I would expect the new strategic plan to have another capital campaign," Leonard said.

Habitat will also work to increase its reserves in the coming years. "The goal is to have a reserve that is three times the average monthly unrestricted cash income" by 2018, he said. That equates to roughly $21 million, using fiscal 2003 numbers as a reference. Habitat is putting aside 2 percent of the unrestricted income until it meets that goal, he said.

As for the concerns about remaining Christian-focused, Ramsey said "that's something we all value." The Christian witness part of the job was stressed at the first meeting of the succession task force, according to Ramsey.

Leonard is scheduled to stay through June 2006. He moved from his home in Davidson, N.C., along with his wife, to become managing director of Habitat in June, and eventually interim CEO. Ramsey just completed an eventful first year as board chairman and sees himself as a "bridge" to the transition and the next strategic plan.

Leonard said he sees his role as improving teamwork at headquarters, holding employees accountable through performance evaluations, strengthening financial and information systems, and playing a significant role in the strategic plan.

"I see us making more of an effort to partner with other groups that can support not only housing but a sustainable community," Leonard said. For instance, Habitat would focus on housing, and work with other nonprofit organizations that specialize in micro-loans or clean water, he said.

Fuller will remain an employee of Habitat and will draw a salary as long as he continues as founder/president. "I am not bent out of shape about how things have turned out," Fuller said. He added that although the process has been convoluted, the point that has been reached "is not all bad."

"Any organization that moves from a founder to the next stage, you encounter some bumpy roads," Ramsey said. "What I feel good about now is that we are united in moving the organization forward."

Sent: Tuesday, March 15, 2005 8:09 AM
From: Don Mosley
Tue, 15 Mar 2005 10:23:47

Re: Resignation

Resignation from the Habitat International Board of Directors—Don Mosley—March 15, 2005

Four days ago I resigned from the Habitat IBOD. I did that at the end of the most frustrating and stressful year I have ever experienced. I also took this step because I am determined to focus my attention again on the exciting work of building homes for "God's people in need" around the world and (for me, at least) the even more exciting by-product of that work—the enhancement of understanding and goodwill across all kinds of barriers separating people. This has been at the center of my own faith and actions for many years, even before I moved to Georgia and helped Millard and Linda Fuller start Habitat for Humanity in the 1970s.

I believe Millard was wrongfully accused a year ago of sexual harassment. This very serious charge launched the conflict that has led to both Millard and Linda's being fired by the IBOD. Millard denied the charge vehemently. Because of my long association with Habitat, I was contacted by at least a dozen Habitat staff people (mostly women) who also felt that he had been falsely accused. In July Millard voluntarily took a polygraph test under the supervision of experts in such matters. The results strongly indicated that he was telling the truth. If the accuser ever took similar or equivalent steps, I would be open to a different conclusion. Polygraph tests are not perfect proof, as everyone agrees, but neither should they be summarily dismissed as insignificant. I argued repeatedly during those early months of the conflict that HFHI should show no less readiness to welcome evidence of Millard's innocence than of his guilt. At the very least, I felt we should say loudly and clearly that we had no firm proof either way. In August a declaration of "insufficient proof of inappropriate conduct" was the best the lawyers would allow—and even that weak statement was very close to being enough.

Unfortunately, Millard and Linda had already failed on several occasions to recognize efforts at reconciliation that I believe were being made by at least some leaders of the IBOD. As time passed, the tempers rose on both sides. With President Carter's help twice, we came very close to resolving the conflict. Then, during another six months of agonizing struggle, I believe we had a resolution of the conflict within reach several more times. I love Millard and Linda like my own brother and sister, but I have to say that the blame for the failure of those efforts must lie at least as much on them as on the IBOD.

We all have to share the blame. Even those many well-meaning friends of the Fullers who bombarded the IBOD with angry letters, frequently insisting that "Millard *is* Habitat!," had the reverse effect from what they intended. I know, because I received each of them. Some were sensitive and eloquent, but many of them did more to alienate and hurt good people than to persuade them.

When the Executive Committee fired Millard on January 31, I begin to reassess how I could best help with this ministry that I firmly believe is a great work of God around the world. God has obviously worked through Millard and Linda to establish it, more than through anyone else—but it is clearly God's ministry, not theirs or anyone else's. I continue to believe that we can all work together in it again, but only if we remember that central fact.

Rightly or wrongly, I have decided that I can do more off the IBOD than on it to promote this ministry. I did not attend the IBOD meeting in Cape Town. I appreciate those on the IBOD who are willing to continue the difficult duties it entails; this has never been simply a matter of "good people" versus "bad people." Nor is it a struggle about whether HFHI should continue to be a Christian ministry. There is a clear, strong consensus on the IBOD that this should be so.

I am already waking up in the morning excited again about getting out and *doing* the work of Habitat, for and among all kinds of people, all around the world—speaking, fundraising, pounding nails, helping Christian and Muslim neighbors dig foundations for each other, seeing young people on university campuses catch the vision, etc. Please don't ask me to comment any further on the past. I have spent enough time on that. I'm turning toward the future. —Don

King & Spalding—Atlanta
3ʳᵈ Quarter Newsletter
2005
"One of Firm's Best Pro Bono
Representations of the Year"

All of us are familiar with Habitat for Humanity International (HFHI) and the firm's long commitment to building Habitat homes. Perhaps not everyone is aware that a man named Millard Fuller of Americus, Georgia, founded Habitat in 1976. Or that the 70-year-old Fuller and his wife were dismissed by HFHI in January in a dispute involving allegations later thought by the board to be "unconvincing," fundamental differences over the direction of HFHI, and the official reason, "a pattern of ongoing public comments and communications that have been divisive and disruptive." Former President Jimmy Carter, Habitat's most famous volunteer, tried to intervene as a peacemaker but to no avail.

Many Habitat donors were outraged by the dismissal of Fuller and his wife and cut off their donations to HFHI. Fuller said he didn't want to see families in need of housing hurt by the controversy, so he came up with a new housing charity called Building Habitat, Inc. to support the work of local Habitat chapters and also to give disaffected donors a new venue for supporting HFHI's work.

HFHI's board filed suit in federal court asking that Fuller be ordered to drop the word "Habitat" from the name of his new charity on the grounds that it was a trademark infringement and would confuse people. Fuller stated that his intention was not to compete with HFHI but to be its partner by independently raising money for local Habitat chapters.

Fuller called Judge Bell to help with the suit HFHI had brought against him and the judge referred the matter to Ben Easterlin who took it as a pro bono case. Ben managed within two weeks to work out an agreement whereby the Fullers would change the name of their organization to "The Fuller Center for Housing" if HFHI would drop its suit. The case was dismissed and the Fullers moved ahead with their new venture; The Fuller Center for Housing dedicated its new headquarters on May 28.

Judge Bell said of Ben's successful efforts, "It was a masterful piece of negotiating and 'lawyering,' on Ben's part, and I think everyone in the firm should know about it."

Ben, himself a native of Americus, had this to say: "I have known Millard Fuller since the middle 70s when we were both practicing attorneys in Americus. We tried several cases against each other. Millard is an evangelist, and he would really preach to the jury. It was always important to not let the outcome of a trial depend on closing argument, as Millard was likely to get the jury to start giving him 'amens' during his portion. Many people in Americus were skeptical of Habitat when it first began in 1976 because of Millard's ties with Koinonia Farm, a Christian commune in the county that was widely considered at the time to be inhabited by communist sympathizers. However, it did not take long for the community to recognize the genius of the Habitat model and the benefit it brought to the underprivileged. Millard went from a pariah to a local hero in a very short time. I have always thought that one of his unrecognized accomplishments is that he almost single-handedly infused an entire community with a greater sense of charity and made it a better place to live not only for the underprivileged, but for everyone. Millard was able to raise Habitat to its present stature in part because he is a risk taker and an idealistic optimist. However, his personality clashed with the mind-set of a corporate structure, which is what HFHI has necessarily become as it has grown to its current size. So, conflict between Millard and the HFHI Board was inevitable and unavoidable. The true purpose of the suit filed by HFHI was to control Millard by limiting his fundraising efforts and his contacts with Habitat affiliates. Of course, HFHI cannot do that, and they had to admit as much in the end. Thus, we settled with Millard agreeing only that he would not use the word 'Habitat' in the name of his new organization. Hopefully, Millard and HFHI will eventually bury the hatchet and work together to pursue the Habitat goal of affordable housing for all."

We appreciate Judge Bell's suggesting this article about what he considers to be one of the firm's best pro bono representations of the year.

# From the *St. Petersburg Times*
A Beacon for Dark Times
By Philip Gailey
Published April 22, 2007

With all the madness in the world, from the Virginia Tech massacre to the carnage in Iraq, Millard Fuller's letter couldn't have come at a better time, a small light breaking through the darkness. He is a good man doing God's work, and he wanted to bring me up to date on what's going on at the Fuller Center for Housing, which he started after he was maligned, fired, and exiled by officials at Habitat for Humanity, the Christian housing ministry he co-founded and led for almost three decades.

Since its messy breakup with Fuller two years ago, Habitat has become more corporate. It moved its top executives from the small southwest Georgia town of Americus to Atlanta and increased their compensation (Fuller had insisted on modest salaries for Habitat leaders). Its new spiritual leader and most famous volunteer carpenter is former President Jimmy Carter, who once wrote that Fuller inspired him to pick up a hammer for Habitat but now rarely mentions his name when talking about the organization. Habitat, an international brand name, continues to raise big money and build small houses, even though it lost some longtime contributors who thought Fuller had been treated unjustly.

The Fuller Center for Housing is not as big or as well-known as Habitat, but it has allowed Fuller and his wife, Linda, to continue to build houses for low-income people in partnership with churches, businesses, and individuals. Fuller, who received the Presidential Medal of Freedom, America's highest civilian award, says his housing center should not be seen as a rival to Habitat but as a partner. Although he disagrees with the new direction of Habitat International, Fuller said he has been working with local Habitat affiliates around the country and speaking on their behalf.

In his latest book, *Building Materials for Life*, Fuller writes: "I pray for all of Habitat, and I hope that it continues to thrive and be a blessing to thousands more people in the years ahead. There is no shortage of need. We are not in competition with Habitat. The Fuller Center is an ally in the struggle to provide adequate housing for all who need it."

Since Katrina's devastating blow to New Orleans and the Mississippi Gulf Coast in 2005, the Fuller Center has been building houses for low-income families who lost their homes in the hurricane. In Shreveport, the center built ten houses in a one-week construction blitz. Last fall, the Bush-Clinton Katrina Fund gave the center a $100,000 grant to continue its housing project for storm victims who have relocated to Shreveport. The center also has housing projects in other areas of the United States and abroad, including El Salvador and Nigeria.

Perhaps the center's most ambitious undertaking so far is its plan to build 500 houses, a few at a time as donations allow, in the Chattahoochee Valley of Georgia and Alabama, an area where the textile industry has been devastated by globalization. The local Habitat affiliate in Americus, where the Fuller Center is headquartered, contributed $25,000 and dozens of volunteers to the Valley project. One of the towns where Fuller Center volunteers will be working to eliminate poverty housing is Lanett, Ala., Fuller's hometown.

After his banishment from Habitat, I worried that Fuller, who was seventy at the time, would let that unhappy experience end his housing ministry. Some of his friends urged him to "hang it up" and move on to the next chapter in his life.

"I couldn't do it," Fuller writes in his book. "By the Grace of God, I was in good health and high spirits. I loved what I had been doing; it was God's calling for me. I couldn't wait to get out of bed each morning. The job was not finished."

Today, Fuller is as busy as ever raising money and recruiting volunteers to translate Christian love for one another into decent housing. When a house is ready to be occupied, Fuller hands the new owners a Bible and tells them, "This house was built by God's love."

That is an inspiring sermon, words matched by deeds that make a difference in the lives of the poor.

# About the Author

Bettie B. Youngs, PhD, EdD, is the Pulitzer Prize– nominated author of thirty-four books translated into twenty-six languages. Dr. Youngs is a former Teacher-of-the-Year and a university professor of administration and management, graduate division. As president of Professional Development Services Inc., she is a consultant to business, industry, and education, and speaks to audiences around the world. She has frequently appeared on *The Good Morning Show, NBC Nightly News,* CNN, and Oprah. *USA Today, The Washington Post, Time Magazine, U.S. News & World Report, Redbook, Working Woman, Family Circle, Parents Magazine, Better Homes & Gardens,* and *Woman's Day* have all recognized her work. The author may be contacted through www.BettieYoungs.com

## A Partial Listing of Books by the Author

*Woman-to-Woman Wisdom: Inspiration for Real Life* (with Linda Fuller and Donna Schuller). Nashville, Tenn.: Thomas Nelson, 2005.

*Teaching Our Kids to Care: Nurturing Caring and Compassion* (with Joani Wafer, Joanne Wolf, PhD, and Dawn Lehman, PhD). Charlottesville, Va.: Hampton Roads Publishing, 2007.

*Oh, Baby! 7 Ways a Baby Will Change Your Life the First Year* (with Susan Heim and Jennifer Youngs). Charlottesville, Va.: Hampton Roads Publishing, 2006.

*Living the 10 Commandments in NEW Times.* Deerfield Beach, Fla.: Faith Communications, Inc., 2004.

*A Teen's Guide to Christian Living: Practical Answers to Tough Questions about God and Faith* (with Jennifer Youngs and Debbie Thurman). Deerfield Beach, Fla.: Faith Communications, Inc., 2003.

*12 Months of Faith: A Devotional Journal for Teens* (with Jennifer Youngs and Debbie Thurman). Deerfield Beach, Fla.: Faith Communications, Inc., 2003.

*Getting Back Together: Repairing the Love in Your Life* (with Masa Goetz, PhD). [Second Edition]. Avon, Mass.: Adams Media, 2006.

*The Moments and Milestones Pregnancy Journal: A Week-by-Week Companion* (with Jennifer Youngs). New York: American Management Association, 2007.

*Helping Your Child Succeed in School* (with Michael Popkin, PhD). Marietta, Ga.: Active Parenting, 2000.

*Gifts of the Heart: Stories That Celebrate Life's Defining Moments.* Deerfield Beach, Fla.: Health Communications, Inc., 1999.

*Taste-Berry Tales: Stories to Lift the Spirit, Fill the Heart and Feed the Soul.* Deerfield Beach, Fla.: Health Communications, Inc., 2000.

*Values from the Heartland.* Deerfield Beach, Fla.: Health Communications, Inc., 1998.

*Stress & Your Child: Helping Kids Cope with the Strains & Pressures of Life.* New York: Random House, 1998.

*How to Develop Self-Esteem in Your Child.* New York: McMillan/Random House, 1999.

*Safeguarding Your Teenager from the Dragons of Life: A Guide to the Adolescent Years.* Deerfield Beach, Fla.: Health Communications, Inc., 1998.

*A Teen's Guide to Living Drug-Free* (with Jennifer Youngs and Tina Moreno). Deerfield Beach, Fla.: Health Communications, Inc., 2003.

*Taste Berries for Teens: Inspirational Short Stories and Encouragement on Life, Love, Friendship and Tough Issues* (with Jennifer Youngs). Deerfield Beach, Fla.: Health Communications, Inc., 1999.

*More Taste Berries for Teens: A Second Collection of Short Stories and Encouragement on Life, Love, Friendship and Tough Issues* (with Jennifer Youngs). Deerfield Beach, Fla.: Health Communications, Inc., 2000.

*Taste Berries for Teens #3: Inspirational Short Stories on Life, Love, Friends and the Face in the Mirror* (with Jennifer Youngs). Deerfield Beach, Fla.: Health Communications, Inc., 2002.

*Taste Berries for Teens #4: Inspirational Short Stories on Being Cool, Caring and Courageous* (with Jennifer Youngs). Deerfield Beach, Fla.: Health Communications, Inc., 2004.

*A Taste-Berry Teen's Guide to Managing the Stress and Pressures of Life* (with Jennifer Youngs). Deerfield Beach, Fla.: Health Communications, Inc., 2001.

*A Taste-Berry Teen's Guide to Setting and Achieving Goals* (with Jennifer Youngs). Deerfield Beach, Fla.: Health Communications, Inc., 2002.

*Taste Berries for Teens Journal: My Thoughts on Life, Love and Making a Difference* (with Jennifer Youngs). Deerfield Beach, Fla.: Health Communications, Inc., 2000.

*365 Days of Taste-Berry Inspiration for Teens* (with Jennifer Youngs). Deerfield Beach, Fla.: Health Communications, Inc., 2003.

# More Praise . . .

When the news reverberated around the world that the beloved founders of Habitat for Humanity, Linda and Millard Fuller, had been ousted, people were in shock. How could this happen? What would become of their beloved organization—and the people who depended on it for an affordable housing opportunity? This book is a huge story about how the Fullers triumphed over the incredible injustice, and went on to create The Fuller Center for Housing as they continue their mission to eradicate poverty housing around the globe. This book is a page-turner from beginning to end.

—Deborah Bridges, Former Board Member,
Habitat for Humanity, Kansas City, MO

Through the course of American history, only a handful of private citizens have pioneered volunteer movements as profound as Habitat for Humanity. Millard Fuller has altered the lives of the million-plus family members he has housed and the millions of home-building volunteers he has inspired. But his impact also transcends that immediate circle. One of the remarkable things about Millard's legacy is the multiplier effect of his work. Reading Millard's story years ago made me realize that he and others like him deserve a place of honor alongside the politicians and generals who have long been memorialized in our nation's capital. This thought started me on a fourteen-year journey that ended when The Extra Mile Pathway national monument was dedicated in Washington, D.C., in 2005. Today, Millard and his wife Linda are among a select group of men and women immortalized there, a group that includes Martin Luther King, Jr., Helen Keller, and Clara Barton!

—John A. Johansen, Founder, The Extra Mile Pathway
national monument, Washington, DC

Most impressive is the foundation Ms. Youngs laid for this marvelous book. Meticulously researched, each fact carefully corroborated, her book is built upon the pure, unvarnished truth of an important story that has yet to be told—until now, and the world will be better for it. The Fullers' story reveals that a person of faith can remain true to himself, even when caught up in the world of corporate manipulation, when his house is cemented with the following wisdom: Keep your eyes on the mission God has given you, and He will see you through. The road will be hard. The end may be far different from what you ever envisioned, but it will be far more glorious.

—Stephen D. Coggins, Attorney,
Rountree, Losee & Baldwin, Wilmington, NC

Through a faithful friend, we asked Millard to spend three days with our Habitat affiliate in Oregon. That step motivated us to expand our annual fundraising weekend. Hundreds of people heard his clear, loving, and transformational vision. This book tells of very human lives; of everyday people who were led and inspired to build affordable housing for a million people; and of a man who is continuing to serve humanity with a singular purpose. Get into a good chair; your heart is about to be warmed, and your values about to be checked.

—Bill Gellatly, Former Executive Director,
Habitat for Humanity, Willamette West Affiliate, OR

This book is one incredible, incredible story! What makes Millard and Linda Fuller's story so special is their unwavering commitment, even through adversity, to people living in conditions beneath human dignity. They have provided a way for everyone to take meaningful action that benefits not only a single person or family but the whole community. Their efforts have forever changed the lives of millions—from a new homeowner moving into an affordable home, to the volunteer who leaves a worksite knowing she has made a tangible difference in the lives of real people. The Fullers are amazing, genuine people as this in-depth and most interesting account reveals.

—Stacey Odom-Driggers, Executive Director,
Flint River Habitat for Humanity, Albany, GA

Millard and Linda Fuller's calling to the ministry, which became Habitat for Humanity, has improved the quality of life for millions. The Fullers' vision is a true partnership, as this book chronicles, empowering those who are most in need. The Fullers modeled their ministry on Christ's servant-leadership, coming to serve, not to be served. It is this refreshing quality of partnering with those that God has called us to serve that has made Habitat for Humanity unique and outrageously successful. I can personally attest to this vestment of empowerment as I am a Habitat for Humanity homeowner who now has the privilege of giving back to my community through the housing ministry that Millard and Linda founded.

—Michelle Connor, Habitat Homeowner, Executive Director,
Almost Heaven Habitat for Humanity, WV

Millard Fuller is a living legend, and an embodiment of unremitting love, compassion, sacrifice, and charity, determined to serve mankind in both word and deed. Thousands of homeless families in my country have immensely benefited from his ministry of Habitat for Humanity. Now that he has founded The Fuller Center for Housing, I am sure millions around the world will be extricated from their substandard housing and provided with decent homes to live in. While I deem it my privilege to be associated with the Fullers and their noble mission, I am proud to call Linda and Millard Fuller the greatest philanthropists of our time!

—T. H. Lawrence, Recipient of HFHI Nehemiah Award, India

Millard and Linda's story is such an inspiration to us all. It is certainly a great example of unconditional love. You hear people talk about making a difference or changing the world all the time. However, there are very few of us who personally connect to those who have. This is a story of love, inspiration, and hope—it is a story of how two people have CHANGED the world—one house at a time. Just think about how many lives are going to be changed by the GIFT of this new book! The world needs more visionary leaders like the Fullers. May God continue to richly bless them.

—Jeff Cardwell, Founder, People Helping
People Network, Indianapolis, IN

As a Congressman, I can think of nothing more important than each citizen committing themselves to community service as volunteers. I admire and support the work and life achievement of Millard and Linda Fuller who reflect the essence of this commitment. The example that they have set for our future generations to follow is extraordinary. The Fullers are the American spirit at its greatest!

—Congressman Brian P. Bilbray,
50th Congressional District,
San Diego, CA

Genuine, faithful, inspiring, the salt of the earth—that's what Linda and Millard Fuller are. At Koinonia Farm, we call them friends. Once you read Bettie Youngs's book, you will feel as though you've always known the Fullers, too. Whether you are new to their story or have shared their path for years, read on and rejoice in their resiliency, courage, and faithfulness. The Fullers truly live the words of their mentor, Koinonia founder Clarence Jordan, who wrote: "The Scriptures should be taken out of the classroom and stained-glass sanctuary and put out under God's skies where people are toiling and crying and wondering, where the mighty events of the good news first happened, and where alone they feel at home."

— Bren Dubay, Director, Koinonia Farm, Americus, GA


Everyone needs to read this book! When I first heard Millard Fuller speak about the revolutionary concept of eliminating poverty housing from the face of the earth, I didn't pay him any attention and I didn't think anyone else would either! However, I soon realized that Habitat for Humanity was a movement of God's Spirit—a vision that everyone could wrap their brain and hands around. Now, young and old, black and white, rich and poor, the powerful and the powerless have banded together in this great work of building lives, homes, and communities. It is the perfect win/win scenario. Everyone is blessed, both the giver and the receiver. Linda and Millard have shown us how to really love our neighbor, and for that, we owe them our love, gratitude, and deepest respect.

— Michael K. Green, Executive Director,
Harbor Habitat for Humanity
(2005 Affiliate of the Year), Benton Harbor, MI


Some years back, I was sitting in an American airport lounge waiting for my flight back to Australia casually reading some magazines, pondering a problem I had in Australia. I had raised several million dollars and built accommodations for hundreds of homeless. Wesley Mission supported the work totally, but we were discouraged how those homeless treated our property. My staff and volunteers were becoming discouraged. I didn't know how to face our donors. Then I saw in the magazine an organization was doing exactly what I was doing. But they were successful because they allowed the people to help build their own places, taught them to budget, and then gave them ownership titles, so the people took pride in what they owned and cared for their own property. I immediately wrote to Millard and Linda to come to Australia. We set up a Habitat affiliate here which I chaired for the next ten years. We built houses, established affiliates throughout this nation, and built hundreds of houses in Papua New Guinea, Fiji, East Timor, and Australia. Anyone who reads this remarkable full account of their lives will be inspired by these two twentieth-century heroes!

—Reverend The Honorable Dr. Gordon Moyes,
State Senator, New South Wales, Australia,
former Superintendent of Wesley Mission, Sydney, Australia

Everyone who knows the Fullers is inspired by them! We each have a memory that is loving and lasting. I got to know them in 1995, when Millard and Linda joined our Wisdom Keepers Forum in Istanbul as part of the United Nations HABITAT conference. We were deeply moved at their story and commitment. When David and I got engaged just after the conference, we even asked Millard to marry us! This book is the extraordinary story of a couple—Linda and Millard Fuller—who, in their lives, lived on true Christian principles, have created a legacy of caring and love in action that has inspired millions. What a story! What a work of God!

—Nancy Rivard, Founder, Airline Ambassadors
International, Moss Beach, CA

This story is an insightful thirty-year history of Millard and Linda Fuller's extraordinary experiences in creating one of the most renowned humanitarian organizations in the world. Millard and Linda put their faith into action every day and with such great caring. This book isn't just a biography, it's a call to service!

—Christopher Crane, President and CEO,
Opportunity International, San Diego, CA

This is an extraordinary book about two unusually extraordinary people whom God has used in a unique way to make life better for thousands of families. Pensacola Habitat for Humanity has been blessed to have them visit and inspire us many times. Millard and Linda Fuller are one of the reasons our affiliate has been so successful, in the top ten affiliates, as to the number of new houses built among more than 1,700 affiliates in the United States.

—Betty Salter, Executive Director,
Habitat for Humanity, Pensacola, FL

Surely, there are few more effective examples of "love in action" than Millard and Linda Fuller. As you'll readily discern in this book, the Fullers have given their time, talent, and treasure for more than three decades to improve the quality of the lives of their fellow human beings around the world with something as basic as simple, decent, affordable housing. Their vision has inspired hundreds of thousands of us to care and to act on God's love to help change the social tide from oppression to empowerment. I am so grateful for the impact they have had on my life and on so many others.

—Ann M. Felton, CEO, Central Oklahoma
Habitat for Humanity, Inc.

"Fuller" has become a household name. This book takes us into the home of that household name, giving us never-before-told details about the love story behind Habitat for Humanity, an endlessly fascinating and extremely well-told account. Read it and celebrate the joy!

—Greg Hunt, Pastor of First Baptist Church, Shreveport
and Shreveport-Bossier Community Renewal Board member,
and Priscilla Hunt, Certified Specialist in Marriage Enrichment
with the Association for Couples in Marriage Enrichment (ACME)

This book sets the record straight on how Habitat for Humanity was founded and led for three decades by two remarkable people—Millard and Linda Fuller—who dared to dream big, to dream of eliminating substandard housing for people worldwide and who have made a remarkable difference for millions. This book will inspire anyone who reads it to follow their own inspired goals to make a difference in this world.

—Wanda Urbanska and Frank Levering,
Producers of the PBS series,
*Simple Living with Wanda Urbanska,* Mt. Airy, NC

As we sit in our comfortable, sturdy dwellings, it seems incomprehensible that many of the world's people are living in squalor. And yet, when Millard and Linda Fuller saw this firsthand, they made it their life's goal to eradicate poverty housing in every country of the world. And, for more than thirty years, they have made great strides in doing so through their creation of Habitat for Humanity and The Fuller Center for Housing. After reading their story, you'll never take your cozy home—or lifestyle—for granted again! A remarkable story, eloquently told. A must read!

—Sean Lambert, International Director, Mission Adventures;
President and CEO, Youth with a Mission, National City, CA

Bettie Youngs's book is a moving account of the blessings and costs of obedience to Christ's teachings for Millard and Linda Fuller—whom in this book you will come to honor. It is encouraging to read these stories and be reminded that in the face of triumph or trials, God is faithful and just.

—Kimberly L. Smith, Founder and Executive Director,
Make Way Partners, Birmingham, AL

I became friends with Linda and Millard when I was president of Huntingdon College in Montgomery, Alabama, Linda's alma mater. The Fullers are caring, decent, unassuming, hard-working people who have accomplished what all of us wish we could do: make a difference in this world. They have sacrificed, labored, and endured. I am so pleased that this remarkable book has been written about their noble lives!

—Wanda Bigham, Assistant General Secretary for Schools,
Colleges, and Universities at the United Methodist Church
Board of Higher Education and Ministry, Nashville, TN

Unlike most, the Fullers were able to take a crucial plunge of faith that set the ball of their existence rolling into an adventure that has spun off into a plethora of directions. The story of the Fullers continues to unwind through all those whose lives have been affected by their amazing ministry to the world. Thank goodness their lives have been set to words for all of history to enjoy.

—Sam Odia, The Fuller Center for Housing, Nigeria

As a new mother, I'm more conscious than ever of the need to make the world a better place for my child—and all the children of the world. That's why, when I hear that another family has been handed, atop the Holy Bible, the keys to a brand-new home—one they would never have been able to afford without Habitat for Humanity, and now, The Fuller Center for Housing—I am so moved by this demonstration of serving one another. I have been a volunteer on building a Habitat home, and members of my family have been on builds for The Fuller Center for Housing. I want to raise my daughter with the same courage and conviction that the Fullers have shown in making a difference in the world.

—Jennifer L. Youngs, Coauthor, *Oh, Baby! 7 Ways a Baby Will Change Your Life the First Year,* and the Taste Berries for Teens: Inspirational Stories and Encouragement on Life, Love and Friendships series, Del Mar, CA

Millard and Linda Fuller are true servant leaders and heroes for humanity. The great news of this most thorough and fascinating book about the history of Habitat for Humanity is that their torch remains bright as they continue to kindle the vision of providing decent homes for our world's families through The Fuller Center for Housing.

—Gary Cook, PhD, President, Dallas Baptist University, Waco, TX

I had the privilege of visiting poverty-stricken homes in rural Georgia with Millard Fuller in the late 1960s, a decade before Habitat for Humanity ever started. Millard and Linda come by their mission and their passion honestly. It has been a pleasure and privilege to know them and observe the blessings of their ministry. Enjoy this meticulous account of the incredible journey of these two remarkable people, their founding of Habitat for Humanity, and growing it into one of the most beloved nonprofits of our time.

—Art DeFehr, Human Rights Activist, Winnipeg, Canada; Former UN Refugee Official

The first time I met Millard was in Shreveport, Louisiana, after hurricane Katrina devastated the Gulf Coast. I listened to Millard sharing his vision to help rebuild those people's lives and homes that had lost everything. By the end of his speech Millard asked everyone to sing the hymn "Higher Ground" with him, twice. At that moment I leaned over to my wife and said, "This is one man I am willing to follow and I am not going to let him go." Since that day my life has been changed—not only because of what Millard Fuller does, but by the power of his example. In my book Millard and Linda are today's modern day disciples, storing their treasures in heaven. The Fullers are the most amazing people that I've ever met in my life—and millions of others in the world can say the same. This book shares the details of these destined lives.

—D. J. Bakken,
Founder of Hope Filled Hands,
Elk River, MN

Knowing Linda and Millard Fuller is loving them. They are examples of love in action. They have lived their lives following the greatest of the Commandments: to love God and others. They never fail to give God the credit for the success of their work. This book inspires and challenges us to think of others and to love enough to serve them.

—Deen Day Sanders, Chair,
Cecil B. Day Investment Company,
Norcross, GA

The Fullers are Heroes! The vision for Habitat for Humanity was a gift from God to Millard and Linda. Unjustly ousted from their beloved Habitat, Millard and Linda Fuller founded The Fuller Center for Housing and continue their commitment to end poverty housing worldwide. This book honors all of us who share their vision.

—Mary Erickson, Executive Director, Imagine LA, Los Angeles, CA

Millard Fuller is a man of great integrity and compassion. Having built houses for some one million people in 100 countries is truly love in action. His Christian service is an example worth emulating. This book will challenge you to open your heart and mind even wider to the great needs of our brothers and sisters in need of a decent place to live.

—Reverend Dr. R. B. Holmes, Jr., Pastor,
Bethel Missionary Baptist Church, Tallahassee, FL,
and President, National Baptist Congress
of Christian Education, NBCUSA, Inc.


Our Habitat affiliate invited Millard to be our speaker for one of our gala fundraising dinners soon after he was ousted by the board of Habitat International. He let it be known that he still wanted to spread the message of eliminating poverty housing and he would visit as many affiliates as would have him. Just before Millard was to come to Pennsylvania, the hurricane hit the Gulf Coast. He decided to come anyway. During his inspiring speech, he mentioned The Fuller Center's plans for Shreveport, Louisiana, and the "Building on Higher Ground" project. We knew Millard would be immensely grateful for any help we could give. Six weeks later, we were building the framing for two houses in the parking lot of our local mall, then packing it up for the trip to Shreveport. Six weeks after that, a large group of us went down and helped erect the first three houses of this new project. There, waiting for us, were Millard and Linda ready to cheer us on. Millard is an amazing thinker and planner, cheerleader and partner. I consider it a blessing to know and work with him and call him my friend.

—Chip Huston, Executive Director,
Habitat for Humanity of Chester County, PA


I had been with Habitat for about one year when the situation arose with Millard and Habitat's board. We had invited Millard to speak at our annual fundraising dinner, but the governing office of our local organization told us in no uncertain terms that we were not to have Millard as our speaker. When I invited Millard anyway, having another organization sponsor his trip,

I was fired from Habitat as the local project manager. Millard supported us when we felt we were in our darkest hours even though he had just been through his darkest hour as a leader. Millard is never but a phone call away with a genteel demeanor, and kind, uplifting words that carry you through the next weeks of your journey. . . . Even when it rains, Millard makes you want to run out and play in the puddles.

—Angela Koncz, CEO, Building Suffolk, Inc., Suffolk, VA

As an author of parenting books, I'm in the business of helping families lead better lives. Linda and Millard have profoundly changed the lives of families around the world, tending to their goal to ensure that children aren't caught up in the deadly cycle of poverty. This life-changing book will inspire you to consider what you, too, can do to improve your community.

—Susan M. Heim, Author, *It's Twins! Parent-to-Parent Advice from Infancy Through Adolescence*, Boca Raton, FL

People want to know how they can make a difference and this excellent book details the process for one couple who from a failing marriage created Habitat, and it is now the largest non-profit home builder in the world! If that isn't impressive, I don't know what is. But adding corporate moneymen on their board would do them in, and Millard would be removed from center stage, and his wife fired for good measure. But like the Phoenix rising from the ashes, they triumphed—now with an even greater mission to serve the poorest of the poor. This is truly an amazing story and not all of it is what most readers will be anticipating. . . . For all its ups and down, we come away knowing that we can begin again. And, we can choose to see each experience laid before us as an opportunity to be a blessing in the lives of one another.

—John St. Augustine, Radio Host, XM Satellite, *Oprah and Friends*, and Author, *Living an Uncommon Life: Essential Lessons from 21 Extraordinary People*, Chicago, IL

If you're still wondering if God works through people, you'll stop wondering after reading this beautiful, and startling, story.

Millard and Linda Fuller made unprecedented accomplishments in founding and building Habitat for Humanity International (HFHI) into one of the world's most successful and respected nonprofit organizations. For them, history is now repeating itself. In spite of their abrupt termination from HFHI, the Fullers never lost sight of their intense conviction that adequate housing for all is a matter of conscience—socially, politically, and religiously. Millard and Linda Fuller immediately started over by founding The Fuller Center for Housing to continue their vision of decent housing for all God's people. Their lives remind me daily that, through faith, all things are possible. That's why this book is a must read for all.

History will record Millard and Linda Fuller as among the handful of individuals who have successfully led a movement to transform the world for the better. I've been fortunate enough to be witness to their compassionate and inspiring lives and the way the lives of millions have been enriched through their vision. This historical book chronicles the Fullers' unbelievable journey from peaks to valleys and ultimately to the triumph only the most resilient of spirits can achieve.

In cataclysmic upheavals one often hears the term "unvarnished truth." In the aftermath of the Fullers' removal from Habitat for Humanity International, we in Americus, Georgia, heard a lot of "varnished" untruth—it was slick, it had a high gloss (media appeal), but it could not hide the real story. Bettie Youngs gets beneath the veneer in this outstanding book. The Fullers are dear friends and are going to continue to live out the vision that God gave them. The name of the organization and the address may have changed, but with God's help, the mission continues.

—Reverend James R. McIlrath, Senior Minister, First United
Methodist Church, Americus, GA; Board Chair of
New Horizons Habitat for Humanity (the home affiliate of HFHI);
and a personal partner with The Fuller Center for Housing

Millard and Linda have done so much to improve the lives of so many people. Their story is one that inspires all who know it. As a result, Dayton Ohio Habitat for Humanity formed the Millard Fuller Society to recognize his exemplary contributions to the affiliate—and to history.

—Ann Charles Watts, Executive Director,
Dayton Ohio Habitat for Humanity

This book sheds profound light on the Fullers' lives and their vision to raise the consciousness of the world. Bettie Youngs has captured their lives and tells the full story of the thirty-plus year journey of two people whom I am honored to call lifelong friends. This book is a testimony to the true faithfulness Millard and Linda Fuller have demonstrated by creating thousands of simple, decent homes across the world. This book will inspire you to put your faith into action . . . to build your own House on Love and Faith.

—Jim Killoran, Executive Director,
Habitat for Humanity of Westchester, NY

From a lonely moment when a TV movie spoke prophetically to the state of Millard's heart, to a heartbreaking moment seeing their marriage in jeopardy, to a moment of discovery when an afternoon visit brought them into the company of Clarence Jordan and Koinonia Farm, a holy spirit seemed at work to draw the Fullers into one of the great service ministries of the past century. Their story is an inspiration, and having Millard and Linda in our church for a week was one of the high points in my ministry. They have given us a blessing for years to come.

—The Reverend Dr. Randal B. Gardner,
Rector of St. James-by-the-Sea
Episcopal Church, La Jolla, CA

This book is a thorough account of Millard and Linda's remarkable journey, one that addresses the deep spiritual underpinnings of the early Habitat and of The Fuller Center and also provides an objective review of the Fullers' last days at Habitat. There are countless Fuller friends around the world who have had to rely on Habitat's accounting of these events and who will be grateful to have a complete understanding of something that has been so troubling and confusing to them.

—David Snell, VP, Programs,
The Fuller Center for Housing,
Colorado Springs, CO

"*My Father's house has many mansions*" and Linda and Millard have built many of them. It is impossible to quantify the impact that the energy of these two people has had on the homeowners and volunteers inspired by their vision. Their legacy is built on such a strong foundation that their millionth home cannot be many years away.

—Chris Scott, Founder, CEO, Profile Lumber,
Author *I-Kology: Practical Ideas
for a Sustainable World*, La Jolla, CA

The first time Millard Fuller was a guest on our show, we were blown away with his amazing story of giving away a self-made fortune to the poor and he and Linda devoting themselves to God's service. Most know the Fullers as the founders of Habitat for Humanity but there is so much more about this extraordinary couple that needs to be told. The Fullers are truly two people who have changed the lives of millions of people and the world forever! We are so pleased that such a distinguished author is telling the full story of our friends Millard and Linda.

—Don and Cheryl Barber, Hosts of *goodnews,* Atlanta, GA

Millard Fuller is fond of saying that the only way for bad things to happen in the world is for good people to do nothing. As an attorney, I couldn't be more convinced of this message. As I've gotten to better know the full extent of the impact that Millard and Linda have had on people through their Christian ministry outreach, I can see how the good they are doing has changed parts of the world and has the potential to change the entire world. Through their mission to build homes for families in need, they have changed the hearts and attitudes of many, demonstrating the importance of lending a hand to others. This can go a long way toward reducing crime, hatred, and the terrible sense of disconnect in the world. This is a most remarkable book about a most remarkable journey.

—Larry Kincaid, Attorney, Adjunct Professor of Criminal Justice and Legal Studies, El Cajon, CA

Millard Fuller's life story proves that one person can make a difference. Because of Habitat for Humanity, millions of people throughout the world have a decent, affordable house that they can call home, and perhaps for the first time in their lives they have hope. Hope to succeed in life and become whatever they want to be and do. Millard and Linda Fuller's spiritual leadership has changed the lives of not only Habitat homeowners but the millions of Habitat volunteers that have been touched by their vision and in doing so, has made this a better world.

—Tom Chagolla, CEO, Mesilla Valley<br>Habitat for Humanity, Las Cruces, NM

After reading Millard's book, *No More Shacks,* my interest grew about building homes in a one-week period of time. I got involved and, sure enough, under Millard's drive, time and time again, homes go up and families move in. I always asked Millard, "Who motivates the motivator?" I have since learned that the answer to this question for Millard is his profound belief in God. I am pleased to call Millard my great friend and deeply respect all he is doing.

—Ron Fisher, Founder and President,<br>Discovery Group, Indianapolis, IN

For the past three decades, Millard and Linda's dream has always been to eliminate substandard housing in the world. An ambitious undertaking, no doubt, but for the Fullers, an achievable objective despite the many challenges they would ultimately face. The brilliant Habitat housing model is Millard and Linda's legacy to this world. It is a concept that pairs altruism with recipient accountability. It's a successful concept that has worked in building homes for one million people at HFH and continues to work at The Fuller Center for Housing today. Bettie Youngs writes a powerful book detailing the "riches-to-rags" story involving the Fullers' selfless service to others, the sometimes uncomfortable details of the betrayal by the board of directors of the organization they founded, and the true "riches" earned by moving on with the work they feel "called" to do.

—Lynda Spofford, Volunteer, Lanett, AL

I truly love Millard and Linda Fuller's ministry. They are a living antidote to self-interest. Linda and Millard exemplify a great spirit of compassion for those in need that goes beyond building houses. It is building hope, not only for today and tomorrow but also for eternity.

—Jan S. van den Bosch,
Executive Producer and TV host,
Dutch National Television,
Netherlands

Is there a more inspiring figue anywhere in the world than Millard Fuller? Just look at what he's done to build decent houses for hundreds of thousands of people who needed them! I'd have to rank him right up there alongside Mother Teresa as a candidate for sainthood!

—Ted Stanley, Philanthropist,
New Canaan, CT

# Bettie Youngs Books

We specialize in MEMOIRS
. . . books that celebrate
fascinating people and
remarkable journeys

Visit our website at
www.BettieYoungsBooks.com

To contact:
info@BettieYoungsBooks.com

CPSIA information can be obtained
at www.ICGtesting.com
Printed in the USA
FSOW01n0332050118
42811FS